Love
After Sex

About the Author

Olivia ia a professional astrologer with over twenty years of experience in counseling clients with relationship problems. She is the author of *Erotic Astrology: About Him, For Her*, a step-by-step guidebook on how to please each sign sexually.

To Write to the Author

If you wish to contact the author or would like more information about this book, please write to the author in care of Llewellyn Worldwide and we will forward your request. Both the author and publisher appreciate hearing from you and learning of your enjoyment of this book and how it has helped you. Llewellyn Worldwide cannot guarantee that every letter written to the author can be answered, but all will be forwarded. Please write to:

Olivia
℅ Llewellyn Worldwide
2143 Wooddale Drive, Dept. 0-7387-0853-4
Woodbury, Minnesota 55125-2989, U.S.A.

Please enclose a self-addressed stamped envelope for reply,
or $1.00 to cover costs. If outside U.S.A., enclose
international postal reply coupon.

Many of Llewellyn's authors have websites with additional information and resources.
For more information, please visit our website at http://www.llewellyn.com

Love After Sex

RELATIONSHIPS BY THE STARS

Olivia

Llewellyn Publications
Woodbury, Minnesota

First Edition
First Printing, 2005

Book design by Donna Burch
Chart for finding your Moon sign from *Llewellyn's Moon Sign Book*
Cover art © by Picture Quest
Cover design by Gavin Dayton Duffy
Llewellyn is a registered trademark of Llewellyn Worldwide, Ltd.

Cover model(s) used for illustrative purposes only and may not endorse or represent the book's subject.

Library of Congress Cataloging-in-Publication Data
Olivia.
    Love after sex: relationships by the stars / Olivia.
        p.   cm.
    ISBN-13: 978-0-7387-0853-9
    ISBN-10: 0-7387-0853-4 (alk. paper)
    1. Astrology. 2. Love—Miscellanea. 3. Interpersonal relations—Miscellanea. I. Title.

    BF1729.L6042 2006
    133.5'86267—dc22   2005051178

Llewellyn Worldwide does not participate in, endorse, or have any authority or responsibility concerning private business transactions between our authors and the public.

All mail addressed to the author is forwarded but the publisher cannot, unless specifically instructed by the author, give out an address or phone number.

Any Internet references contained in this work are current at publication time, but the publisher cannot guarantee that a specific location will continue to be maintained. Please refer to the publisher's website for links to authors' websites and other sources.

Llewellyn Publications
A Division of Llewellyn Worldwide, Ltd.
2143 Wooddale Drive, Dept. 0-7383-0853-4
Woodbury, Minnesota 55125-2989, U.S.A.
www.llewellyn.com

Printed in the United States of America

Other Books by Olivia

Erotic Astrology: About Him, For Her

Contents

Preface

In my first book, *Erotic Astrology: About Him, For Her*, I guided lovers in the art of seduction, surely one of life's most exciting adventures.

Now I assume that you and your lover have been joyfully seduced, that you are committed to each other (legally or otherwise), and that you are now ready to embark on your second great adventure: living together!

Make no mistake, this second journey is more dangerous than the first. It promises emotional risks, hairpin turns of temper, and perilous currents of jealousy—emotions you might never suspect of that calm and together person you see in the mirror. One minute you'll scale great heights of passion, only to lose your footing and plunge into the darkness of second thoughts.

But ah, the heights! Those moments of euphoria when not just your bodies but your hearts and minds merge. When compassion and love flow between you; when you begin to speak what is in your heart and your lover whispers, "I know." The communion between you is silent and complete. Once those sweet rewards are tasted, the thought of a solitary life seems like a starvation diet.

However, just as seduction is an art, so is living together. Now, I don't mean relationships of convenience. We all know couples who stay together simply not to be alone. They end up like The Odd Couple, barely tolerating each other and paying for it with strange rashes and hard-to-diagnose stomach cramps. No, what I'm talking about is having the union we all dream about—when the passionate connection between lovers grows into a deep bond. However, it's the nitty-gritty, the everyday give and take in a relationship that teaches us to grow mentally, emotionally, and spiritually. So, the road to a perfect union may be uphill, but with a little astrological push, you'll make it just fine.

Heaven only knows!

Astrology helps you to understand the multifaceted being you love (whose underwear is decorating your bathroom). Too often we wake from the honeymoon in shock. Where did that nasty temper come from? Tight-fisted with money? Lack of imagination in bed? No, this cannot be the perfect person with whom I signed a two-year lease!

Fortunately, astrology gives you insight into the full spectrum of your lover's soul. Just by knowing your lover's birth date, you can understand his or her Sun sign and the planetary energies that rule it.

The magnificent Sun represents the ego and your need to individuate, *to be your own person*; it represents your need for creativity, self-expression, and a positive self-image. The Sun also shows how you go about creating that impressive, smart, dynamic god or goddess you dream of being.

It's important to realize that you're either an evolved soul or still in kindergarten. Yes, there are many lovers "on the path" between those two points, but for those who have been around the cosmos a few times (in various incarnations), they're now in the "graduate school" of life. These lovers hold the brass ring on life's merry-go-round: real honest-to-goodness adults, accepting responsibility even when life tests their souls. At the other end of the spectrum is the kindergarten class posing as grownups. They wreak havoc in any relationship with their infantile needs, turning love into a romance of whine and roses!

This book is about the emotional problems you might encounter with your lover, but remember, these problems can be minimized (even totally eliminated) with a *mature* soul mate. If your lover's still sucking on an emotional pacifier, be brave if you *really* care—the going may get rough.

There's more of you to love than your Sun sign!

I've also given you the chart to find your lover's Moon sign (see appendix). While the Sun is termed masculine in astrology and represents the father, so the Moon is its feminine counterpart and signifies the mother—the lunar yin to the solar yang. It's the Moon that speaks of our innermost feelings and how giving we are in nurturing our lovers.

While the Sun and Moon give great insight, they by no means give us the whole astrological picture. Imagine a wheel (the horoscope) composed of twelve houses, each signifying a different part of our lives: work, love, children, health, friends, relationships, and so on. Only by knowing the exact time and place of birth can we determine what sign is placed in the first house, known as the Ascendant, or Rising Sign. It represents the "face" we show to the world, confirming that what you see is not necessarily what you get! The Ascendant also determines, to a great extent, one's health and physical appearance.

After reading this book, you may say, "Wait a minute! My Cancer lover's personality really fits the Capricorn profile." Once you have your lover's personal horoscope, you may discover that his or her Rising Sign is indeed Capricorn, or multiple planets are in Capricorn. Add to this astrological puzzle the exact placements and aspects of all the other planets in the heavens, and just imagine the endless configurations, the fascinating possibilities. Astrology is a never-ending adventure of discovery—just like love.

What was it that you didn't say?

Communication is what this book is all about. It's the biggest stumbling block you'll face on that uphill climb to a great relationship. Naturally, it's easy to communicate when times are good . . . there are long talks in bed, whispered secrets. It's your lover's shoulder you cry on, your lover's voice you long to hear when you're apart. But! When problems arise and hurt raises its wounded head, you'd rather die (or at least lie) than admit how crushed you are. Pride gets in the way, and it's not easy confessing how insecure you feel. Your most important words go unsaid. Your deepest feelings are never expressed.

Most of us have little experience communicating during an argument without angry attacks. Often, the best we can do is simply shut down, close off our emotional connections, and stew in the sour juice of hurt feelings. The other person isn't a mind reader, so he or she reacts negatively to the arctic drafts. A typical reaction (unspoken or not) is, "Oh, so you're not talking? Well, two can play that game." Suddenly, both of you are silent and frustrated, each one feeling righteously indignant and waiting, just waiting, to be approached, to feel the touch of a hand, to have it all made right again.

Unless the unspoken hurt and anger are healed, they can slowly undermine the foundations of love and trust.

What lies at the bottom of it all? What are the underlying tensions that were never brought into the light? I call them the Triple-Headed Hydra: Sex, Money, and Power. No matter how deeply in love or personally enlightened you are, at some point in your adventure of living together you'll confront this nasty beast. I'm here to help you discover its hiding places and *off with its heads!*

So, let's begin our journey through the twelve signs to see how each of us approaches a long-term commitment, the challenge of love after sex. I promise this will be a guidebook unlike any other, and when you get to the last page, it will be time for a new beginning. You'll return to your relationship revitalized and wiser, with a new sense of who you are and who it is you really love.

"*The art of love is largely the art of persistence.*"
—ALBERT ELLIS

———————————————→

Aries

March 21 to April 20

Sex and Aries

Ruled by the explosive energy of the planet Mars, those born under the sign of Aries are dynamic and often impulsive lovers. They'll turn your world upside down with excitement, and you'll never want it set straight again. Since Mars is also directly associated with testosterone, the hormone that stimulates sexual arousal in both sexes, it makes perfect sense that fiery Aries love to love.

In the beginning of your relationship, try to curb your own aggressiveness and allow Aries to play the hunter or huntress. Aries are in their element when they take the lead, and besides, they do it so well! Be prepared to be seduced with intensity and ingenuity. It's only when they savor the sweet taste of conquest—be it on the battlefield, in the boardroom, or in bed—that Aries feel truly alive.

Doesn't sound bad at all, does it? As a matter of fact, for that kind of primal sexual energy, most of us would be willing prey, indeed. However, you'll find that the light of an immature Aries shines most brilliantly in the beginning of a relationship. It frequently dims to twenty-five watts when mundane routine sets in. In short, when the honeymoon is over, all too often, so is the passion.

Flirting with danger

With the battering Ram as its symbol, Aries are aggressive in seeking the variety they love. They're also quick to follow their impulses. Put those two together in the less than mature mate, and you have a very exciting but dangerous combination: an impulsive lover who's easily bored and ready to risk the known for a mouth-watering maybe.

What makes our Ram thirst for new seductions? The answer might surprise you. Very often both sexes flirt simply to see the effect. They need feedback that they are sexy and desirable because they fear they may not be! If they could get away with it, they would probably hire a focus group! That's right, underneath their super-confident facades are lovers who are ego driven, and those egos need stroking on a regular schedule.

It's all a matter of perception, of course. Aries is probably a lover par excellence, but if your Aries *feels* inadequate, he or she may require more than a "Gee, that was great honey," followed by "Can you reach the remote?" in order to boost his or her ego. Now, since you're a supremely intelligent lover (or soon will be), it's you who will build up your lover's sexual ego. This is definitely a job you do not want to farm out! Aries lovers don't need you to praise their courage, initiative, or boldness—they're secure in those attributes—but they love it when you communicate everything you admire about them, from the neck down.

"God, you're fabulous"

My intention is to make sure the flames of passion do more than flicker—so remember to compliment Aries before sex. Better make that before and during sex. Well, all right . . . *before, during, and after!* An Aquarius lover might become impatient with this overboard flattery, but since Rams go out of their way to bring passion and excitement into the bedroom, is it too much to give them a *lying down* ovation? Plus, remember that this drama is also being played out on a subconscious level, and Aries are never sure of being sexually fantastic. They want, and usually merit, immediate verbal confirmation.

The male wants to hear about his incredible technique, how your orgasm imploded on every molecule in your body. In the same vein, try telling the Aries female how exquisite her body is. Are you protesting that you show her how much you admire it every night? It doesn't matter, because in this case words speak louder than action. Tell her! Once you feed your male or female lover these compliments on a daily basis, trust me: he or she won't go shopping elsewhere for ego nourishment.

Bed and bored

In *Erotic Astrology* you learned that when sexual variety disappears, the immature Ram can soon follow. Nothing pleases this sign more than a lover with spontaneous passions—and the imagination to ignite them. If you suddenly have an appetite for sex, why wait? Most of us are controlled more by inhibition than imagination, and we need the privacy of our bedrooms before enjoying sex. How dull! In the throes of passion, Aries will happily pull over to the side of the road, meet you in the airplane's bathroom, or satisfy your desire in the church rectory! Now, as I explained in the preface (if you haven't yet read it, please go there right now!), your Aries may have many planets in the shy sign of Pisces. This creates someone less aggressive than the pure breed. Or, if your lover's planetary scale tips in the favor of multiple planets in the sensible sign of Capricorn, he or she might have to plan to be spontaneous. I hope you will be inspired to get your lover's full horoscope so you will understand all of his or her fascinating facets.

Of course, as your relationship progresses, these aggressive traits of the Aries Sun will make themselves known. With the pure 100 percent, undiluted, dynamic Aries lover, you won't have to wait a minute. The more shocking and dangerous the sexual setting, the more chance of being discovered, the more Aries will be turned on. This is definitely a sign that likes to love on the edge!

Also, remember, the Aries female is every bit as passionate and aggressive as the male. Virgo, if your idea of the perfect female is someone who waits for *you* to make the first move, with her legs demurely locked at the ankles, don't waste this lady's time.

It's been said by astrologers who have done their research (they're the ones smiling, of course), that an Aries female can even like indulging in sexual shock therapy. To her lover's astonishment—and eternal gratitude—she may dress up in black leather, take a dainty fistful of her partner's hair, and order him to perform something he's only seen on late-night cable.

Who's at the controls?

On their way to adulthood, Aries have great potential to be total control freaks. In everyday life this may translate as a little bullying, ranging from the subtle to the overt. If you have a female Aries lover, never let her push you around, no matter how she sugarcoats the pill! If you don't happen to agree with her, don't compromise your own beliefs, even if she becomes overbearing. The Aries woman will *only* respect you if you stand up to her. She may also test you to find out how far she can push you before you begin to push back. One thing is certain: there's not an Aries female alive who really wants a submissive man . . . well, perhaps in the bedroom, but only when playing games that have Mommy giving baby the sexual equivalent of gold stars!

If your Aries lover is male, and still on the path to becoming a real grownup, then be on the lookout for how much he wants to control you. It can manifest in harmless theatrical play, à la the film *9½ Weeks*, with silk scarves around the wrists, a blindfold, and a few gentle slaps on the bottom to heighten the excitement. Or it may simply begin with flattery ("I wish you'd buy that blue dress, because I love you in blue") and progress to where you begin to feel programmed ("What are you doing wearing that white dress when I specifically told you that we are having dinner with my boss, who loves blue!").

Now, we all know the difference between something that is just a little scary—a lot of excitement and nothing to worry about—and something that makes us want to run home to Mommy and our blanky! What's important is to let your partner know your limits. A mild slap on the bottom is fine, but if your lover approaches the bed with a hairbrush or cat-o'-nine-tails, you might prefer to spend the evening with Jay Leno. Of course, I offer this advice to lovers of all the twelve signs and every nationality and religious persuasion: the moment you feel that your partner's sweet tooth for a little pain is turning into a gourmet dinner, yell "Stop!"

Three is a crowd

Variety is the name of Aries' favorite game. You know how easily your lover gets bored, and if you do the same thing five times, that's four times too many. With a mature Aries, that simply means enjoying a delicious smorgasbord of sexual variety with one person. However, for the less mature, a play with only two characters becomes boring. He or she starts imagining the fun of auditioning supporting players! For Taurus, who cherish one-on-one relationships, this fantasy will cause acute acid discomfort. However, before you pounce on your lover with, "Why didn't you tell me that you invited the neighborhood?" it's better to subtly poke around in his or her psyche to see how your lover might feel about a third party joining you. If a *ménage à trois* (or quatre, or cinq, or whatever number) is also your preference, then all is fine, but if it isn't, a sexual thrill-seeker may not be either.

When Aries sees red

Of course, red is Aries' favorite color—the carnal color of passion. But that isn't the kind of red I'm talking about. I'm referring to the famously explosive Aries temper. Astro-psychologists (people who blend the sciences of psychology and astrology) equate Aries with a child's developmental phase of birth to eighteen months. This is when pure impulse is felt, along with a sense of omnipotence. I am here! Me, me, me! Hear me roar!

One sure way to trigger that temper is to catch an immature Aries in the act of flirting . . . or worse. Because these less-than-grownup lovers are so prone to lust before they look, their libido often leads them into compromising situations. How do they react? Pisces, you're a sensitive soul who might assume they drop to their knees and beg for forgiveness?

(A moment while I chuckle at the thought of a humble Aries!)

Oh no. When an Aries is caught with his or her hand in the cookie jar, what follows is total bravado. He or she feels dumb, is defensive, acts self-righteous, and gets real, real angry. The result can be a good old-fashioned temper tantrum.

Aries rules the head, so watch for temper tantrums to implode on your poor lover. Headaches can run the gamut all the way to migraines. Now you have an indignant Aries with a guilty conscience and a splitting headache. Trust me, this isn't a pretty picture, and not the time for constructive communication.

When Aries uses the energy of Mars to whip anger into a crackling storm, the first thing you must do is wait it out. That often means allowing your own inner storm to pass, realizing that the harshest words are said when tempers are flaring. We don't always mean those words, but we can never take them back. Remember to give Aries what they often lack themselves: sublime self-control and tact.

Any lover of Aries would do well to enroll in a Tai Chi class, where he or she can learn the art of deflecting assaults by simply stepping out of the way—a very unusual and effective technique! Tai Chi practitioners never use force to combat force. However, if your plate is too full for martial arts, then apply its wisdom and let your lover's anger pass you by; just allow it to dissipate in the wind. Then step in and calmly demonstrate how communication is a lot better than a temper tantrum.

This doesn't mean you have to let Aries get away penalty-free. Oh no, it's important that Aries understands just how seriously you were hurt by his or her cheating. So, Pisces, don't try to hide it. Leo, don't dramatize it. Virgo, don't analyze it. Just speak from the heart. *Caution for all signs:* if Aries feel that you're trying to control them (as opposed to sharing your innermost feelings), the Rams will only butt up against your efforts. Lead them gently and subtly by the nose—and isn't it fitting that the nose is ruled by Mars, the planet that rules Aries?

The good news is that although these lovers explode easily, they calm down just as quickly. Unlike Scorpio, who never forgets and rarely forgives, Aries doesn't hold a grudge. So I promise that the making-up part—the sexual passion that explodes with even more intensity—will more than reward you for heroic bravery under fire.

Soul mates

If your Aries, at this stage of evolvement, still worships the god of Me-ism, then we have to face the reality that you've found yourself a self-centered and selfish lover. Is this condition terminal? Can you call 911? What can you do?

The first thing to do is to realize that life never was—and never will be—that Hollywood musical. People simply don't find their soul mates and miraculously overcome every problem in two hours flat. As a matter of fact, soul mates were put on earth to help each other grow emotionally and spiritually. It's a fact of love: there's simply no growth without growing pains.

Want to understand more about your Aries lover's potential? Begin by understanding his or her opposite sign—Libra. It's an educated guess that as your Aries grows in maturity, he or she will begin to express some of Libra's qualities. In the same way, those born under the sign of Libra, in order to be well-rounded souls, will struggle in their lifetime to manifest positive Aries qualities.

Libra, your lover's opposite sign, has an innate understanding of the needs of others. Libras care deeply about other people, and they want to share everything. They usually succeed at this because they have a built-in talent for communication and the art of compromise. They have patience. They know how to listen. Now do you see how Aries might benefit from these qualities?

Libra's symbol is the balance scale, symbolizing their eternal search for just the right balance in a relationship. Aries must learn this balance too. They have to take their lovers into consideration, learning to think in terms of "we" and leaving the altar of Me-ism. They must learn what Libra intuitively knows—communication is everything. Without it there can be no balance. Without balance there can be no harmony. Without harmony there can never be real happiness in a relationship.

Your Aries lover must begin to understand his or her own nature. Aries lovers are often too aware of their strengths, but too impatient to deal with their weaknesses. The wonderful thing is that even when this sign is scared silly of something, they have the courage to tackle it. Remember, these are the heroes and heroines of the zodiac. They might be shaking in their boots, but they'll never turn away from a challenge. In this case, once they understand what can make them formidable human beings—and even better lovers—they'll take on the challenge and use their energies to transform themselves.

But think about it: it's always less painful to recognize our weaknesses when we discover them ourselves. So why not begin by reading this book together? Talk a little. Laugh a lot. Remember to stroke both body and ego. Gently help your lover along the path.

Yes, it all means work. It means a lot of love and support from you. It also means that *you* get to play two fascinating parts: teacher and lover. And just between you and me, they have always been one and the same!

Money and Aries

Red may be Aries' favorite color, but you can be sure that green is a close second, especially when it's imprinted with Ben Franklin's picture.

Isn't it nice to know that you've attracted a sign with an innate talent for making money? Aries invests a lot of mental energy into thinking about money—scheming about how to get it, dreaming about how to spend it! When that kind of creative energy is released into the universe, things happen. In this case, most of Aries' dreams alchemize into gold.

Both males and females are blessed with the Midas touch. They love the thrill of the chase, that exciting moment when the coin flips and it's either heads ("Sweetheart, call the airlines!") or tails ("I don't want to talk about it!").

Money is freedom

Even more than the sense of security it brings, Aries desire money in order to feel free, unshackled. It's that million-dollar sensation of being able to pick up and take off when the mood strikes. It's the luxury of having some "f-you money," so when they feel like biting the hand that feeds them, they can still pay the rent.

Money is control

Both sexes are more than willing to work and fight for what they want. The females are usually too energetic to stay home for long, plus their boredom threshold is about two inches from ground level. Most of them can be found juggling both home and career.

Women who find themselves in a relationship with *mucho* macho Aries might discover that he definitely expects to handle the checkbook. Even though he may be generous to a fault, he still intends to have control of the finances. Now, if you prefer the passive role—and don't mind being handed an allowance—then this relationship will be ideal for you. However, if you're more independent, then it's necessary to set things right, right away!

Gemini, your tolerance level isn't your strongest point. Before you throw in the towel and telephone that old lover, talk it out. And Cancer, don't smile bravely while you grow a third ulcer: talk, talk, talk! Keep reading, because I will get into the nitty-gritty of that talk further on.

Men married to a fiery female might be surprised to learn that even if she stays at home with the children, when it comes to handling the money, she intends to play a major and very vocal role.

But what if she doesn't want to stay home? What if she has a dynamic career and—hold on to your egos, fellas—she makes more money than you do? This female is the prototype of the liberated woman, and chances are she won't be satisfied in the typing pool. Oh no, she has her eye on that plush corner office.

To test your love even further, once she nabs that corner office, her ego will not permit her to be quiet about it. As far as she's concerned, the word "humble" describes the guy who *lost* the corner office! She'll strut her success and loudly shout it to the world.

Of course, I know that all you men are liberated and progressive—well, in theory anyway—and that's when problems start. Even though you're supposedly no longer threatened by career women, think about how you'll feel if your partner brings home most of the bacon. Leo, could your ego swallow it? Taurus, will it destroy your own cherished sense of security? Capricorn, will your ambitious Sun be outshone by someone who's just as driven as you are?

Play now, pay later

Although you've found yourself a very adventurous and exciting mate, impulsiveness also comes with the package. "What's wrong with a little impulsiveness?" you ask. Absolutely nothing when you're dealing with a mature Ram. However, there's a certain breed that sneaks into the flock every now and then. These lovers never learned the meaning of "moderation." They are *very* impulsive, and perversely, they manage to destroy the very freedom that Aries craves. How do they do it? By piling up a staggering amount of bills.

The problem begins with their devotion to self-image and status. You know by now that Aries are acutely aware of how they appear to other people. Some less-evolved Rams walk around as though everything in life (including people) exists only to reflect their own magnificence!

Since these Aries movers and shakers are devoted to image, they never just "throw something on," even for bowling. Most are impeccably groomed in designer labels. They want the fastest fire-engine red sports car on the lot. Naturally, they consider their home an extension of themselves, and even though they get antsy and don't spend too much time there, they want a secure and impressive nest to come home to.

Me first

I want to remind you that not all Aries are immature, status-seeking, and self-centered. Many lucky lovers out there will find an authentic adult with the patience to put money in the bank and watch it grow. These Aries have overcome the negativity of their stars and are no longer prey to being unduly impulsive and impossibly self-centered.

However, since most of us, alas, haven't completely overcome the negativity of our stars (it is our life's work, after all), you'll probably encounter these unfortunate traits to some degree. Isn't it better to know the worst so that you can make the best of it?

In the same way that optimism is a predominant Aries strength, a definite weakness is selfishness. This can really become an albatross if Aries is the only partner working outside the home. Remember that female with her eye on the corner office? Today you'll find the weaker (ha!) sex heading corporations while their husbands stay home with the kids and play Mr. Mom. But whether the bread-winner is male or female, Aries feel they deserve to have what they want when they want it. After all, they're the ones earning the paycheck!

Well, what about their partners who work from 6 a.m. to 11 p.m. at home? Yes, the Aries breadwinner appreciates what they do, and in an unguarded moment, even admits that it *might* be defined as "work"! However, they still think that whoever gets the paycheck deserves the bigger financial say. That kind of thinking should have gone out with the hula hoop, but unfortunately, it's still alive and as frustrating as ever.

Again, if you're a passive partner, then you might be very content being married to this more "primitive" type. For the majority, who want to contribute to a relationship on all levels, then immediate therapy is needed.

Role playing

Now here's where communication comes in. If the two of you haven't sat down and discussed money—how to make it, spend it, and save it—now is the time to start. If you're already having problems, don't think things will work themselves out, because statistics prove they won't. Remember hearing about the couple who never discussed what religion their children would be, and two years later one of them screams: "I never heard you say Holy Roller!"?

So, whether you're just starting out together or have been bearing financial frustrations for a while, now's the time to clear the air. If you don't, then you might find yourself exchanging this dialogue:

> *Aries:* What do you think, honey? I saw this sitting in the window and couldn't resist it. [It doesn't matter what it is, just imagine something flashy, overpriced, and totally unnecessary.]
>
> *You:* [In a state of shock] It must have cost a fortune!
>
> *Aries:* [Defensively] Don't worry about it.
>
> *You:* [Frustrated] Have you seen our checking balance lately?
>
> *Aries:* Why are you putting a damper on it?
>
> *You:* I'm just trying to be sensible about money.
>
> *Aries:* [Angrily] Let me worry about that!

And that's precisely the problem. Never let Aries have total control over the money.

There's a famous saying that goes "power corrupts, and absolute power corrupts absolutely." So, it makes sense to share control when it comes to money . . . it's the only way to make sure that your relationship doesn't become corrupted!

Selfish isn't sexy

It's true that bickering over money is definitely a sexual turn-off. After all, we do have better places to concentrate our energies, hmmm?

So, start your discussion by pointing out that fact. Trust me, it will definitely grab their attention. Then open the door to communication and boldly go where no other lover of theirs has gone before . . . into a frank discussion of partnership!

Even though we women have the right to vote and can even ride a horse without sitting sidesaddle, there are still scores of us who take a back seat when it comes to finances. Not only do we *not* pay the bills, we don't even know how much money we owe or to whom. Insurance policies? Safety deposit boxes? Stocks? For some, these subjects remain totally foreign and frightening. Hard to believe, isn't it?

So, Pisces, don't be afraid to open this can of worms with your lover. It may be unpleasant, but trust me, worms do not kill. Libra, you've got a built-in talent for compromise and negotiation . . . use them both! Capricorn, nobody beats you when it comes to a keen eye for financial investments. How about showing Aries what an asset you can be as a real full-time partner?

What about you men? I told you that an Aries female can be very opinionated. She can flare up like the Fourth of July. She can become loud. Sometimes you might feel it's easier to let her spend recklessly than to enter combat. Leo, any female who upstages you risks getting a one-way ticket to her mother, but how about talking it out? Virgo, you hate scenes, but wait until she calms down and then let the lady know—in your quiet, rational way—that your relationship needs a transfusion of communication.

Now that you've bravely raised Aries' blood pressure—then calmed it down with gentle talk—let this irresistible, aggressive, passionate, self-involved, and impulsive lover know exactly what you want: a fifty-fifty partnership. That means you discuss major purchases *before* the check is written, not after it bounces. If you're just starting out and haven't already put money into a savings account, open one immediately. This is vital, so don't wait until the bank offers a free toaster. If you have a true type A, impulsive lover—one who might tap that savings account in a wild moment—then discuss that tendency frankly. Don't leave the room until it's agreed that you hang on to the checkbook, at least until your lover becomes more disciplined.

These days, career people making big dollars might decide to have their own checking accounts. They might split household expenses while contributing to a shared savings account. Or they may decide on one checking account and more than one savings account. There are many variations on the partnership theme . . . the important thing is to talk about it *before* a crisis hits.

There is a Chinese symbol that means "crisis," and it also means "opportunity." So, when you discuss your financial relationship, take a deep breath and don't lose your temper, even if your lover does. You can transform even the most heated discussion if you retain your cool. Above all, whatever you say . . . always, always, come from love.

Remember what the Chinese tell us about crisis. In this case, you are being given two opportunities: to help your lover grow in maturity, and to make sure that not even Tom Jefferson can come between you.

Power and Aries

We all know people who must exercise control in a relationship—and make no mistake, control is power to a lot of insecure lovers. We also know that an immature Aries craves control. We know this because although Rams may be the most exciting bit of humanity on the planet, they can also be the least subtle. So, how does the less mature lover take control? For starters, Aries doesn't simply take control, they *grab* it, and your independence is gone before you can file a missing person's report!

Hell hath no fury

When it comes to seeing red and indulging Aries' tempers, we might look to fiery, aggressive Mars, the ruling planet of Aries, for the source of that energy. However, your lover is solely responsible for often turning that energy into anger in order to manipulate and control.

At their least grownup, both sexes can turn into bullies; unlovable lovers whose tempers make life miserable. It's a case of Aries wanting something and not getting it, then screaming, stamping their feet (figuratively speaking, I hope), and talking into your ear as long as it takes to get their way.

Now, when dealing with children, few of us will put up with all-out temper tantrums. We try to reason with them: "Mommy will listen if you just calm down and stop screaming." We ignore them as they flail about in the supermarket aisles. We threaten to withhold goodies: "Daddy will not buy you that bicycle if you keep biting his nose!"

We talk, we plead, we do anything and everything . . . but we do not put up with it!

Isn't it interesting how we tolerate behavior from our lovers that we wouldn't think of accepting from a toddler? Why do we do it? Even more than our instinctive need to retreat from force, we're simply afraid of losing love. We're petrified that anger will propel them out the door and they'll never come back. It's that fear that an immature Aries senses and gleefully manipulates.

Now, when your lover raises his or her voice, you have one of two choices. You can either yell back and step onto the Ram's playing field—where you'll probably be outmatched —or you can refuse to play. The first scenario leads only to a dead end, where no communication is possible. We've all known lovers who become sexually aroused at this kind of confrontation (remember Richard Burton and Liz Taylor in their headline-making battles?), but be warned, you'll be playing with fire. When passion overrides reason, all too often these arguments lead to physical violence.

In the latter scenario, even with a bedroom door between you, you'll suffer everything from headaches to raised blood pressure while listening to your lover's tirade. Maybe Aries will feel better after the storm is over, but your stomach will resemble the insides of a kaleidoscope.

Virgo, are you just going to back off, keep quiet, and become a willing victim? Pisces, will you do anything to keep that temper in its place, including compromising what you really think? Libra, since you hate confrontation, will you put up with this nonsense long after quitting time?

If you do rationalize and say, "Oh, I'll give in this time, it's not so important," you will have lost the battle as well as the war. Of course, Aries will be very sweet after you give in . . . very, very sweet.

So sweet, in fact, that you'll remember it the next time your lover gets angry. It's a little like Pavlov's dog. Every time Aries wants something in the future, the Pavlovian bell will ring (anger), and you will immediately react (intimidation). This kind of pattern, once set in concrete, is there to stay.

But wait! This pattern can also be used to turn the tables on Aries' anger. Let's get back to our toddler who's discovered that Mommy and Daddy refuse to indulge his or her tantrums. Dennis the Menace eventually learned to say what he wanted without screaming. He learned that communication gets him respect, love, and attention. That's exactly the lesson Aries must learn. So, if your Ram uses outbursts of temper to control you, speak to him or her as you would to any irrational two year old.

You: Sweetheart, why don't you just calm down and we'll talk about this later.

Aries: I want to talk about it now!

You: Let's do it without any yelling, okay?

Aries: WHO THE HELL IS YELLING!!

You: [Leaving the room] When you calm down, I'll still be here.

Don't give in, don't indulge that puerile temper, and *never* stop coming from love. If you can manage all that, your Aries has found someone whom they might possibly one day deserve!

Selfish is not sexy

I've told you before that selfishness is a sexual turn-off, but it's worth repeating. You see, we're about to delve into one of the worst traits of Aries. Yes, the immature Rams have a tendency to make everyone else's needs secondary. In business, this attitude can spell success; in a relationship, it spells disaster. You can find yourself giving in, following your lover's desires, ignoring your own, and assuring Aries total control and power.

Remember baby Aries' devotion to Me-ism? Well, it can raise its ugly head at very inappropriate times. A sexual itch has to be immediately scratched. Career moves must be ruthlessly made—whatever it takes to get what he or she wants now, and not a minute later.

"Grab all the gusto" was a term created for impatient Aries, but at what cost?

Cancer, don't give up before you give it your all. Aries' selfishness will be physically hard for you to stomach (did you know Cancer rules the stomach?). You'll have to force yourself to crawl out from under your shell and actually tell your lover how rotten selfishness makes you feel.

I have a friend who is a typical Aries lady when it comes to the art of Me-ism. Every time I talk to her she sighs and says, " I think it's time I really started looking out for myself." Now, between you and me, my nearsighted chum has been thinking of no one else for years. Will I tell her that? No. . . . I don't have a death wish. I'll just give a copy of this book to her next lover, along with a pair of combat boots!

The infernal triangle

Yes, in a relationship with Aries, you'll definitely be confronted with a dangerous triangle . . . you, Aries, and your lover's ego.

The ego of the Ram should be held up as a manifesto for every class given on self-confidence. It's humongous. It's unshakable. It's a pain in the posterior. However, it's as much a part of Aries as their sense of adventure, heroics, and charisma. They're simply born knowing they're superior human beings. This certainty gives them control over partners who are less sure of their own infallibility.

In some circles, they might be considered "know-it-alls." After all, since Aries believe that if you've got it, flaunt it, they're not shy about letting you know how intelligent they are. That doesn't sound too terrible, but don't breathe easily yet. You see, in their mind, their superior intelligence only produces superior opinions, and they fully expect their partners to adopt the same views. After all, it's *their* opinion. Translation: it's better!

Now, if you live with this kind of brainwashing long enough—and you see this in someone who married young and enrolled in the "don't do as I do, but do as I say" school (Edith Bunker from *All in the Family* was a definite graduate)—then it's hard to find your own individuality. Let's face it, if somebody continuously yells about how superior he or she is, after a while somebody who missed assertiveness class is going to believe it!

Hey you "somebody" out there, it's time you began thinking of yourself as a Somebody! If up to now you've lacked a strong sense of self, and have yet to take that course on self-confidence (probably taught by an Aries), then how do you begin to assert yourself? How do you get Aries to drop that superiority complex?

First things first. Sit down and get a large piece of paper, because you're going to write down all of your assets. No, not those stocks and bonds from Aunt Shirley; I'm talking about assets such as kindness, talent, intelligence, humility, generosity, and caring. Also, don't forget the fact that you play a mean hand of poker and make a sinful lasagna. Everything counts!

Think about the assets you bring to the table, and chances are it will be more of a picnic than you thought. List all of the things about yourself that you're proud of, and then meditate on them. Don't get up until you feel very, very good about yourself. Actually, in this case it's all right if you even feel a little *superior* . . . you've earned it.

If you've put up with an immature Aries posturing for too long, then it's going to be harder to help the Ram down from the proverbial pedestal (notice I didn't say "knock down"). After all, your lover has gotten used to breathing all that rarefied air. So, think about the kind of specific talents you might have that can help.

Sagittarius, you can use your humor to give Aries a little perspective on the matter. Capricorn, I know you're not about to waste precious time polishing anyone's ego. However, you can shed light on the problem in your pragmatic, take it or leave it way. Scorpio, you can do the same with your talent for analyzing, just be careful not to open a few arteries while dissecting your lover's psyche. Cancer, you're capable of unconditional love, and now *you'll* even need to stretch your capacity to help Aries.

If your lover is more adult than not, then real talk is going to hit home. However, if he or she is still sucking on the flattery pacifier, then drag out your arsenal of verbal strokes. Example to be used if all else fails: "Honey, I wouldn't even bother telling you this, but you're so smart you've probably known it all along . . ." This is to be delivered with absolute sincerity and no shame.

The sweet part about this tactic is that Aries are usually convinced (and rightly so) of being able to do whatever's necessary all by themselves, and in half the time it takes somebody else. So you might be very surprised to find your lover actually accepting the challenge and working to better your relationship.

Never forget that you can do it! You love your lover, don't you? Love works miracles, doesn't it? I want you to remember that we can indeed rule our stars—that's the true lesson of astrology. You can help your lover grow up and grow strong. Although you may give your lover many gifts in your lifetime, this will be the most precious.

The power of potential

Keep in mind that most Rams can be helped because they have that irrepressible quality that spells "youth" no matter what their age. That quality is enthusiasm! They're never too old to begin something new. They might be volatile, self-centered, and selfish at times—even too much of the time—but they're always brave with a divine sort of courage. That courage can be used to look inward and recognize their weaknesses—with the same clarity with which they admire their strengths.

It's your lover's potential for greatness that will help him or her learn the hardest lesson: to grow spiritually in this lifetime. Instead of using intelligence, determination, and aggressiveness in a negative bid for control, your lover must harness those strengths on a more spiritual level.

So, the next time you're both relaxed, encourage your lover—male or female—to become involved with yoga or martial arts (or how about both of you taking Tai Chi, as I suggested earlier?). It's a lot different from just "working out at the gym," because these arts involve more than just physical strength. Explain that not only do they discipline the mind and body, but they demand a high degree of openness, courage, and determination—just the qualities Aries possess. Attaining skill in these arts is a slow, patient process, and that in itself will be lesson number one for this lover who wants everything yesterday.

If your Aries does it (and remember to offer it as a direct challenge), he or she can attain the kind of disciplined mental and physical power that's been known to break through walls—one that will let them touch the spiritual source of their fiery energy.

The end result will be my early Christmas gift to you: a more powerful lover who knows how to control passion, temper, and aggression, and thinks before exploding. All it takes is loving your Aries as much as your lover loves life . . . completely and with every ounce of your being.

Decanates

Take two lovers born under the sign of Aries and they can be radically different. One is able to work for compromise in a relationship, the other is so self-involved that an attempt at communicating ends up being a monologue. Why are they like day and night? Studying decanates can explain a lot of the differences.

You see, every sign in the zodiac is divided into three parts. Each sign spans thirty days, and is divided into thirty degrees. Each decanate encompasses approximately ten degrees. While the first ten degrees reflect the pure nature of the sign itself, the other decanates have different planets as sub-rulers. So, while Aries is generally ruled by Mars, some Aries people can also be sub-ruled by the Sun or Jupiter, dependent on the date they were born.

Is your Aries a mirror-image of the sign? Is there a sub-ruler that is playing an important part in your lover's behavior? It's all right here . . .

March 21 to March 30

These lovers are ruled by Mars and are 100 percent pure, undistilled Aries. Ambitious and dynamic, both sexes have tremendous enthusiasm and seem to get the attention they crave without even trying. They're on a nonstop ride to the top—wherever that destination leads—and nothing and nobody can get in their way.

Women of this decanate are very assertive, and possess what used to be identified only as *masculine* qualities: drive, arrogance, and so on. I don't like to define the sexes so narrowly, but this lady does tend to act from the head more than the heart.

In a relationship, both sexes want to be dominant and won't take kindly to being told what to do—that's how they'll perceive a well-meant suggestion. Advice is a little less attractive to them than a diagnosis of herpes, so it's important that you sugarcoat what you say, and feed it with an eye-dropper. If you haven't signed any legal documents as yet, you might want to live with this lover first. Just a test drive to make sure that you've found an honest-to-goodness grownup whose impulsiveness is under control. More importantly, someone who is open to communication. If not, you may find yourself living with a lover who can resist anything but temptation!

March 31 to April 9

The Sun is the sub-ruler of this decanate, making Aries somewhat less combative, but even more success-oriented and egotistical! Since these lovers usually achieve whatever fame and fortune they seek, their religion of Me-ism calls for daily worship. That's difficult to take! However, it's vital that you don't attack Aries' self-image directly. Although the strength of their ego can move mountains, that ego can also be crushed by a lover's brutal truths. These are true idealists, far more sensitive than they appear, and at a loss if they think they're losing face.

Again, "tact" is the keyword. It's your job to teach Aries a profound truth: if they can get beyond their egos and really give equal time to someone else's feelings, then their image will only be enhanced in their lover's eyes.

After all, Aries relates their own self-worth to their success and grand achievements. All you have to do is convince your lover that your relationship will be the greatest achievement of all, and you won't be lying.

April 10 to April 20

Sub-ruled by mighty Jupiter, these lovers are far less aggressive and more philosophical. A lot of the aggression that motivated the other two decanates—and usually expelled in highly competitive careers—is now released onto the playing field. These lovers love sports as much as travel. I mean travel of the mind as well as physical travel. Ideas consume these Aries and transform them into eternal students.

We know that people who take themselves too seriously also rob themselves of humor. However, humor is what this decanate has in abundance. In short, this Aries is highly idealistic, fun, easy to talk to, and charming. They only fall prey to the less flattering aspects of Aries when it comes to flirting. In this case, the flirting has more of a chance of being harmless, simply because they usually *think* before acting. This means your lover has more of a chance of growing up and attaining maturity before social security.

So, even if you find that it's necessary to discuss the downfalls of less than faithful behavior, be happy knowing that your lover is basically very honest and is really *open to communication*. Those three little words should take you all the way to the chapel.

The Aries Lover

March 21 to April 19

The Good

Courageous

Sexual

Passionate

Innovative

Dynamic

The Bad

Impulsive

Flirtatious

Dominating

Defiant

Self-centered

The Ugly

Violent

Cheating

Egotistical

Combative

Selfish

*"Love has nothing to do with what you are expecting to get—
only with what you are expecting to give—which is everything."*
—KATHARINE HEPBURN

Taurus

April 21 to May 21

Sex and Taurus

A warm puppy's tongue licking your neck . . . a roaring fire on an icy winter night . . . the luxurious feel of fur against your skin. These are simply sensual metaphors for the earthy love of Taurus. Even this sign's symbol reflects the essence of a powerful sensuality—the symbol of the Bull.

Ruled by Venus, those born under this sign have one thing in common: they feel they've died and gone to heaven once they're in a committed relationship. The key word here is "committed," because both sexes crave security—emotional security in all the love, passion, and affection you can give, and material security in all the stocks, bonds, and pork bellies they can get.

I believe that you've truly found the quintessential sensualist. Not only will both sexes whip up gourmet delights to tease your taste buds, but your mate will take the time to expertly tease other parts of your anatomy as well. Yes, Taurus is known for knowing how to love, taking long, lazy hours to lick, nibble, and, finally, devour you (when it comes to sex, Bulls are definitely carnivorous!). Taureans are indeed lovers who understand the art of sensuality. However, like every true artist, they have their dry periods.

Usually, one of those periods comes after they're comfortably settled into a relationship. You see, immature Taureans tend to treat everything they love as possessions, and the danger is that once something is considered owned, it risks being taken for granted.

Play it again, Sam . . . and again . . . and again

Taureans are resistant to change because they're creatures of habit. Sticking to the tried and true gives them the security they need. However, that need can spill over into the bedroom, and if it could speak, it would say something like:

"Hmmm, yummy, sex in this position is good. It feels good every time. That's why I've been doing it this way for thirty years!"

See what I mean? Now, I'm not saying that chocolate sundaes are not delicious, but once in a while we like to sample vanilla or sherbet, don't we? And heaven help us, let us sometimes dip into the decadence of chocolate-raspberry-nut fudge ripple!

So, although Taurus will create a home that's a veritable cocoon to shelter you from life's harsher realities, even cocoons can become stifling if fresh air isn't allowed in. The same can happen to your sex life.

As I speak to women around the country, I've heard the same complaint over and over: "My sex life with him has fallen into a rut!" "He seems to have lost his imagination in bed." "I'm thinking of moving, just so I'll have another ceiling pattern to memorize!" I'm not saying that all those lethargic lovers are Taureans, but this sign does have a tendency to fall so deeply into a rut that their toes wiggle in China.

Remember, it isn't because Taureans aren't intelligent, it's simply that security issue again! They need established patterns in order to feel secure, and new territory represents a definite disturbance of the status quo.

This problem can be quite acute for a Taurus mate, no matter how sensational the Bull's lovemaking may be. Leo, for instance, craves change and won't put up with a lack of drama in bed. Scorpio will love Taurus's sensuality, but wants a more varied sexual repertoire. Gemini seeks variety as naturally as a flower turns to the Sun—and if this air sign feels claustrophobic, he or she will turn elsewhere for sexual nourishment.

The Taureans' old "stick-in-the-sheets" attitude is doubly frustrating, because they're not only great lovers, they're magical lovers. Nobody better understands the emotional nourishment of a sensual touch. Nobody knows how to set the scene for seduction quite as well. Nobody takes your breath away quite as completely with unbridled lust. Besides, even though they may have feelings of inferiority about themselves in certain areas (don't we all?), that rarely carries over into their lovemaking. They know how good they are!

So, if your Taurus has been in the missionary position for so long that you fear his or her limbs will atrophy, I urge you to introduce sexual variety slowly, just to see what happens. If Taureans suspect they are being told what to do, they'll turn against you . . . so tease, tempt, tantalize. To get you started, did you know that Taurus knows all about the joys of masturbation? They may even fantasize about doing it with you! Of course, whether or not they can make the leap from fantasy to reality is yet to be seen . . . and felt. Give all the encouragement you can, including stroking the throat of your lover with soft, wet kisses (it's the Bull's erogenous zone). If nothing works and Taurus refuses to enhance his or her repertoire, then it's time to communicate verbally.

Two disclaimers: Remember that astrology points out *potential* problems. Now, if your mate has planets strategically placed in more experimental signs (Aquarius for example), then you might happily discover that this Taurus is a lot more innovative. Or perhaps your Bull might have learned some new dance steps from a previous Leo bedmate who did the leading. But the potential is there to sink into a sexual rut, so be aware of it.

Also, because of society's still archaic double standards, collecting cobwebs in the missionary position usually bothers the male partner of the Bull. Males are always under more pressure to bring sexual variety into the bedroom. However, the typical immature Bull meets change with the same enthusiasm with which he or she prepares for an IRS audit.

Whereas another sign might suspect what's coming when you say, "I think it's time we laid down and talked"—this lover is always the last to know. Both sexes will listen to your dissatisfaction in disbelief. Their eyes will be full of innocent hurt and confusion.

Taurus: But, but, I thought you were perfectly happy!

You: It's not that I don't love you, it's just that, well, our sex life has gotten sort of stale.

Taurus: [Going white] Really?

You: I think we should try different things.

Taurus: [Going whiter] Really?

You: Sweetheart, let's try to be more spontaneous.

Taurus: [Now albino-colored] Sure, how about tonight, say around ten?

You're going to feel *really* guilty.

But don't let an adorable, totally innocent, hurt Bull put you off. Nobody said that relationships are easy, and communicating sexual problems with Taurus takes consummate skill.

Whether or not you approach Taurus wearing kid gloves, you're still going to totally shake up your lover's world. You're presenting this insecure and vulnerable sign with a frightening possibility . . . losing you. Your mate already has a deep-rooted fear of rejection, and the Taurean version of a Stephen King nightmare is being pushed away by the one person in the world they trust not to hurt them. Are you ready to turn into Cujo in order to save this relationship?

For a Bull, this conversation is worse than a natural disaster, because in your lover's mind there is nothing *natural* about it! "Natural" to Taurus means constancy, stability, lack of problems. It means keeping everything the same, keeping stability intact!

However, it may inspire you to understand your lover's potential. Taureans have to explore many of the qualities of their opposite sign, Scorpio. In the Bull's attitude toward sex, these missing qualities become very apparent. You see, Scorpios might not have invented sex, but they're constantly improving upon the art form. Your lover's opposite sign is experimental, and there's no area of erotica that is off limits. Actually, the more off limits it might be, the more Scorpio wants to experience it. Of course, it works both ways. In their lifetime, Scorpios must become aware of the positive qualities they lack, but which are inherent in their opposite sign, Taurus. So, you see, it doesn't make sense to place a personal ad "Scorpio Wanted Immediately!" because there's no sign that has everything. We all have our lessons of growth and development. If you already have pretty much what you want, then you're way ahead . . . just keep polishing the potential.

When talking to your Taurus, make sure he or she understands that discussing a problem doesn't mean rejection. If you wanted to reject your Taurus, you wouldn't be rapidly growing old trying to communicate, would you? The point is, you care enough to communicate. Get this message across immediately, or Taurus can lapse into a silence so intense you might mistake it for a coma.

Silence is not always golden

The silent treatment that Taurus imposes can be lethal. Those born under this sign are so afraid of rejection that they hide their fears and vulnerabilities behind silence. However, silence can cause the last thing your lover really wants: the beginning of the end of your relationship. Taurus must be told that when there's no talk, there's no change, and when there's no change, stagnation sets in. The prognosis is fatal.

Also, repressed hurt or anger is bad for us physically. It brews, it stews, and, with Taurus, it can erupt even years later! You've heard of the raging bull, haven't you? Well, for Taurus, rage doesn't build up overnight. The Bulls' biggest problem is learning how to communicate their feelings *when they feel them!* So, it's vital to get Taureans to articulate their anger or hurt.

These repressed negative feelings can manifest in ways even more harmful. One way is depression. Psychologists tell us that depression is just anger turned inward, so if you're depressed, instead of turning to alcohol or drugs to ease the pain (or in Taurus's case, an eating binge), talk, talk, for goodness sake, talk!

Next, convince your lover that he or she is not solely to blame. I know the temptation to play the martyr is irresistible, but resist! After all, your Taurus takes everything personally and feels responsible if a link in your relationship weakens. But a relationship is comprised of two feeling, thinking human beings. It still takes two to do that proverbial tango—and it's going to take two to bravely confront problems. Of course, if lovers continue to hide hurt egos behind a concrete wall of silence, then taking all the blame is the least they can do!

Stubborn as a you-know-what

Now that you've gotten past unnerving silence and your lover's ready to communicate, you run into the next problem: stubbornness. You're going to need steel headgear to get past this one.

Yes, the immature Bull can be inflexible and rigid. Astro-psychologists measure an infantile Taurus around the developmental phase of a child eighteen months to around four years of age. At this stage, children display rigidity of thought, and are mainly concerned with security and their attachments. So, that mental groove Taureans settle into is darn comfortable—they're not going to leave it without a fight. Getting your lover to see your point of view takes patience, because many Taureans can also be quite dogmatic. Add that trait to their iron flexibility and you've got your work mapped out for you.

Try to approach the subject as pragmatically as possible (charts and graphs are acceptable!). Remember that your lover tends to think in black and white, so keep your red hot temper at a low.

Remind your mate that he or she goes crazy with insecurity when getting mixed signals. Pragmatic Taurus will recognize this truth. Then, with all the caring in your voice that you can muster, explain that you want to be honest—and that it's pure love motivating you. "Motivating you to do what?" Taurus asks.

You take a very deep breath.

"Well, darling," you say, "motivating me to discuss the sameness in our sex life" (get the smelling salts ready) "and the fact that your overeating has created love handles so big they deserve to be named!" (Call the paramedics!)

An interesting aside: It's ironic that both sexes love beauty, but while they admire a sleek thigh or muscled bicep, too often food gives them that needed sense of comfort when they're feeling down. If they don't learn how to talk about their feelings, double fudge desserts will play havoc with their self-image. Then they seek more comfort, which leads back to the fridge, and poor Taurus is trapped in a downward spiral. They're miserable, but diabolically, it's a familiar pattern and oh, so secure.

Oh yes, while you're introducing Taurus to the no-pain, no-gain joys of communication, perhaps you want to venture into another subject that's been giving you hives—your lover's jealousy!

You belong to me

Taureans tend to treat loved ones like prized possessions. It should come as no surprise that they experience jealousy when seeing someone else's goodies, and have multiple orgasms (figuratively speaking, we hope) when someone admires their own. Wouldn't it be interesting to know how many older, affluent men with "trophy wives" were born under the sign of the Bull?

Next to Scorpio, Taurus is the most possessive and jealous lover in the zodiac. If their sense of security is threatened, be ready to move over in bed, because that old, green-eyed monster is climbing in!

Hopefully you've found a Taurean who's overcome the urge to hold on to your love with white knuckles, but if you have a natural tendency to flirt (Gemini, are you listening?), then by all means curb it. Taurus is 100 percent monogamous and doesn't understand how lovers can betray each other's trust.

Only infidelity and broken trust can evoke a rage in Taurus that will literally take your breath away. Their anger is slow to build, but when it erupts, it's devastating.

However, Aquarius, if you feel that your lover's extreme possessiveness is needlessly clipping your wings, then sit down with those smelling salts and talk it out. Both males and females of the Taurus species have to be told (and shown) that your love is for them alone. That might not cure their jealousy, but it will keep it under control.

> *You:* Sweetheart, can I really trust you? [Naturally, you will be bombarded with assurances.] Well then [continue gently],why can't you trust me?
>
> *Taurus:* But I do trust you! [Taurus swears indignantly.]
>
> *You:* But you don't trust me not to have an affair. Why are you so possessive?

That should be an eye-opener for your mate, who, naturally, spends half the day worrying about someone stealing you. If this conversation is successful, Taurus will understand that people can admire you, flirt with you, even offer you six months in St. Tropez—but that doesn't mean they're going to get you!

In communicating, don't forget that you have love working for you. Never underestimate its power. Plus, you have your lover's own inherent assets: determination, stability, and the obstinacy not to let life's difficulties triumph.

No self-respecting Taurus will leave a relationship just because it runs into stormy seas. This sign, if anything, is guilty of hanging on to a mortally wounded relationship while desperately trying to resuscitate it with immediate CPR (for the Bull that means Caring, Presents, and Romance!).

With enough loving communication from you, Taurus will become ready, willing, and open to new sexual horizons. He or she won't seek the security that food brings, hide fear behind sullen silence, or indulge in extreme possessiveness. Instead, your lover will become a creature of *many* fascinating habits—and, if you do it right, your love will be the most addictive of them all.

Money and Taurus

Money buys different pleasures for different people. It also fulfills needs on a deep psychological level. For Taurus, that need is primal, and one that you'll have to satisfy as long as you love this lover.

Money is security

Yes, Taureans are motivated by a strong need for security. It colors everything they do. Unfortunately, for some less evolved souls, it makes them *mucho* materialistic.

Since possessions bring Taureans the security they crave, it makes sense that having enough money to purchase the good life is very, very important.

Thanks to their ruling planet Venus, they're usually creative, with a highly developed aesthetic sense. Gifted with an innate understanding of beauty and value, both sexes lust after luxury. They appreciate craftsmanship, fine texture, and subtle design; they might have been born into a polyester world, but they'll work two jobs to leave it. They want to own what they admire, and to play out their artistic imaginations on lavish scales.

Happily, Taureans have a natural talent for making green stuff grow. No dear, I am not talking about alfalfa. They know how to use every God-given resource they possess to make money, and they know how to save it and invest it. With the Bull's solid pragmatism and eye for value, most investments reap high rewards, and it's not unusual for this earth sign to profit from real estate.

On the downside, we all struggle to gain an ounce of maturity, and heaven knows (and *only* heaven knows) how long it will take us to become wise enough to control our stars. In this lifetime, your Taurus has lessons to learn about possessions . . . what's truly important and what's just shiny with a high price tag.

Now that we've established that your lover's emotions are tied into an intense need for possessions (translation: security), you might have to lend a little perspective.

Buy, buy, baby

The next time you want to witness a fascinating phenomenon, watch your lover's face closely when viewing a beautiful, expensive *objet d'art*—be it jewelry, furniture, or, yes, a striking member of the opposite sex.

If there's such a thing as an orgasm *imploding* on Taurus, you'll witness it. Your lover is incapable of admiring this beauty for its own sake . . . it must be touched, stroked, owned!

It's not unusual for our Earth Goddess to possess multiple sets of china and enough designer shoes to make Imelda Marcos look like a Kmart shopper. Closets and drawers are stuffed with finery that bring a snug (or is that *smug*?) sense of ownership. Plus, our Bull never builds a palace merely to sleep in it! Oh no, Taurus wants to entertain, to serve the finest food and liquors. Most importantly, home is a backdrop for original oil paintings and Oriental carpets. Everything that says, "See how much I'm worth?"

On another financial level, Taurus may simply show off a bargain pool table or widescreen television with surround sound. It doesn't matter how much the Bull can afford to spend, the purchase will be tirelessly shopped for, prices relentlessly compared, and Taurus will revel in ownership.

Now, there are those among you who might find this materialism a little oppressive. As always, patience is needed, because eventually your lover will learn that true emotional security comes only from *within* ourselves. It's a hard lesson to learn, but with the Aquarius Age before us, more people will turn from materialism to spirituality. Soon, even your lover may take a long look inside himself or herself for emotional security, and hopefully, not come up empty.

Taurus is found wanting

Buddhists assure us that the root of all pain is desire. Their philosophy teaches that if you don't have what you desire, you're miserable. If someone else has what you desire, you're jealous. When you do have it, you risk feeling superior. Then you must spend precious time guarding your possession, living in fear that someone will steal the bloody thing!

When you communicate with your lover about possessions and acquisitiveness, remember to explore the subject (gently, gently) that the hoarding of things usually breeds selfishness. It sure isn't spiritual. It definitely isn't sexy.

Now, your mate doesn't have to become a Buddhist seeker of truth (orange isn't everyone's color!), just someone who knows when to stop depending on possessions as a reflection of self-worth. Someone who's familiar with the word "moderation."

Whatever your sign, consider using some of Libra's talent to communicate this need for moderation. Librans have an innate understanding of moderation because they're always seeking balance in life. Since most born under this sign are gifted in the art of communication, it might be interesting to shed our own astrological skins for the moment and assume Libran identities. Now we're ready to communicate with quiet patience, gentle love, and calm objectivity. (Aries, please stop laughing and at least try!)

You: I think we should try for more moderation in our lives. For instance, we spend so much money on material things.

Taurus: Having luxuries makes us happy. What's wrong with that?

You: I read recently that acquisitiveness is lethal. It just breeds selfishness and . . .

Taurus: That's stupid!

You: Well, let's talk about it. If you lost all your possessions tomorrow, would you know who you are? Could you be happy?

With honesty, the answer would be "no." What you've done is question your lover's value system. Though your Bull may read the *Wall Street Journal* with religious reverence, there are simply no guarantees in this world that financial fortunes will last. If Taureans identify self-worth with possessions, they risk falling apart emotionally if they lose them.

So, the road to psychic health starts with, "Let's talk!" And as long as your lover doesn't feel that you're going to push (no *radical* transformation, please), the Bull can be gently led to a meaningful change.

However, on your way to happiness ever after, be prepared for that bullish silent treatment. Taurus might need to withdraw to nurse the wounds you've inflicted—attempting to raise someone's consciousness can hurt! Just remember about that silence erupting into a delayed rage. Don't allow the anger to fester. Give your lover a chance to cool down, then, after a while, try to talk. With gentle persistence, your mate might even do some profound thinking about what self-worth really means and where inner security really comes from.

Needy is greedy

If your Taurus is too far gone down the road, and believes that only money spells success, then does he or she judge people by their financial status as well? If left untreated, this condition can turn a healthy respect for money into terminal greed and social snobbery.

Then there's never enough. So Taurus spends more and more time making money, obsessing over it, and being envious of others who have even more, all the while spending less and less time with what's important, namely you! This obsession may produce financial moguls, but it also supports thousands of high-priced divorce lawyers.

George Carlin does a classic routine about greed and materialism. How some of us are compelled to accumulate more and more meaningless *stuff*. Then we've got to buy bigger and bigger houses . . . why? To store our stuff!

When you try some honest communication, begin by asking what "stuff" really means to your mate. Whatever you do, don't use the word "greed" unless you want to be speaking to an empty chair. You'll hear the word "investment." Okay, investments are wise, but is there a point when acquiring things becomes wretched excess? If your lover answers "No way!" to the last question, start brewing coffee. This could take a while.

It's rare to find the greedy giving to the needy. However, if you've found one of the rare few, then you indeed have a winner. The other Bulls will usually repeat one phrase whenever you bring up helping others financially: Charity begins at home.

If you're more of a humanitarian, like Aquarius, then you may be totally turned off by a lover who thinks only of self-gratification. A spiritual soul like Pisces probably believes acquisitiveness makes Taurus a more selfish human being, and a far less attractive one.

There's only one recourse if greed has swallowed up the person you once knew . . . bite the bullet and confront him or her.

You're in a top bargaining position because, never forget, you're the most important possession your Taurus has. Since your lover is every inch a pragmatist, when you speak honestly, your mate will hear the message: Learn to become less greedy, less materialistic, or you will lose my respect.

In a strange way it seems fitting that in order to help Taureans release their grasp on possessions you must trigger the fear of losing their most prized possession: you! Sort of poetic justice, isn't it?

Yes, Taurus will do almost anything in order to keep your love, even if that means confronting the most terrifying dragon of all: a change of attitude!

On the other hand, if you're both on this level, then by all means buy a big house, hang original art on every inch of wall space, stuff every closet, load every shelf, fill the yard and garage with Mercedes Benz's and boats, have a summer home in the South of France and a winter compound in Jamaica, and call me!

Going for the gold

Too many Taureans are seduced by another's money and status. An emotionally young Earth Goddess can be drawn to a man's wealth not only because of the luxuries his money buys, but because wealth offers her emotional security. Remember, for Taureans, a sense of security doesn't always come from within (hopefully that will arrive with time). It comes from being able to have and to hold what they can see.

Perhaps the wedding vows were written by a typically romantic and security-minded Taurus way back when . . . *to have and to hold from this day forward.*

The man who places an expensive necklace around a female Taurus's throat is performing not only a time-honored ritual, but a very symbolic act. He's giving her a possession she craves (translation: security), but he is also touching her most erogenous zone: her throat. Taurus women and oral sex are legendary—and if our lover didn't know that salient fact before he touched her lovely throat with diamonds, he may yet.

In the worst scenario, both sexes might play the role of stereotypical gold-diggers, judging lovers by how much they can afford to lavish on them.

If you're a male who is in the honeymoon stage, I suggest you find out what's expected in the way of your financial contribution. How important *is* money? Will there be less love with less of it? Resentment with little of it? Will you be shown the door with none of it?!

Both sexes, of course, are open to the temptation of being seduced by another's possessions. Both must learn that although money can give them power over their own lives—it cannot buy love. It can rent, but that's another chapter.

Stingy isn't sexy

There are times when Taurus can be positively generous; however, it's often a wrenching experience to part with money. Most don't mind spending on something they consider an investment. Stamp collections, absolutely. Jewelry, of course. But they'd have to be crazy in love to splurge on a dinner in an expensive French restaurant. The hefty bill might ruin their appetite for sex later. But the truth is, only *buying* the whole restaurant could ever sexually deflate the Bull!

Of course, they'll still love every gourmet minute since they're the haute cuisine experts of the zodiac. The practicality of le doggie bag was created for them.

Since Taurus finds unpaid bills as unsettling as an empty freezer, it's wise to avoid this trauma. If your lover is tight-fisted—and you're a girl who never turned away from a "final sale"—be smart and arrange for separate checking accounts along with one to pay household bills. Financial independence will save you from explaining why you bought something that *only* gave you pleasure, but wasn't a wise investment!

If being tight-fisted is a real problem, you're about to find out how committed you are to Taurus, because only the deepest love can weather the upcoming storm. The storm I'm referring to is what these words forecast: "I think it's time we talked."

I have already given you some openers for this dialogue about the power money has over us. Now it's up to you to follow through.

Leo, you believe that money is meant to be spent (and how you love to spend it!), so you might already have one foot out the door. Gemini, put aside your aversion for anyone who belongs to Bankbook-of-the-Month Club and see what your unconditional love can accomplish.

Aries, please stop laughing or at least try!

Most lovers, no matter what their sign—even pragmatic Capricorn—are definitely turned off by a stingy lover. It's just *not* sexy. After all, isn't the very meaning of love "giving with both hands"?

I fully believe that someday there will be peace on earth, no one will go hungry, black will love white, will love yellow, will love red, Johnny Carson will come back to the *Tonight Show*, and every tight-fisted Taurean, with angelic smiles of true enlightenment on their faces, will take their most treasured objects and give them away as gifts of love.

Until that happens . . . communicate!

Power and Taurus

The saying "power corrupts, and absolute power corrupts absolutely," which I mentioned in the chapter on Aries, is even more meaningful for Taurus.

The Bull has a karmic lesson to learn: the true value of possessions. If the Bulls don't learn how to give with generous and loving hearts—without always anticipating what they'll get in return—they're in trouble. If they try to control you with possessions in order to wield power, you're both in trouble.

Love for sale

At their worst, Taurus can turn the very people they love into objects—prized, spoiled, possessed. Naturally, I am all for a little spoiling. Well, make that a lot of spoiling! However, I don't like to feel manipulated by money and I'm sure that you don't either. The minute we suspect that someone is trying to buy our affection, the warm glow we feel is quickly replaced by an icy chill.

Of course, a really mature Taurus can be extremely generous and give from the heart. It's our less evolved Bulls who give us problems. Their generosity springs from pragmatism first, treating gifts as calculated investments. But what do they expect as a return on those investments? Quite simply, their lover's loyalty, devotion, and libido . . . and not necessarily in that order.

A symphony of strings

With our investment-minded Taurus, every gift comes beautifully packaged with invisible strings attached. Our lover might not consciously be trying to buy affection, but whether the crime is premeditated or not, the victim will still suffer. In this case, those invisible strings will eventually feel like a noose around your neck. I have sympathy for all you mates who are bathed in luxuries and made to feel like coveted booty. Am I crazy? Isn't there something inherently delicious about being treated like one of Ivana Trump's diamonds? No, you've got to trust me on this, it *sounds* a lot better than the reality plays.

You: I can't believe you put a down payment on that condo without even asking me!

Taurus: I just loved it so much that I knew you would too.

You: How could you do such a thing?!

Taurus: It's perfect for us.

You: Doesn't my opinion matter?

Taurus: I know what you like; you like what I like!

You: Like hell!

Taurus: Honey, you can decorate it from top to bottom. The sky's the limit! [For the male lover, a new sports car or gym equipment does the trick.]

You: [Weakening] Well, I know you didn't mean to upset me. I guess it's all right.

Guess again, because you just got bought! Your lover treated you like a non-thinking object. However, since you were still a *talking* object, Taurus shut you up by placating you with *stuff.*

Of course, we must be honest and recognize there are those who don't mind feeling like they have a price tag attached to a body part. These mates are simply in the game for the goodies. We've all known supposedly respectable married folk, male and female, who are light on values and heavy on personal property insurance.

However, you don't have to be mercenary to find out that you actually like being treated as a possession. Being masochistic will do just fine. There are those who might submit to Taurus's ownership because of their own deeply buried feelings of inferiority. If you secretly think that you're nothing, it's amazing how good being treated like a mere object can feel.

Insecure Virgo, intellectually you know your own value, but too often (like Woody Allen's classic line in *Annie Hall)* you emotionally question the worth of any club that would accept you as a member! Having your worth validated by Taurean possessiveness will feel good for a while, but trust me, you're going to hate yourself in the morning!

Leo, your Achilles heel is flattery, and expensive gifts from Taurus will certainly stroke your ego. You'll also bask in the Bull's possessiveness, which you'll interpret as intense love. Some of us just take forever to learn this lesson: *passion is not love, and intensity is not depth.* So Leo, let yourself be fooled for a while, but your innate pride will eventually rebel. You don't like to be dominated, and you think too much of your own worth to be treated like a commodity.

Believe it or not, there are even those who match Taurus when it comes to craving security. Cancer, how much are you willing to pay for the security you love? You'll have all the luxuries you adore, but if you suspect your lover's hard-headed calculations, you will be crushed.

Sagittarius, you might be the hardest lover for Taurus to control, and you are the sign voted most likely to have the Bull seeing red! You require freedom above all else—and you place a low pricetag on material possessions. Bravo! You simply refuse to be anyone else's possession.

As for you, Gemini, I pity the Taurus who tries to treat you like a possession. You'll take the gift, flash a charming smile, toss a witty remark over your shoulder, and then skip out without paying!

You other signs, think about how much you really value yourself. Are the cynics right and does everyone have their price? Or is your idea of love too valuable for any price? Finally, even before you sit down with your lover to discuss love versus ownership, get out your shears and cut those strings. Taurus is smart and won't be fooled by mere talk or posturing. Being truly your own person—mentally independent and free—will be the first thing that will communicate itself.

War of silence

In the same way that Aries may use verbal temper tantrums to intimidate and control, your Taurus can use deafening silence.

Think about it: there's something very scary about a lover who's cold as ice and twice as quiet. Their silence has a message: "I am hurt, you have hurt me, and I am punishing you."

Silence = intimidation = control = power!

These lovers will either give you the punishment for a capitol offense—total silence—or, if you're lucky enough to have gotten away with a misdemeanor, you'll get one syllable answers, punctuated with shoulder shrugs.

You: Are you still angry?

Taurus: Yes.

You: Will you talk?

Taurus: [Silence]

You: I love you. Do you still love me, or do you hate me, or will you forgive me if I kill myself and die at your feet?

Taurus: [Shoulder shrug]

There is obviously no way to communicate with a lover who uses the intimidation of silence. I strongly suggest ignoring the tactic. Speak to your lover as though he or she was approximately eight years old. Okay, I don't want to be insulting, make that twelve.

Remember our "come from love" philosophy, because you're now in the teacher mode. A lesson really hits home when the love behind it can be felt, and you can't fake this kind of real feeling. So don't be the type of lover who speaks with kindness and concern, but whose eyes project all the warmth of a Wall Street commodities trader. Be as gentle as you would be to any child with a pouting lower lip. Remember when your own child used silence to pay you back for not buying that choo-choo train? The little darling hadn't learned how to properly communicate then, and guess what? Your big darling hasn't learned now!

It's time to explain to Taurus what Mommy never taught him or her:

1. Silence will only intimidate someone who's very weak and naive, and you are neither, thank you very much.

2. It's time he or she learned how to communicate with an exchange of ideas, and stop indulging in adolescent behavior that embarrasses you and is a shame for the neighbors.

3. He or she will get a lot more respect from you when treating you with the respect of speech.

4. You're fighting for your relationship because, dammit, it matters to you!

Then tell your lover to please think over what you have said, and that you'll be back later to talk more. If your Taurus lover will permit it, reach out and stroke and hug him or her, and let your lover feel the warmth of your hand. You know that your stubborn baby is one of the most tactile creatures alive . . . just the feel of your warmth might be enough to break through the sound barrier.

Try until your patience stretches to its limit. Then try again. Give it everything you have. After all, this is the love of your life, isn't it? If the silence is still deafening around midnight, your local operator can give you the number of all major airlines.

Bullheaded to the end

After you get your lover to stop intimidating you with silence, you must confront other Taurean means of control: stubbornness, rigidity, and a righteously dogmatic attitude.

Put on your teacher's hat again. The next lesson is that stubbornness may indeed conquer, but it can also destroy. After you've pierced the iron curtain of silence, and actually heard the human language once more, that doesn't mean real communication has occurred. What it probably means is that Taurus has just left silence for unrelenting stubbornness. You're tired, and you still can't seem to breathe fresh air into the Bull's stuck-in-a-rut thinking. "What's the use?" you ask yourself . . . and then you give in. Now Taurus has what he or she wants and what do you have? You have a small, hard kernel of resentment in your stomach that will grow and grow and breed revenge.

So, while Taureans gloat over victory—yes, by God, they've gotten their way—they've actually sown the seeds of endless future arguments. And you—you have sown the seeds of future breakdowns, be they mental or physical. Remember, the word "dis-ease" is just that—lack of ease and peace in our own souls. That's why disease often attacks people who have nursed resentments for years.

Most importantly, and in all sacred seriousness, please know that changing lifetime patterns, especially those ingrained in the negative aspects of a sign, takes time. I don't want you to think that the first time you try and fail, you should throw up your hands and quit! Remember, Taurus isn't a quitter, and you can gain a lot of inspiration from this sign's formidable tenacity.

There's a Hindu term called *vritti*—the name for the little groove formed in your brain when you start to learn something new. The first time you point out to your lover that control can be destructive, that's just the first little millimeter of the *vritti* being formed.

The next time Taurus uses silence or stubbornness to control, you must again reinforce the lesson, thus making the *vritti* just a little longer. Hang in there, because eventually this concept of teaching will form a good, solid imprint in your lover's brain.

If you can get Taurus to a stage of communicating and understanding that "take me as I am" behavior is just not acceptable, and even kills sexual desire, then you will eventually see the light at the end of the tunnel. That Taurean inflexibility will loosen and expand. All you need is love, determination, unlimited patience . . . and the certainty in your heart that your lover is worth it all.

Decanates

Take two lovers born under the sign of Taurus and they can be radically different. One is able to work for compromise in a relationship, the other is so self-involved that an attempt at communicating ends up being a monologue. Why are they like day and night? Studying decanates can explain a lot of the differences.

You see, every sign in the zodiac is divided into three parts. As each sign spans thirty days and is divided into thirty degrees, each decanate is figured at approximately ten degrees. While the first ten degrees reflect the pure nature of the sign itself, the other decanates have different planets as sub-rulers. So, though Taurus is generally ruled by Venus, some Taurean people can also be sub-ruled by Mercury or Saturn, dependent on the date they were born.

Is your Taurus a mirror-image of the sign? Is there a sub-ruler that is playing an important part in your lover's behavior? It's all right here . . .

April 21 to April 30

These lovers are ruled by Venus and are pure, loyal Taureans. Extremely security-minded, they are driven by a fear of not having enough, ever! Extreme cases keep cash under the mattress.

They worry over every purchase. Did they get the best quality? Should they have shopped more? Could there be a more attractive deal down the road? When it comes to a mate, they worry even more. Taureans have to make sure they have the absolute top candidate for the job (if they could get away with it, they would ask for your resumé!). However, their motivation is the best. Your Taurus lover is faithful to the core and intends to celebrate your golden wedding anniversary, hopefully with you still there!

Whether or not you get there depends on how much Taurus can overcome his or her extreme possessiveness and jealousy. As a matter of fact, Taureans worry so much about losing their lovers, they often don't make the commitment in the first place!

While they are very romantic and sensual, this decanate is likely to treat a mate as an object. If you're just starting out in this relationship, look for the warning signs: a lover who goes around the house humming "You Belong to Me" and having a blatant disregard for your opinion on just about everything. This decanate should be encouraged to develop their strong artistic skills, because that in turn will sensitize them, making it easier for them to empathize with your feelings.

Change doesn't come easily for these Taureans because they are also very judgmental. Once they fall into a certain mental rut, it takes extreme devotion and a bulldozer (appropriately named, don't you think?) to get them out. If you're already a casualty of this relationship, read the previous chapter again and then read it aloud to your mate. It will be an eye-opener!

May 1 to May 10

Welcome Mercury! Here is a sub-ruling planet that can help our Taurus sort out confusing emotions and communicate feelings.

Unlike the typical Taurus, this decanate might actually *enjoy* sitting down and communicating with a partner. They're not as rigid or self-righteous about their opinions. They're willing to climb out of a mental rut if you can show them it's a destructive pattern. They might even question their own conclusions, something unheard of in the typical Bull.

So, with Mercury as your helper, you can present sound reason to your lover and it will not be taken as a personal affront. The one thing this decanate needs is feedback—a real thinking exchange from you. Remember that Mercury is the planet of ideas, not emotion, so in order to make progress you have to be able to articulate what you want to change. Since Taureans like to know exactly where they stand, and Mercury likes things in writing, make a list of hoped-for changes under the heading of "My Fantasy List"—and good luck!

May 11 to May 21

This decanate is sub-ruled by Saturn, making them the most materialistic and status-conscious. They are ambitious and hard-driven, with a tendency toward stinginess. Remember the word "tendency," because they might have already worked through this weakness.

Saturn also intensifies their need to communicate while making it twice as difficult. There are times when this lover's aloofness will send chills up your spine. If hurt, angry, or confused, they're most likely to recede behind that formidable silence. It's perverse that they choose the exact time when they need human love the most to make themselves so unlovable. Isn't it true that nobody knows how to torture us as well as ourselves? This decanate, unlike the previous one, doesn't have Mercury to help open up communication. Loneliness and depression are suffered in silence.

In truth, they want to reach out and speak. They want a warm stroke to make everything all right. But it's as though they're imprisoned in a block of ice. What's it going to take to melt it? Well, you and I both know the answer. Love and real caring is the only thing that can warm the soul of this Taurus.

Saturn indicates that perhaps this decanate suffered from a lack of love or parental approval (usually from the father), and now you're both feeling its effects years later. If you haven't discussed this possibility, try bringing up the subject. It might open doors to a past that you and your mate can explore together.

You may never get this decanate to lighten up and take life less pessimistically, but you can help Taurus locate deep-rooted anxieties, talk about them, feel your caring, and lean on your optimism while your Taurus cultivates his or her own.

The Taurus Lover

April 21 to May 21

The Good

Strong

Practical

Protective

Determined

Calm

The Bad

Stubborn

Materialistic

Possessive

Opinionated

Phlegmatic

The Ugly

Immovable

Stingy

Jealous

Self-righteous

Lazy

"Love is like quicksilver in the hand. Leave the fingers open and it stays, clutch it and it darts away."

—Dorothy Parker

Gemini

May 22 to June 21

Sex and Gemini

Gemini is an air sign ruled by Mercury, and propelled through life by a love of variety and learning. There's no sign as entertaining, and so relentlessly charming. Gemini is the great seducer, using irresistible mind play to tempt and tease. However, it can be said of too many that getting there isn't half the fun—it's all the fun!

The former madam Sidney Biddle Barrows remarked, "We're becoming a country of couples with one foot out the door." Her words are descriptive of Gemini's biggest problem in a relationship—staying power. After the relationship settles into the known, Gemini might might not have one foot physically out the door, but mentally he or she is long gone.

The Twins in the heavens, Castor and Pollux, symbolize this sign's dual personality. Until Geminis learn to control this duality, they're always being tugged in two directions. They love you and in *theory* they want to live in faithful bliss forever, but there's that foot dangling out the door—just itching to explore virgin (pun intended) pastures.

Life is not a surprise party

Gemini's quest for variety keeps them incredibly youthful. Astro-psychologists equate Gemini's developmental phase with a four- to seven-year-old's unbounded curiosity and explosion of learning. The only problem is that when it comes to seeking constant romantic variety and surprise, the less evolved Gemini peaks emotionally somewhere around puberty.

Give your Twin a plethora of sexual scenarios to look forward to and you'll have a happy lover. Foreplay in the bathtub, orgasms on the carpet, a variety of sexual toys to play with, and, since Gemini is ruled by Mercury, the sign of communication, phone sex is a delicious way to tease and intrigue this sign.

However, no matter how imaginative you are, sooner or later every relationship settles into the familiar. For Cancer, this can equate with warm and wonderful. For an unevolved Gemini, it means that some big, bad adult—mainly you—is going to burst his or her balloon.

For real grownup lovers (now on the endangered species list), solid relationships let them relax and explore the fascinating facets of their partner. Geminis are used to skimming people the way they skim books. After all, it takes quieting down one's mind to concentrate on someone else. Gemini is constantly carrying on an inner dialogue, and has trouble concentrating on anything longer than ten minutes at a stretch.

When this immature lover gets bored, it leads to the need for immediate diversion. A prescription to cure Gemini's boredom might read: "Have two orgasms and call me in the morning!"

Sex relieves boredom

The road to immediate orgasms, however, is paved with thorns, and sooner or later you'll find yourself trekking down that thorny path looking for your lover. Oh yes, there goes Gemini behind that bush, flirting outrageously and indulging in verbal foreplay.

But wait! Your lover isn't with the best-looking or even the sexiest person at the party. That's right, for Twins of both sexes, looks are secondary. It's what's between the ears and not the knees that tantalizes.

I told you in *Erotic Astrology* that when it comes to making love and using our five senses, the mind makes the most sense of all. It is Gemini's most erogenous zone. The Twins need to feed their minds with communication: words, quotes, puns, witticisms, gossip! There are two things in this world this lover will never, never do in silence—suffer or make love!

Now, when you catch Gemini flirting outrageously, you cannot simply look the other way, because that's all the time he or she needs to book a room at the Ramada Inn. You must confront your mate with the reality of what's happening.

Scorpio, your jealousy can consume you to the point where communication is impossible. It's better to back off until your blood pressure cools. Just remember that for Geminis, flirting is in their DNA; it's nothing personal. However, your job is to make it personal, to make your lover see that compulsive flirting carries risks. Specifically, losing you.

Virgo, don't immediately think you must have done something wrong and go off in a corner to hate yourself in private. Gemini is a split personality, remember? Just because your mate is thinking lewd thoughts about someone doesn't mean it's the end of your world.

Capricorn, you're much too conservative to put up with the social embarrassment of a flirting partner. But read on before you deliver that ultimatum.

Whatever your own block to communication might be, when you finally overcome it and sit down with your lover, get ready to confront some slippery maneuvering on Gemini's part.

Who, me?

Gemini rarely takes responsibility for messing up. To begin with, this lover doesn't want to appear vulnerable—something Gemini equates with weakness. So, self-righteous anger will be first on the menu, served with a diatribe of rhetoric. Remember how glib Gemini played with words in order to play with you? Now words (your lover hopes) will be the way out of the corner he or she is backed into.

Talk, talk, and more talk. It's the Twins' equivalent of "I'm dancing as fast as I can!"

Somewhere along the line, Gemini even manages to twist a noun here, an adverb there, and suddenly it's all your fault! What's more, don't be surprised if this self-righteous monologue turns from defensive to offensive. What began as caustic can become down-right cruel. After it goes on for a while (forget about getting half a syllable in), you'll learn a few things:

1. The Twins seem to filter everything through their intellect and not enough through their feelings.
2. They often lack empathy with *your* feelings.
3. At times, that split personality can translate as being two-faced, especially when the Twins resort to deception to squeeze out of an argument.

Unlike Taurus, who can sink into stony silence when angry, Gemini aims for frigid coldness, then lets loose a stream of icy barbs like well-aimed missiles! When this guilty rhetoric hits its mark, it's intimidating enough to make a Scorpio back off.

Does Gemini hope your anger will justify even more indignation? Well, fool him or her and wait it out. This will be doubly hard for you, Cancer, because your sensitivity may not survive your lover's lethal tongue. However, even Gemini has to run out of script material after a while. In the meantime, be prepared for anything. Some female Twins even work themselves up to a point of hysteria. Gemini rules the nervous system, and those born under this sign are expert at knowing how to abuse their equilibrium.

Your lover finds humor irresistible, and the more sardonic the better. I realize that at this stage you're in no mood to be funny, but as the French advise, *sois sage!* Be smart and consider the use of humor as a weapon. Also, feel free to use it at Gemini's expense. For instance, you might quip, "They put a big A on poor Hester's chest in *The Scarlet Letter*. I was thinking about something a little more modern for you . . . how about a tattoo?"

Okay, we have a little smile now. Gemini realizes that you're not headed for either the kitchen knife or your lawyer. It's time to begin teaching our restless lover how not to ravage a relationship.

For starters, ask Gemini to really listen. It's important that your mate quiets that constantly active mind, which blocks out half of what you're saying and interrupts the rest.

Again, it's all in the approach. Make your frustration and hurt felt, but above all, make your *love* felt. Then have a talk about feelings. Bring up a hypothetical situation, perhaps one in which your lover might catch *you* flirting, or worse. How would he or she feel? What you'll probably hear is what your lover would *think*. So start again . . .

> *You:* I want to know how you would *feel*—bad, sad, angry, disgusted? [Your lover is too smart not to try to escape this trap.]
>
> *Gemini:* Well, I might be angry at first, but I know that you love me and . . .
>
> *You:* But what if your anger turned to disgust? What if that turned you off from wanting to touch me again? [That would be an interesting question, wouldn't it?] I don't want it to get to that point because I love you. It would kill me to lose my desire for you, but I can't guarantee that that won't happen if you continue to step on my feelings.

Now go back to your original question, "So imagine catching me with someone else. How would you really feel?"

Don't stop questioning until Gemini actually talks about feelings—and not just what he or she thinks about feelings.

Say that you understand Gemini's need for variety. In fact, you want to share more variety. You want to learn new things together, learn new languages (Gemini also rules the tongue, and is probably bilingual), travel together, and so on. Whatever happens, don't even whisper the word "routine"! Explain that you're not about to sign up for unisex belly dancing classes every Thursday at 4 p.m. And this doesn't mean that you want your mate to start carrying a beeper. The idea is not to make Gemini feel less free, so make it plain that you both need your space.

A reality check: be advised that Geminis can become truly distraught. They can swear to change—after all, they do love you—but the Twins have a very short attention span. More often than not, *they mean it when they say it,* but you can't take that to the bank. Look for repeated good behavior before you breathe a sigh of relief.

Impatient Aries, stop checking your watch, you might have a little waiting to do before Gemini's maturity catches up with his or her intellect. But once the two finally merge, I promise, so will you!

To give you encouragement on your quest for a more grownup lover, consider Gemini's opposite sign, Sagittarius. Here are many positive qualities just waiting to raise Gemini's consciousness. While Gemini just sips a subject and goes on to the next taste, Sag tastes, swallows, and thoroughly digests. Sagittarians are also lovers who derive great spiritual meaning from sex, something that Gemini (up to now anyway) has probably never contemplated. Most Sag people live life with a sound philosophy. Yes, it's true that in youth Sag can be almost as flighty as Gemini, and it's only later on that Sagittarians really begin to focus on what it's all about. So take heart, your lover may still grow into his or her polarity potential.

In the meantime, what about those merciless words that Gemini flung your way during that argument? You haven't forgotten them, but you may believe that your lover has. It was all just innocent play and he or she doesn't remember any of it. Oh yes, the Twins are slippery! So you might as well forgive the words. But the next time you hit the battlefield and words are hurled as weapons, stop Gemini in mid-vowel and make him or her listen to what is being said.

Now, about the quieting of Gemini's mind. You can try getting your lover to practice a mind-silencing meditation used for centuries in Eastern cultures. The nice part about this is that you can do it together.

"What do you mean *stop thinking*? I think from the moment I get up to the moment I go to bed. It's impossible to stop thinking!" Gemini argues.

At that point, explain that what your lover is really saying is: "I get no peace from myself, no quiet, no calm. My mind is like a dog constantly chasing its tail!"

Quieting the storm

Here's a little experiment. What you've got in your favor is Gemini's love of self-improvement. Besides, the Twins are the ultimate mind-game players, and you're about to introduce one of the most difficult mind games of all. Find a quiet spot in the house and light a single candle in the dark.

Both of you sit in front of the candle and focus on it. You can even hold hands. Tell your lover to think of nothing but the candle. You'll see that within seconds, Gemini's mind is whirling with the mortgage, the boss, and any available trivia.

This is when you point out that Gemini is just repeating the same thoughts over and over again, watching the same old movie. In order to stop that constant inner chatter, tell Gemini to cut the sentence they're thinking in half—*do not finish it in their mind*.

Of course, within seconds your lover will be back to mind chatter and they'll have to learn to consciously stop the sentence in mid-thought. If Gemini simply can't handle this radical concept of no thought, it might help to give a word like *love* to keep repeating like a mantra, replacing the mental chatter.

Another effective and much easier path is to have your lover visualize his or her thoughts as a stream, chattering and babbling by, in constant motion. Now tell your lover to imagine himself or herself sitting next to that stream, watching it go by. There's no longer any need to stop the endless thoughts, only to recognize the quiet, calm, self-composed being sitting beside the stream as the true Self.

Too much . . . too soon

Gemini's nervous energy fuels his or her need for sex. However, with the male Twins, the swiftness of their response to sex can sometimes manifest in their performance—many Gemini men experience premature ejaculation. Now, other planetary influences in a horoscope may prevent this problem, but if it occurs, remember there are many scientific cures available today . . . and some not so scientific.

Read the Libra chapter in *Erotic Astrology* and you'll learn a Chinese technique for holding back the orgasm. It consists of using the fore and middle fingers of the left hand to exert pressure on the point between the scrotum and anus. It's done for about three seconds while taking a deep breath. Plus it's far more fun than having your ready-to-explode lover trying to concentrate on Margaret Thatcher!

Expect the unexpected

The Twins don't understand their own sudden impulses, so it's understandable if you walk around half the time muttering, "I never would have believed it!"

When it comes to sex, there isn't much that Gemini hasn't fantasized. Their vivid imaginations have probably pondered group sex, and they might even have enjoyed a party or two or six. Naturally, it's your choice whether you want to participate. My advice is to do what feels good, but only if it will leave you feeling good about yourself.

Also, as Gemini is usually drawn in two directions, a liking for bisexuality isn't uncommon. If you're the experimental type, this might not bother you at all. Aquarius, as another air sign, you tend to filter everything through your mind, too, so you might take an intellectual curiosity in your lover's dual likings.

At the other end of the spectrum, Pisces, you'll be in pieces, if not totally destroyed. Even if Gemini just *dabbled* a bit—had the experience and is ready to move on—you definitely will not be. Your deeply emotional nature will never understand Gemini's detached sexual experimentation.

For most lovers, having their mate attracted to their own sex seems to be the final insult. In truth, Gemini may simply be an equal-opportunity lover—just very pleased with the sexuality both sexes offer. However, for the ego-wounded mate, the unspoken cry is: "I just wasn't woman enough (or man enough) to satisfy my lover!"

But is this a permanent preference? Or just a one-time experiment? Does Gemini even know the answer? If you're just starting out together, then discuss bisexuality and get an understanding of where your lover stands (and hopefully, hasn't as yet lain) on the matter.

If you suspect a real problem, then run, do not walk to the nearest sofa. Sit your mate down and do what Gemini loves to do best—talk! Getting sexually delicate situations out into the open doesn't guarantee a solution, but not talking guarantees a disaster.

Most importantly, don't panic. Your mate may have impulses that you can't understand, but remember that we all have our wild side. What about yours? Have you ever really discussed your deepest fantasies with your lover? You have one of the most imaginative partners on earth. Gemini's mind can imagine all sorts of scenarios, whether acted upon or not, and most Twins have a wild fantasy life. I fervently believe that if more lovers would learn the art of erotica, including acting out sexual fantasies—at least talking about them!—fewer would experiment with third parties.

So, consider fulfilling your female lover's need to feel more aggressive—or your male lover's need to feel more submissive—and anything in between. Let Gemini express the facets of his or her personality (while you express yours, of course). Once you explore each other's fantasies, your Gemini's need for experimentation and variety may never go farther than your bedroom door to be wholly satisfied.

Money and Gemini

You understand how impulsive your Gemini can be when it comes to escaping boredom, so you're not foolish enough to believe that Gemini will suddenly be a paragon of stability with money, are you?

I was afraid of that!

Well, it looks as though you're in for a shocking revelation. Not only does money slip through the Twins' fingers like fairy dust, but they couldn't care less. As a matter of fact (you practical Capricorns will shudder at this heresy), Gemini even *likes* the cataclysmic jolts of "now-we're-rich-now-we're-broke" finances.

Down but not out

Why would Gemini get a positive rush from unstable finances? Is there a psychological disorder here? Well, Gemini may have a split personality, but don't confuse that with being crazy. Our Twins love having money because they get to outrun boredom by hopping over to Europe, or adding to their gizmo collections with the latest Japanese computerized things.

Your mate is also generous and loves to share the good life. Easy come, easy go, is Gemini's motto—and let's enjoy it while we've got it. Nobody knows better than Gemini how fleeting that timespan may be!

However, *easy go* for the Twins isn't viewed as a terminal situation. It's temporary. They don't whine. They don't head for the corner bar or their shrink. You might be on your fifth Excedrin (or first fifth), but your lover will already have put the loss out of sight and out of mind. Gemini is already looking for the next possibility.

How do the Twins know it's only temporary? Because these dreamers—and sublime schemers—have complete faith in their ability to make money. After all, didn't a Gemini sell a refrigerator to a guy in Nome with the offer of free ice cubes? Isn't being entrepreneurial in the Twins' blood? Don't they have an uncanny sixth sense of what the public wants—and time and time again, prove they can turn doo doo into dollars? Even a zero bank balance gives them just the challenge they need to use their wits (always in ample supply) to come up with new money-making schemes. So, you see, the financial instability that would have most of us chewing our fingernails creates what Geminis live for and crave having, and if they can't get it, they invent it for themselves: *Change!*

What rainy day?

The good news is that you won't have to argue with your lover about who controls the finances. Gemini really doesn't want to be bothered with a checkbook and has no desire to become a member of Taurus's Bankbook-of-the-Month Club. So, it's not only a good idea that you take charge of the savings, it's vital. Otherwise, when that rainy day comes around, you'll be lucky if you can afford an umbrella! (This reminds me of a movie poster I once saw about two schemer-dreamers crouched under a big umbrella. It said "They finally got their heads above water—and it's raining!")

Also, be prepared to watch Gemini spend whatever money he or she has impulsively, and not often wisely. They usually walk around with bills stuffed into all pockets. Ask Gemini, "How much money do you have on you?" and you might as well have asked what cell produces haploid spores.

Gotta give them credit

The Twins seek immediate gratification, and that's why sooner or later you should have a deep and meaningful conversation about credit cards. (When it comes to confronting something painful, my philosophy is to always do it sooner.)

Credit card companies were created with Gemini in mind. See something you like? Can't afford to lay out the cash right now? Well, why not get yourself into serious debt and total embarrassment by using this pretty little card with the attractive shiny gold decal on it?

Whether male or female, Gemini might hesitate for a sane second, but most will succumb, following Scarlett O'Hara's famous philosophy: "I'll think about it tomorrow!"

If you dig a little deeper, you might discover your lover's hunger for this purchase is also motivated by envy. It's the "My brother-in-law's got it!" syndrome. That's right, many Geminis covet what they haven't got, and they're going to get it or go broke trying.

Now, as a mate of one of these capricious creatures, you know that Geminis can do without checkbooks—but taking their credit cards away is like cutting off their oxygen supply. If your lover has already shown complete irresponsibility in overusing credit cards, then you'll have to brave Gemini's self-righteous arguments and caustic tongue—but if you share finances, don't give in or give up.

Of course, it's all about immediate gratification (translation: immediate relief of boredom), and our goal is to get Geminis to ask themselves, "Do I *really* need this?" Especially when they have four varieties of the same thing at home.

"Well, I don't *need* it, but I *want* it!" Gemini protests.

If your mate has unlimited funds, then just say: "That's great, get me one in green!"

But if what's in your shared bank account will only put a few months (weeks?) between you and welfare, then suggest:

"Why not sleep on it? If you still want it in a few days, then get it."

"Are you serious?" Gemini sputters, "That's like telling a kid to wait until New Year's to celebrate Christmas!"

Put it in writing

Now, that conversation isn't going to do much but frustrate your Gemini. I got you started, but it's up to you to appeal to your lover's intellect, not emotions. It's only through logic that Gemini will see the light. Remember that feelings run second to ideas with this sign. The quickest way to lose their attention is with a flood of emotional bitterness, guilt, and self-pity. You can indulge yourself, of course, but be prepared to get nowhere. You'll only have to come back later and start the conversation all over again.

If you can't control your anger, then consider putting your logical, reasonable arguments on paper. That isn't as silly as it might sound. As Gemini is the sign of communication, the Twins usually do a lot of writing, reading, and clipping out newspaper columns to give to friends. They have great respect for the written word.

Besides, trying to get your point across to Gemini, who isn't going to hear half of what you say anyway, whose mind is racing faster than a speeding bullet—well, it's an exercise in masochism that you can do without.

So instead of facing a flood of tears or wrath, Geminis might very well prefer the safety of the written word. Let them read about their impulsive spending. Let them digest their envy of what others have. Let them make big ugly X's over their irresponsibility. Then, get them to sit down and talk about it. If they balk, threaten publication.

Keep in mind at all times that you've got yourself the salesperson *par excellence* of the zodiac. When Gemini gets through selling you on how important it is to have what caught his or her eye, you just might end up buying His and Hers matching refrigerators—and wasn't free ice cubes a terrific deal?

It's all in the cards

However those born under this sign earn money, it has to give them the freedom they crave. If you want to see a really pathetic sight, catch a glimpse of a Gemini in the seventh hour of an eight-hour day at the office. If you do see one briefly inside any office, you can be sure that for the better part of the day he or she was doing outside sales.

No, Geminis are not meant to be confined. They'll pace that psychological cage back and forth, forth and back, until the boredom becomes excruciating. And you've already learned what impulsive methods they adopt to relieve boredom, hmmm?

Your mate, lover of immediate gratification that he or she is, has no intention of climbing the corporate ladder to collect a watch at the top. That's why Gemini spends so much time dreaming and scheming. It's the big windfall they're after. Sometimes they can actually pull it off. Other times you'll have to step in before your hard-earned money backs a really implausible scheme.

Be forewarned: just as Geminis are superb salespeople, they're also suckers for other great salespeople. Call it *professional courtesy*, but they're easy prey for get-rich-quick deals. Or maybe it's just poetic justice? Whatever the reason, while your Twin's head is way up there in the clouds—and unreachable by logic—it's still your job to keep dragging him or her down to earth.

I know this is easier said than done. Being with a Gemini is like carrying around your own amusement park—all colorful excitement and dangerous thrills. Gemini's enthusiasm for a new project is contagious. "C'mon, let's do it now or else the parade will pass us by!" or the ever-compelling, "Sweetheart, this is a once-in-a-lifetime opportunity, I can feel it in my blood!" It's difficult to act as a wet blanket (that's how it will be perceived anyway), but there will be times when you'll just have to lend some objectivity to the moment.

It's the idea of a big score that also makes gambling so appealing. With just a turn of the cards, they can change their lives. And they do it again and again—sometimes for the better, often for the worse. But the thrill and quickening of the blood is addictive. Edna St. Vincent Millay might have written this ode to a Gemini:

My candle burns at both ends, it will not last the night.
But ah my friends, and oh my foes,
it gives a lovely light!

Now while most burn that candle at the blackjack table, within the normal bounds of vacation play, too many Twins lose too much, too often. I have personally witnessed a go-for-broke Gemini do just that—losing ten thousand dollars in less than ten minutes at a blackjack table in the Bahamas. The airplane ride back to Miami was like being on the Hindenburg *after* the crash.

Naturally, if this behavior surfaces, then groups like Gamblers Anonymous might have to step in. That's why it's important to be aware of potential problems before they develop—so you can talk about them and harness them. Remember though, I stress that astrology points out *potential problems*. Geminis may have other stable planetary influences in their charts that can impact the whole picture. In fact, we're talking about the fairly immature Gemini who's still fighting his or her own impulses. Ideally, the person who's in your bed will have gained insight into himself or herself. Those grownup Twins have enough courage to face whatever weakness needs changing.

But think about yourself. If you're a typical Capricorn, as noted before, the thought of a mate who's reckless with money will be terrifying. Or, perhaps you have strong Gemini placements in your own horoscope? Just how responsible are you with a credit card? Or does the blackjack dealer greet you by name?

Very often, due to planetary placements in our charts, we are far from what our Sun sign says we should be. In fact, it's not unheard of to find a Gemini with very strong Capricorn aspects, and this person will be far more pragmatic and conservative. Now, what happens when they meet a Capricorn with strong Gemini placements? The roles might very well be reversed!

In the end, astrology can only make us aware of our mate's potential strengths and weaknesses. None of us is perfect—we only have excellent parts of ourselves to offer each other. As for those less excellent parts, if one of them is the tendency to be totally irresponsible with money, then talk about it, understand it, structure a better way to deal with it . . . together.

Power and Gemini

The Twins are blessed with quicksilver minds that not only make them fascinating, but make them supreme manipulators. A dubious blessing indeed.

As you probably know, your Gemini is an artist at word games. In its most innocent form, you spend hours bent over a Scrabble board, or doing the Sunday crosswords together. At its worst, you'll spend those hours in a mental ping-pong game, playing against a world champion who will never admit there's a game going on!

Mind games, anyone?

Gemini's *modus operandi* in mind games is simply to keep you off guard. That way your mate keeps control of the relationship, and control is power.

You don't need words in order to play one of Gemini's most devastating mind games—keeping you unsure of where you stand. Just when you think you're on a firm footing,

Gemini nonchalantly reaches one foot behind his or her back and kicks you off balance. Mind you, this is a subtle tactic and not one with which you can easily confront them.

In the same way that Geminis use flirting to relieve boredom, they can also use it to disconcert you, to make you feel insecure, to play with your mind. A Gemini at this low level of development will get two goodies for the price of one: a) a big charge out of the excitement of your jealousy (translation: relief of boredom) b) the resulting insecurity will make you try all the harder to please your lover.

It might happen when your lover flirts a little too long with a friend of yours. On the Twins' part this is all innocent stuff. They may not even consciously admit to themselves what they're doing. But you can be sure they're testing, and waiting for the reaction they know is coming.

So you don't disappoint. You react.

You: Why were you flirting like that?

Gemini: I was just having a little fun.

You: No, what you were doing was totally embarrassing me in front of my friends.

Gemini: Nobody noticed anything. There was nothing to notice!

You: [Talking more to yourself by now] You just made me feel like an idiot.

Gemini: Believe me, sweetheart, it was completely innocent!

Funny how Gemini's quick denial still leaves room for doubt. Was it the amused look in his or her eye? The disingenuous tone? You just can't be sure if your mate is being totally honest with you. Of course, that's exactly the point of mind games, isn't it?

Aries, we know how much you hate mind games, and you won't put up with them for long. Cancer, having your lover play with your mind plays havoc with your sense of security. Scorpio, using this tactic on you is really hitting below the belt, because Gemini knows all too well how possessive and jealous you can be. But any Gemini using this tactic on Scorpio must have a death wish, too. I also know how vengeful Scorpio can be!

In truth, most of us are going to react with an array of emotions—and none of them show our best qualities. We'd simply much rather have our mates play with our bodies than our minds.

I've read astrological advice urging lovers not to show a jealous reaction. The reason? It would only give Gemini the exciting (to them!) reaction they want. Another author suggested pretending to being sexually turned on by Gemini's flirting. Then, the mate who probably feels like strangling Gemini is instead advised to whisk him or her away from temptation and take him or her home for instant sex! Male partners of a mind-playing Twin, hopelessly trying to suppress hurt and rage, might have more trouble rising to the occasion.

Oh, this kind of childish manipulation does turn you on? Then you might find it great foreplay. However, if you don't (and most of us definitely don't), then ignoring it isn't going to make it go away. How about disguising your true feelings? Well, realistically, it's pretty hard to disguise a hit and run injury. Besides, I firmly believe in being *honest*. That's what real communication is all about, otherwise it's just more game playing. Yes, I advocate communicating gentleness, humor, and love (or at least trying), but then the truth has got to come out and there must be a real and honest exchange of thinking.

The warning shot

You're about to sit down with your mate and, for the first time, discuss what's been keeping you up at night: Gemini's flirting, mind playing, and dishonesty.

We know that Gemini isn't going to readily admit pushing your buttons by flirting. You can expect that swift shuffle your lover always does, giving you half truths, twisting words, and sticking to arguments in the face of all logic. So, at this point, I will make an exception to insisting on what you *know* is the truth. Instead, let's give your lover the benefit of a big doubt.

You: Perhaps I misread what was happening. I'm sorry. [Just when your Gemini is about to throw back his or her head and crow, you add]: But that kind of thing is so open to misinterpretation. I think you have to be more aware of what you're doing in the future, okay?

Gemini: What are you so insecure about?

You: Well [you pause, tempted to deny that you're feeling insecure at all, but opting for truth], I wouldn't be insecure at all if you didn't make me feel that way.

Gemini: Darling, you're the one who's making a big deal out of nothing. I'm not doing it!

Oops, where did you take a wrong turn? Gemini has gone and done it again, shifted an adverb, rearranged a noun, and suddenly, you appear like an emotional basket case!

Remember that conversation you had with Gemini about cause and effect? About taking responsibility for one's actions? Well, your lover might have filed that away under "Later" and promptly forgot about it. It's worth repeating again, and again, until Gemini understands that being responsible is what being a grownup is all about.

Now, you're a certified adult lover, are you not? That means that you abhor mind games. If your mate continues to play with your head, then you have my full permission to be less nice. After half a dozen times, go ahead . . . get downright ugly! After all, if you wanted to feel insecure, unloved, and nervous every time a better looking body walked by, you would have stayed single!

Give till it hurts?

What happens if you're unblessed with a mate who just can't handle the truth? It all depends on how much you love this person, and how much of your blood, sweat, and tears you think he or she is worth. If this is the closest thing you've ever come to deep love, then keep trying. But you won't have a chance of curing immature Gemini's fatal flaw—love of destructive mind games—if you haven't the courage to communicate how you really feel. Geminis have to face reality and the repercussions of what they've done, your bloody, but unbowed head, for instance!

So the first truth to communicate is that you are hurting. You're hurting because of the Twins' immature mind games. Whether they indulged in them consciously or not—if they love you, they won't want to keep hurting you.

Please reread that last line. It is a truth worth repeating. Too many of us put up with destructive behavior from our mates with the rationale: what can I do, I love them! But love is not a license to mistreat someone, or for that matter, it's not a contract forcing you to keep suffering mistreatment. The line between giving unconditionally and giving unthinkingly is not always clear. When you cross that line far enough, you're into the realm of masochism. That's a place that you might want to visit, but you don't want to live there!

We're all familiar with physical abuse and how it can escalate in a relationship. But few of us consider the truth that mental abuse is still abuse . . . it can still be classified under domestic violence for both sexes! The results of it may not be as evident as a black eye, but there's still a lot of pain involved. The mate suffers a constant lowering of self-esteem, and finally, after accepting this treatment for a while, the mate can also lose his or her self-respect.

What's more, by continuing to play the victim, in a sense you're giving your lover permission to continue. What's that again, you ask? Well, this sign, above all others, knows that words don't always say what someone means. So Gemini hears you, but does your lover really believe you?

If these games continue—and you have told your lover in every language but Swahili the pain you're going through—then please think about the depth of his or her commitment. The answer you get may be all you need to think in terms of hard time limits. If telling Gemini that you've had enough wasn't enough, perhaps your mate will understand actions better than words.

Consider an ultimatum on your part. It may mean insisting on talking to a therapist if the mind games continue. It may even mean threatening to walk out the door. Whatever your ultimatum, be sure you follow through with it.

What's the alternative? Will you let yourself be mistreated for six months, a year, forever? Hey, we're talking about the person we love here . . . you! Well, you should love yourself—and you should never forget how much you owe yourself, either. You owe yourself respect and tender loving care. Most importantly, you owe yourself protection. That's right, be smart enough to keep yourself safe from avoidable pain.

So, you might have an immature partner who, because of his or her own problems, can't give you the kind of love you need. At least you can depend on yourself for some needed love and respect. Never underestimate the value of having yourself for a friend!

Stirring the pot

Too often, Gemini's love of manipulation can be used to create diversion that, in turn, will cure boredom.

"Oh, things are a little quiet around the house? Nothing good on television? Let's see what trouble I can stir up."

I used to know a Gemini who loved to play a diabolical game she called *Bull Session*. Everyone had to tell everyone else what drove them crazy about the people in the room. If you disagreed with the charge, you could yell "Bull!" Her reasoning for this sado-masochistic play was, "You'll feel better once you get it off your chest!"

Oh sure! Within minutes the room was reeling with angry cries of *Bull*—denials, hurt feelings, and feuds developed that lasted for years. Our Gemini sat placidly in the middle of all of this, her eyes lit up like Christmas, and not a bored muscle in her diabolical brain.

The Twins' tendency to *stir the pot*, to rip the scabs off old resentments, can cause havoc. Of course, they also get everyone running around in a state of emotional stress, while innocent Gemini keeps their cool . . . and their control.

If you have a Gemini who's still on that bottom rung of emotional development, who's a born instigator, don't let him or her get away with it for a minute. It's a sadistic pastime that if left to grow will eventually turn people against your mate, and, basically, your mate loves people. The last thing gregarious Gemini wants is to end up a hermit.

However, to live with other people, the Twins have to learn to respect the intelligence of others, and to realize that in many cases, that intelligence can even surpass their own! Most importantly, after Geminis learn to concentrate, they should start concentrating on other people's *feelings,* beginning with their partner's.

Gemini is surely the great communicator of the Zodiac. The enlightened among them use words to express themselves, to be creative, to give inspiration to others. Only the less evolved use words to manipulate and control. However, keep your faith, because even your Gemini will someday mature—and realize that in the human vocabulary, "love," "compassion," and "respect" are the only words that really matter.

Decanates

Take two lovers born under the sign of Gemini and they can be radically different. One is able to work for compromise in a relationship, and the other is so self-involved that a try at communication ends up being a monologue. Why are they like day and night? Studying decanates can explain a lot of the differences.

You see, every sign in the zodiac is divided into three parts. Each sign spans thirty days, each day equals one degree, and each decanate encompasses approximately ten degrees. While the first ten degrees reflect the nature of the sign itself, the other decanates have different planets as sub-rulers. So, while Gemini is generally ruled by Mercury, people can also be sub-ruled by either Venus or Uranus, dependent on the date they were born.

Is your Gemini a mirror-image of the sign? Is there a sub-ruler that will modify your lover's behavior? It's all right here . . .

May 22 to May 31

Ruled by Mercury, these Geminis are driven by a formidable intellect. They might be skilled, or even professional in writing and communications. You fell in love with their charm, humor, and ability to spin words into magic! They also have a nervousness and restlessness that keeps them in constant motion.

If they're smart, they're into tennis to work off their energy and yoga to quiet their minds. More than anyone, they need to light that candle I talked about, to meditate and escape their incessant internal chatter.

When it comes to you—and I bet you thought I would never get there—your Twin is truly pulled in two directions. He or she loves you, but balks against commitment. If you're in the beginning stages of a relationship, don't push, because Gemini will only push harder in the opposite direction.

Like Virgo, your mate tends to be a perfectionist and this can translate into being downright picky. Gently remind these Geminis of their own imperfections and they'll ease up on you.

In an argument, logic will win out. Again, don't push for an instant solution. This Gemini likes to think about the situation and analyze it. He or she will eventually come around. You can live happily ever after, but only if you're bright enough to keep your Gemini fascinated . . . anyone else is just a snack.

June 1 to June 10

You are truly fortunate! Your Gemini is sub-ruled by Venus, the planet of love and beauty. This partner will be a happy camper and make your life really enchanted if you make sure he or she has all the outlets needed to express his or her considerable talents.

Yes, this Gemini can write and even realize success as a professional author. There is a love of beauty in all its forms: decorating, design, painting. However, most of them are frustrated musicians and composers. Is your mate often thinking aloud about picking up that guitar again or getting the discipline to go back to the piano?

These Geminis will go crazy if confined to a routine of any sort. They're restless and they demand change. However, for all their talents, they can be lazy. If they're not careful, all that brilliance is going to die from neglect. You can't nag them and win. However, you can motivate them. What they need is your inspiration and applause. Given that, they won't mind a little verbal push from you now and then, and they'll thank you for it later.

June 11 to June 21

With Uranus as the sub-ruler, both sexes may leave their mark on this world. They are unconventional, restless, erratic, and many times brilliant. Metaphysics fascinates them and few are ignorant of astrology. They can excel in any of the communication fields, and they're in their element working closely with large groups of people.

Unfortunately for those who fall in love with them, these Geminis find it almost impossible to commit themselves to a monogamous relationship. Their philosophy is that life is just one big experiment, and sex is a vital part of it.

For the unevolved Geminis, what's new is fascinating and what's old is to be discarded. Unfortunately, that works with people too. They have paranoia about being fenced in. So, if you want to know where your mate is at all times—if you like things done in the same old, comfortable way—this is not the Gemini for you.

However, the more mature Geminis take their lucky partners to dizzying heights of adventure, as long as they can maintain a feeling of freedom. And if they're really in love, sometimes even the *illusion* of freedom is enough.

The Gemini Lover

May 22 to June 21

The Good

Witty

Adventurous

Charming

Versatile

Youthful

The Bad

Gossipy

Restless

Flirtatious

Capricious

Impractical

The Ugly

Caustic

Noncommittal

Deceitful

Scattered

Irresponsible

"Immature love says: 'I love you because I need you.'
Mature love says: 'I need you because I love you.'"
—Bertrand Russell

———————————————————>

Cancer

June 22 to July 22

Sex and Cancer

I'd like to introduce you to one of the most fascinating and complex lovers in the zodiac, the water sign Cancer, ruled by the Moon.

To be happily mated to a Moon Child is to realize why some biblical seer thought monogamy was the only way to live. Cancerians of both sexes love the security of a relationship. Their devotion demands your total loyalty in return. For this happiness, they will carve out a little piece of heaven for the two of you. Sensitive to your every whim, they'll make slow, artful love to you, cook gourmet meals, massage your head, run a hot tub for you . . . and totally ruin you for anyone else.

Astro-psychologists equate the Moon Child with the developmental phase of a child eight to twelve years old. That time of life when children no longer "act out" as much as discover their inner selves. They're more quiet and receptive. You'll find these qualities in your lover, too. Moon Children have the ability to reflect on themselves, to possess an inner calm and a deep empathy for others.

Sex and love are one

For Cancers, love means everything, and nothing ignites their sexual passion more than love. Not *like*, not *lust*, but *love!* Of course an unattached Cancer may have numerous affairs, but somewhere in the background Peggy Lee will always be singing "Is That All There Is?"

That's why I am going to discuss Cancer's love and sex life in the same breath.

Once in a relationship, the female Cancer blossoms like a magnolia on a hot Charleston night. The male of the species will gently instruct his lover in the fine art of sex, his vivid imagination in full play as both teacher and lover. You, the mate, become Cancer's total world—until there is an argument—then that world rocks with an 8.5 earthquake.

Again, it's important to understand that *every* sign has its strengths and weaknesses. Often, we have to live with someone for quite a while, and see them in different situations, before weaknesses make themselves known. Happily, we can prevent a potential fault line from destroying a relationship if we're aware of how our mate can self-destruct. Then we're able to do something about it when the first red flag appears.

The red flag

In Cancer's love and sex life the giving is constant and unconditional. But too often there is a high price to pay! Not only do Cancers demand total devotion, but your devotion is often tested. Is it as all-consuming as they dream? Will you love the Moon Child when he or she is clingy, depressed, a victim of his or her own moods?

A sign like Aquarius, who demands freedom, both physically and mentally, might feel claustrophobic in a relationship with our Moon Child. Even Scorpios, who will adore Cancer's constant affection, have a secretive side that doesn't allow lovers access to their every thought.

Also, many Cancers live in the highly romantic (and highly unrealistic) world of fantasy, where every heart is young and gay, love never fades, and nobody messes up a two-step. But what happens when reality visits?

The shell game

A Cancer female, who likes prolonged foreplay, is hurt because her Aries mate glanced at his watch. Will she talk to him about it? A Cancer male feels wounded because his Capricorn lover forgot his daily dose of kissing, hugging, and touching. Our Moon Children cry, "Love me, hate me, but don't ignore me!" If they *perceive* a slight on your part, their security is threatened. Don't forget that like the ocean tides, these lovers are ruled by the Moon. Their emotions run deep—are quick to surge—and they have to be careful not to drown in them! Often, insecurity clouds reality and they can become suspicious, jealous, and possessive. "Gee," their neglected lovers think, completely unaware of the demonic look in Cancer's eye, "whatever happened to my bath and shoulder rub?"

If your lover has fought for insight into his or her own psyche, if they've learned to control their emotions, then they might even communicate and talk to you about *feelings*. Sounds simple, doesn't it? However, we're learning in this book that most lovers are blocked when it comes to discussing feelings. They'd rather drive toothpicks under their fingernails than show vulnerability.

When upset, too many Moon Children allow emotions to paralyze them. Even their incredible intuition and sixth sense seem to desert them. In extreme cases, they can make themselves sick.

At this time, when communication is so vital, they're literally unable to speak. Instead, they retreat under the shell they carry around on their backs. Remember, the astrological symbol for Cancer is the crab. If they come out of the shell at all, it's to greet you with a mortally wounded look.

Now, a Pisces mate may have the intuition to *read* a Cancer without Cancer saying a word. These two signs usually have a strong psychic rapport. However, the longer the rest of us take guessing what's eating them (and they're usually eating themselves alive!) the longer Cancer will sulk. Then, when you can't take it anymore and you force a conversation, Cancers can turn defensive and angry, blaming you for making them feel so terrible it literally made them sick!

What's the martyr with you?

"Now wait just a minute," you protest, "you made *yourself* sick." In reply, Cancer retreats further inside the shell. So repeat it louder because it's the second lesson Cancer must learn. Here's the first: Lovers are not mind readers!

Cancers have to learn to communicate, because only then will they save themselves from having to learn the second lesson: Emotionally stable people do not torture themselves to the point of becoming sick.

What is Cancer trying to gain by becoming sick? Your sympathy, of course. Moon Children are easily lured into hypochondria by their need for sympathy. If you're sympathetic and worried about Cancer, then you won't be angry with them, simple as that. Or is it? If they've done something wrong, are they actually side-stepping responsibility by developing a bad back or a hernia? If you're the guilty party (in their eyes anyway) are they punishing you by making you worry about them?

If you're new at this game, then you will probably feel guilty about being a catalyst in your lover's bed-ridden state. Consciously or not, that's exactly how your mate wants you to feel. It's mind control at its most lethal.

Mommy dearest

In astrology, Cancers are believed to have very strong ties to their mothers, especially the male of the species. Maybe that accounts for the breasts being such an erogenous zone for both sexes of this sign—they miss all that sensual suckling they enjoyed.

If you're just entering into a relationship with a male Moon Child, understand that he'll always have two women in his life, you and his mother. Now, Mom may live across the street or across the ocean, it doesn't matter, he'll still be wrestling with the impact she made on his life. Whether that impact was for better or for worse remains to be seen . . . mainly by you!

If Mom lives across the street, it would be wise to try to form a good relationship with her. Hopefully she will view you as a friend and not as competition. However, if she visits without calling, walks in, takes one look at her baby boy and asks: "Oh my God, haven't you been eating?"—well, some moving companies are open on weekends!

It's very possible that your lover's emotional and physical collapse after an argument can be traced back to childhood. What happened when his parents were angry with him? Did he often become sick? Did Mommy rush to his bedside with chicken soup and forgiveness?

In order to break any destructive behavior pattern, try to show Cancers how their lack of communication plays out—the whole theatrical scenario—beginning with their feeling insecure and then:

Insecurity—illness—guilt—forgiveness.

Even if your lover can't remember this kind of passive-aggressive behavior from childhood, you can certainly point it out now. It's *not* necessary to point out how self-centered and selfish it is . . . that enlightenment will come in time. Right now, the goal is to get your lover to recognize that it's highly destructive for his or her health and your future together. *Cancer must try to change it.*

The ocean tides are controlled by the Moon, and the oceans can't do a thing about it. It's totally out of their control. However, your lover is a thinking human being and so has the power to change direction.

The more I study the endless variety of human relationships, all mirrored in the twelve signs of the zodiac, the more convinced I am that our downfall is not being able to break patterns. The majority of us even recognize our destructive behavior as we approach it—*Oh yes, here comes that pit again with the venomous snakes in the bottom, guess I'll just fall into it.* Invariably, we seem powerless to take a needed detour—to change the pattern! That's why I hope you'll study the astrological profiles of the people close to you, and help them to avoid a head-on collision with their own emotions.

At the next crisis when Cancer opts for retreat inside his or her shell, point out the pattern. Don't say something less than wonderful, like: "Sure, now you're going to act like a big baby and refuse to talk. What's going to happen next? Are you going to get sick and call Mommy?" Ouch! If your lover didn't have plans for a 102-degree fever, that last line might cause it. No, I stress that you must *come from love.* Cancer, more than any other sign, will appreciate that caring and respond to it. So, when your Cancer is emotionally upset, talk about the possibility of him or her making a conscious decision to filter emotions through intellect. In other words—put the brakes on emotions and reason it out.

Mommy/lover dearest

The Cancer female also has a strong tie to her mother, but less intense than her male counterpart. Just watch out for her tendency to *become* the mother herself! Like any other trait, this is wonderful when you're feeling down and want to be babied. But after a while her maternal attentions can become stifling. She wants to eat, sleep, and drink you. She wants to know that you're thinking about her all the time. She's a bundle of insecurities that demand constant reassurance.

So, your female Moon Child needs every ounce of emotional security you can give. Sagittarius, that means your lady might not understand your desire to go off on your own. Explain that at times you need your space as much as she needs to share hers, then go out of your way to include her as much as possible in what you do.

Virgo, you might relate more to Cancer's deep-rooted insecurities, but Aries, you should sign up for some intensive sensitivity training before becoming involved with a Moon Child. Your hit-and-run bluntness can leave a lover gasping on the corner while you, oblivious to it all, swerve off in another direction.

Gemini, your flirting will cause Cancer to become more jealous than a scorned Scorpio. You won't hear about it, of course, but you'll catch a glimpse of it as your lover retreats inside her shell. Watch out for that Full Moon, the time when Cancers are at their most emotional, and be prepared for an even more intense reaction.

To create the basis for a strong relationship with a Cancer female, take the time to build up her self-image. The more confident she becomes about herself and your love, the less possessive she'll be.

In time, both sexes will express the more positive qualities of their opposite sign, Capricorn. This earth sign isn't as needy as our Moon Child (some lovers of Capricorn might wish they were a lot more needy!)—but they are definitely more independent. As Cancer lovers mature, their egos will toughen up, and they'll stop simply *reacting emotionally* to every experience. Instead, they'll start playing more of a dominant role in their own lives. Not in the old passive-aggressive way, but as adults communicating what they need without creating a fever to get it.

Read more about Capricorn and you'll see how this sign's positive qualities will help your lover become a more secure adult. Think of it as an astrological journey into adulthood—and you get to be the guide!

Psychic sponges

Both sexes are so sensitive that they soak up your vibrations like a sponge and feed them back to you intensified three-fold. However, just because they're sensitive to your vibrations doesn't mean they always interpret them correctly.

A Moon Child I know is undergoing a trauma because she's gained weight lately (Cancerians retain water and have to watch their weight). Her new husband innocently remarked, "Perhaps you should exercise more."

Well, our hyper-sensitive lover isn't buying the *innocent* part. She's convinced that her weight gain really bothers him. Not only that, she feels it's responsible for his recent lack of interest in sex. Perhaps she's right, but will she talk to him about it? It could be that his lack of passion reflects a totally different problem. Besides, if she admits that she's put on too much weight, why doesn't she simply go to a gym and take it off?

In response to that question, I received the martyred look of all time as our Moon Child hissed, "No, I don't even want sex anymore—he's ruined it for me!" (On second thought, maybe it wasn't she who hissed . . . could it have been those snakes in the bottom of the pit, hmmm?)

But our crablike Cancer has definitely side-stepped responsibility. Instead of doing something positive, like finding out if her weight is the culprit, she opts to move her wounded psyche inside her shell and suffer in silence. But you can bet that her wounded eyes speak volumes.

The pity is that her new husband is Aquarius, an air sign who feeds everything through his intellect, not his emotions. He's not one to give our Cancer the babying she wants. So unless she manages to act maturely and communicate (or just go to that gym), she's making a very uncomfortable bed that she might lie in all by her lonesome.

We all need our daily doses of TLC. Some of us get enough and some of us go around with our noses pressed up against the candy store window. The saddest are the people who are getting more than their daily allowance, but are so driven by their own insecurities that they can't even see it.

Seeing is believing

One way to get Moon Children to appreciate what they've got, namely you, is to deliver your love in the way they crave. Gemini, you love to *talk* about it. Virgo, you love to *listen*. Scorpio, you want someone's love expressed in *intense sexuality*.

Cancer wants love delivered with kissing, holding, and cuddling. You must know by now that Cancers are not only the most devoted of mates, they are also the most tactile of lovers. Touching is almost more important than sex itself. Well, just as important anyway. If they don't get enough of it, they will interpret your behavior as a lack of interest, or worse, rejection! That will cause insecurity, and you know the rest of the famous shell game.

So, remember, in order to get Cancer to hold you in a looser emotional grip, hold the Moon Child as tightly as you can. Over time, as you hold this lover in your arms, you will bring him or her closer—literally and figuratively—to your heart.

Money and Cancer

When it comes to needing financial security, Cancer gives Taurus a serious run for the money. Those born under this sign work hard for their bank accounts, basically for the same reason they cling tenaciously to a relationship—security!

Cancers have a common dream: to wrap themselves in a mink-lined security blanket and watch their money grow. Stocks, okay, bonds, even better! The really security-minded keep money in more than one bank account. If possible, they invest in real estate and land, because the only thing better than knowing they're secure is evidence of it in lots of green acreage.

Cancers who stay at home (today they could be either male or female) are still intensely concerned with financial security. They want to know their mates are out there working to feather the nest. We're talking about pure down feathers, baby!

For a sign like Pisces, romantic love mixed with capital gains is not exactly poetry. However, what's romantic and what's not is very subjective. For the *very* romantic sign of Cancer, loving someone without giving him or her financial security is paramount to spousal abuse. Love, marriage, financial security—Cancer never wants one without the other.

A need to succeed

Their overwhelming need to feel secure drives their ambition. They know that only in a position of authority can they relax and no longer feel threatened.

When they finally reach that corner office—furnished with wall-to-wall prestige and perks—they can really begin to enjoy their talents. For Cancers, that means using their profound intuition to give the public exactly what it wants, or to make it *think* it wants it, anyway. Since this sign rules mass consciousness and the public, and they have an uncanny feel for what will sell, success usually comes sooner than later. Many a Moon Child has excelled in the fields of advertising and public relations.

Money is recognition

Cancers may wear love on their sleeves, but they keep their ambitions well hidden. Most people never suspect how important money is until they really get to know them.

However, astrology gives us an interesting insight: money is not only important to Cancers for the security it provides, it's also necessary because it enables them to *shine* among friends. Yes, this sign, so retiring and often shy, still yearns to be in the spotlight. The same way the Moon reflects the light of the sun, so your lover seems to radiate in the admiration of others. (Perhaps it's the theatrical sign of Leo on the cusp of their second house, which rules finances!)

Also, what people think of them is very important. That's why money is pure magic—it makes feelings of insecurity disappear! Money gives a guaranteed ego boost that Moon Children don't get often enough.

Money is love

When Cancers love someone, they automatically want to protect and take care of that person. Nothing is too much to ask when their hearts are involved. Nicest of all is that you usually *never* have to ask. Cancers are so intuitive they not only guess what you want, they know the second color of your choice!

At the same time they're working to protect your financial security, they're reveling in recognition. Your mate will take great pleasure in buying expensive gifts—gifts that tell the world not only of their love for you, but of their success in being able to afford it in the first place.

Pisces, you may not relate to Cancer's need to concentrate their efforts on secure finances, but you'll appreciate how your compassionate lover uses money. Although a firm believer in the credo "charity begins at home," once they're secure, Cancers take pleasure in helping others. Remember, this sign is like a psychic sponge, soaking up everyone's vibrations. It makes sense that they'd have an immediate emotional response to the needs of others.

Never on impulse

Are both sexes fairly cautious in spending money? Well, at certain times they can even be tight. This is a strange quirk in the Cancerian nature that pops up, I am happy to report, infrequently. It's usually triggered when they read about a financial crisis in some remote part of the globe. Shares of Yak butter dropped in Tibet. Yikes! Are my stocks safe? Have the pork bellies bellied up? It might take a while for them to settle down and realize everything is secure. Until they do, frightened Cancer could start cutting back on cheese dip.

For the most part, though, this sign is very giving. They're more than willing to spend money on what *they* love best . . . their homes and loved ones. Like Taurus, they take the long view and expect what they purchase to be around as long as they are. You can expect to be indulged royally every now and then; Cancers will even spend money on something beautiful and foolish just for you . . . but their hearts won't be in it.

Capricorn, while you're a great admirer of Cancer's thrifty nature and respect their business success, it's you, Taurus, who will dream about happiness ever after with a Moon Child. Since Cancers are the last to raise their hands when someone asks: "Who wants to spend a lot of hard-earned money in a totally irresponsible way?"—a great impulse buyer like you, Leo, might be left hungry for a really satisfying shopping binge. Sagittarius, you won't fall in love with Cancer's bent for security, because the Moon Child lives for the future and you live for today. Oh yes, I musn't forget Gemini: your relationship may prove to be financially beneficial (Cancer rules the second house of money in Gemini's chart), but you may still grow impatient with Cancer's inability to go with the flow, which to Gemini means spending money like the well is never going to run dry.

Actually, because they're so shrewd in amassing money, Cancers usually keep the well filled to the top. Again, like Taurus, they not only have the ability to make money, they have the talent to triple their original investment.

On the debit side

Having money still won't convince Cancer to remove the umbrella stand from inside the front door. Moon Children know that rainy day is coming just as sure as Nostradamus predicted the floods! It's that irrational fear that they might be caught with their portfolios down that makes them work all the harder to stash it away.

Their goal is to make money quickly, retire early, and have all the time in the world to play. Perfectly reasonable dream, don't you think? To this end, Moon Children work diligently—but they won't be having Chinese dinners delivered to the office. They enjoy their home, and you in it, much too much to stay away for long.

I only mean they will bring their work home with them. When hot on the trail of money and sweet recognition, your lover doesn't know the meaning of *relax*. In the same way they're attached to your relationship—body, heart, mind, and soul—Cancers will tenaciously attach their all to the project at hand. Expect them to wear a path in the carpet—worrying, planning, plotting—until you demand that they get some sleep.

Let's talk about it

Yes, fear is a great motivator, but if *you* fear that Cancer's ambition is getting out of hand, and it's taking some of the joy out of your lives, then I hope you'll be motivated to talk about it. When the round-the-clock drive for financial security upsets the emotional equilibrium between you, things have to be put in balance.

Balance in life (remember Libra's eternal search) is an art form in itself. With your help, Cancer will learn to balance work with play. As lover, partner, and friend, it's up to you to get your Moon Child to stop and smell the bloomin' roses!

How do you do that? With Cancers you don't have to be the great psychological manipulator. You don't have to plead or coerce them into relaxing. You simply have to tell them it's *you* who needs the diversion. Remember, you're the light of their life and they'll do just about anything to make you happy . . . even skip a deposit!

Is that all there is?

Remember the song "Is That All There Is?" by Peggy Lee? It's what Cancers start humming when real love isn't in their lives. In the same way, they'll work their tails off if there's someone to share a joint bank account. If not, the thrill is definitely gone. They can become millionaires, and, alas, it will be an empty success.

Isn't it nice to know that your lover has the talent and ambition to make money, but only *your love* can make him or her feel like a million?

Power and Cancer

We've learned a lot about Moon Children: how they're too often controlled by their emotions, and how they can use those emotions to control their mates. As I have pointed out, whoever has control in the relationship has the power!

Now, there are cynics who insist that all couples engage in constant power plays. However, I believe it's possible for lovers to share dual controls—and cooperate in the best way to steer their relationship. Continuing this mechanical metaphor, what happens when the relationship goes off course from time to time? Well, every relationship is constantly being tested, and mature lovers use *communication* to find their way home.

That's what I hope this book inspires—the motivation to really communicate. To share what's on your mind and in your heart. It's definitely a no pain, no gain situation. It may not happen overnight, but you're not doing anything for the next twenty years, are you?

Now, in the case of Cancer, the power play may be more subtle and harder to detect. When Cancer plays the victim and attempts (consciously or not) to manipulate your feelings, it's to make you feel sympathetic toward him or her, or—let's be totally honest here—*guilty.*

Packing for a guilt trip

We've all watched children manipulate grownups with the skill of Machiavelli. Well, just as they can twist Mommy into a guilt-ridden pretzel, so Cancers can employ the same childlike manipulations in a relationship.

Cancer: The Victim.

You: The Heartless Lover.

Supporting players: Guilt and More Guilt.

It's just a more passive-aggressive version of a temper tantrum. If previous lovers have allowed your mate to get away with it, then Cancer is no doubt an expert at putting you on the defensive. The female Moon Child may add a flood of tears to heighten the drama. The male might miss work because of a bad stomach. If they really concentrate, they can even work up a good case of ulcers! After many hours (days?) on this uncomfortable guilt trip, you can react in a few ways:

1. You begin to feel a lack of psychic freedom. That's something not too many of us even think about possessing, until someone takes it away. Who was the first person to raise his or her face to the heavens, clutch his or her fist, and cry, "I need my space!" It had to be the Aquarius lover of a Moon Child.

If the feeling gets uncomfortable enough, you may decide to:

2. Become angry, especially if you feel that you're being manipulated. Somehow you let your own emotional response get carried away. (Leo, are you listening?) The next thing you know, the room is filled with passionate cries of hurt feelings, rantings, and a general emotional deluge. Nothing is accomplished except the stock of Kleenex goes up on Wall Street!

3. If you feel guilty because you believe that somehow you're at fault, then you might be willing to do anything to stop the emotional upheaval. (Pisces, this one's for you!) Will you apologize for something you never meant? Of course! Forgive Cancer for something he or she did and hasn't yet owned up to—and may never admit to in your lifetime? Naturally!

You get the idea. By assuming the role of victim, Cancer has succeeded in manipulating you while avoiding the responsibility of what he or she did wrong in the first place. And remember what I asked: Is your lover really punishing you for something they think *you* did wrong, but they don't have the courage to talk about?

Just as the toddler makes a note in his or her psychological database that Mommy or Daddy gave in exactly two minutes and one-tenth of a second after the tantrum, so your Cancer mate will use the same tactic the next time he or she feels threatened.

Up until now, your lover has played the victim, hoping it would not only bring sympathy, but all the affection, love, and passion he or she craves. But honestly now, does loving a victim turn anyone on? Well, perhaps someone who walks around the house in black leather and keeps whips in the garage. However, for most partners, it's a definite sexual turn off.

Virgo, I know that your healing and compassionate nature is a comfort to an upset Cancer. But how often does that comfort turn to sex? Probably not often. It's difficult to segue from being maternal—no matter what your sex—to being a passionate lover. Red-rimmed eyes lead more often to separation than orgasms. Libra, you'll take a long look at Cancer in victim mode and start looking for someone else. As for you Aries, Cancer's very emotional dependence and stance of victim might totally backfire and bring out the bully in you. However, a Scorpio partner might have just the protective instincts Cancer needs, and also the investigative talents to find out what's going on under that shell!

If you've played this scenario a few dozen times, the wear and tear on your own psyche will begin to show. It's time to talk sense to your lover, but please wait until he or she has calmed down. You might think that's simple logic, but it's surprising how many people don't have the control to wait, and when Cancer's emotionally upset, trying to communicate is like shouting down a wind tunnel!

All right, now that we're relatively calm, let's tiptoe into the danger zone.

Love for sale

Be prepared for Cancer to slip into an immediate state of denial. How could your lover mistreat you, because—as your lover will be quick to point out—he or she loves you so much!

However, as I have shown, an insecure Cancer's love can quickly become smother-love, and the emotional price you pay is way too high.

I remember when a female Virgo friend showed me a poem sent to her by a male Cancer lover. It went something like, "You are the trip I did not take . . . you are my blue Italian skies . . . you are the book I did not write . . ." and so on, listing all the wonders she represented to him. At first glance, it was oh so sweet and touching! But somehow Virgo was unsettled by it and couldn't figure out why. Let's read between the lines:

Cancer was telling his lover that she not only meant the world to him, but that she *was* his world! He was totally dependent on her to replace everything he never had or might never have. Virgo felt uncomfortable because she was feeling the weight of responsibility that came with this.

Now, we all want to be needed, but do we want to be needed to that extreme? It's the difference between being needed like a warm coat or like a lifejacket! And isn't it healthier and even more of a compliment to be wanted by someone who can also survive very well without us?

Yes, there is definitely a certain amount of blackmail inherent in that kind of love. It says, "because I love you so much, you have to love me back, no matter what!"

Cancer: How can you upset me by becoming angry with me? I love you so much.

You: [Rejecting the immediate feeling of guilt] I'm not saying this to upset you. I love you, too.

Cancer: Great, then everything's all right?

You: No! Sweetheart, we have to discuss the lack of communication between us.

Cancer: Wait a minute, I think we communicate!

You: [Gently] No, we role play. You behave like a victim and I react like a guilty criminal—

Cancer: [Interrupting] I would *never* make you feel guilty. I love you!

You: I know, but you're not loving me the way I need to be loved, and that's what we have to talk about.

That's a good start. However, right now Cancer is experiencing a high level of insecurity. It's that moment of fight or flight when they usually want to disappear inside the shell they carry on their backs. This is when you have to freeze the frame on the scenario—stop their emotions in mid-flight and say—"Now, don't let your hurt feelings take you away from me, talk to me!"

Victims are not sexy

Very, very gently (especially if it's a Full Moon!) start communicating by relating how you feel. Talk about the habit your Cancerian developed by playing the victim. When Cancers become indignant and tell you that being a victim is the last thing they want to do, believe it. Cancer knows only too well that being seen as a victim is just a little sexier than dandruff. So simply explain that it *seems that way*, and it's making you miserable.

Explain that you would be far happier if both of you talked things out. Ask what the problem is. What unhappiness are they not talking about? Have you made them feel rejected in some way? Have you hurt them without realizing it? Let your love communicate that's it's all right to trust you with their feelings. Repeat at intervals how much you care about them. Make sure that love is in your voice and in your eyes. Lean in close to them and let your body language speak as well.

Okay, now take two steps back, a deep breath (and a stiff drink if necessary), and give your lover time to recover. The Moon Child is probably in a state of shock, horrified about being seen by you—the person he or she most wants to impress—as a victim. Ah, what better motivation to change behavior than a blow to their vanity! If you've done it right, you have communicated with love and sincerity. You have given your lover the *gentle* encouragement to bring repressed emotions and dark thoughts into the light. They have begun to communicate honestly, to confide, to trust, and are actually out of that damn shell for the first time since Labor Day! Miraculously, Cancer has gotten the message at last: all the love they have ever wanted from you can be theirs—without having to burst one single solitary ulcer to get it.

It may take a long while before your lover changes, but then again, it might not. Each individual is different, a complexity of many planets and aspects. It all depends on how mature and introspective a person is. How much courage does he or she have to confront the unknown—the unknown of his or her own nature?

In a positive light, Cancer has a lot more courage than many other lovers. Think about it: how many other signs are brave enough to wear their hearts on their sleeves? Not many. As a matter of fact, that might very well be the ultimate test of courage in any relationship. So take your time helping this compassionate, sensitive creature. After all, every victim, real or imagined, deserves to be rescued by someone who truly loves them.

Decanates

Take two lovers born under the sign of Cancer and they can be radically different. One is able to work for compromise in a relationship, the other is so self-involved that a try at communication ends up being a monologue. Why are they like day and night? Studying decanates can explain a lot of the differences.

You see, every sign in the zodiac is divided into three parts. Each sign spans thirty days, and each day is one degree. The decanates each represent ten degrees. While the first ten degrees reflect the nature of the sign itself, the other decanates have different planets as sub-rulers. So, while Cancers are ruled by the Moon, they can also be ruled by Pluto or Neptune, dependent on the date they were born.

Is your Moon Child a mirror-image of the sign? Is there a sub-ruler that will modify your lover's behavior? It's all right here . . .

June 22 to July 1

Your Cancer is ruled by the Moon, and that means your mate has an urgent need for love. To secure that love, the Moon Child will totally indulge you. This lover can cook up a storm, and they seem to have a sixth sense (most have some psychic ability) that tells them how to please you. When they're happy, they're outgoing and generous. Their myriad talents never cease to amaze you. However, watch out for their extreme sensitivity fueled by a deep-rooted feeling of insecurity. Their thin skins bruise easily. They can nurse a grudge forever or even longer! Unless they learn to think objectively, they can easily become a victim of their emotions. Read everything I wrote in the last chapter about helping your lover to communicate what's hurting, because you can't help him or her fix it if you don't know what's broken!

July 2 to July 11

The emotional range of this Moon Child makes our first Cancer seem almost rigid! Sub-ruled by Pluto, your lover is deeply intense, can be possessive, and definitely demands privacy. Don't dig into this Cancer's secrets until he or she is ready to share (holding your breath is not advised!). It's easy to be in awe of his or her penetrating intellect. Combined with psychic ability, the effect is fascinating. You may not hear it articulated, because emotions are not easily expressed, but believe me, your relationship means everything to this Pluto-influenced Cancer. Also, if you're just beginning this partnership, find out about your lover's feelings toward his or her mother. If it's healthy, full speed ahead. If not, think twice, because it will definitely affect your Moon Child's relationship with you.

July 12 to July 22

This lover, sub-ruled by the planet Neptune, is the dreamer of the three. Your mate may be fascinated by metaphysics and probably has bookshelves crammed with every tome from the Buddhist Sutras to Madame Blavatsky. Do you sometimes have a hard time understanding what makes this Cancer tick? Don't worry, your lover is just as much in the dark. These Moon Children are enigmatic even to themselves—emotional, psychic, and highly romantic. They can also be quite artistic, with a talent that has elusive, spiritual dimensions to it. Perhaps their biggest fault is being too passive and just letting life happen to them. If you're an inspiration for them to act on their dreams, you will be the perfect partner. Your friends might think there's something a little strange about your lover, and you know that's true—wonderfully strange and strangely wonderful!

The Cancer Lover

June 22 to July 22

The Good

Sentimental

Sensitive

Intuitive

Nurturing

Creative

The Bad

Clinging

Thin-skinned

Moody

Possessive

Impressionable

The Ugly

Smothering

Victimized

Fearful

Passive-aggressive

Irrational

"Will you still love me when I'm sixty-four?"
—Paul McCartney

Leo

July 23 to August 23

Sex and Leo

Leo is the zodiac's most dramatic and generous lover. Like their ruler, the Sun, Leos warm the bodies and souls of all they touch. The astrological symbol for Leo is the lion—proud, regal, and luxuriating in its own power.

While it's true that I am concentrating on problems encountered with less mature lovers, it's not exactly a black and white situation. As you might suspect, we're all fascinating combinations of the mature and immature, the wise and the foolish.

No sign better than Leo illustrates how mature lovers become regal queens and kings —and if they're immature—royal pains in the astrophere.

Leos love the drama of love. They consider romance their royal birthright—along with being the center of everyone's attention. While Jacqueline Onassis used her leonine appeal to capture two of the world's most powerful men, other Leos have to be content with drama on a lesser scale. However, famous or not, you can be sure that in sex with Leo, the spotlight in the bedroom will be shining fifteen-hundred watts on stage center!

Yes, inside every Lion and Lioness is a big piece of juicy ham. They're always actors at heart. During a long-running sexual performance they project the essence of love, generosity, charm, and charisma . . . and lucky you has been chosen as an audience of one! Remember though, performers are sensitive about their talents, and they take every review to heart. When humiliated in any way, the Lion becomes as despairing as an actor with a two-minute walk-on.

It's no laughing matter

Some of Leo's deepest wounds are the result of an innocent tease. Both sexes have great humor, but never when the joke is at their expense. Write down these words and memorize them: "Never, *never* step on Leo's dignity!"

Sagittarius, you lived to regret that hilarious comment about your Lion's premature roar the other night. Aries, you actually delivered a quip to the Lioness containing the word "cellulite"?

"But," you protest, "it was all in fun!"

Yes, *you* thought it was funny. It might even have been funny to the cast of *Saturday Night Live*, but not to this proud sign that takes itself very seriously. Naturally, if Leo's ego is bruised, the Lion seeks reassurance, and that leaves him or her wide open to the one temptation he or she cannot resist . . . *flattery!*

Flattery will get you everywhere

There may not be an applause sign over the bed, but notice how Leos radiate when complimented on a sexual performance. They want to feel unique and special. Take them passionately, take them impulsively, take them in the back seat of your father's Chevy—but *never* take them for granted.

Western psychologists tell us that if someone has a big ego, it's because they're super confident, and all that self-adoration has gone to their head. However, Eastern philosophers believe the more confident someone becomes, the less ego they have. According to this theory, giant egos are just working overtime to make up for hidden insecurities.

Whichever way you look at it, if your Leo isn't mature, you can expect to face major ego problems. Leo's ego needs to be tended to, stroked, and nourished on a regular schedule. Depending upon his or her maturity level, this could turn into a feeding frenzy!

I have been telling you how astro-psychologists equate signs of the zodiac with a child's developmental phase. Fascinating stuff, isn't it? Well, Leo represents the teenager from twelve to eighteen years. That's adolescence with all its self-awareness, self-absorption, and posturing.

So, although our lover (like his or her fire sign cousin, Aries) is the outward image of inner confidence, in actuality, the egos of less mature Leos should be stamped "Handle With Care—Fragile!" If bruised, intentionally or not, they'll lose their star quality and Leo's famous *joie de vivre* will be no more. They're simply out of their element when they're not in the spotlight (a metaphor, of course, for their ruler, the Sun!) We all know the image of the unhappy, frustrated lion, stalking back and forth in the shadows of his cage, swishing his tail and dreaming of escape!

The eternal romantic

Gemini, you may yearn for a relationship with a million surprises, but Leo dreams of a union that's eternally romantic. Watch your mate's eyes during an old classic love film. Leo will be totally lost in the romance of it all.

But what happens when their eyes finally focus? After all, there are a few million moments in life that are less than romantic—all those memories we'd like to drag to the trash compactor! If your lover hasn't grown up and grown past romantic *illusion,* then every relationship is bound to disappoint.

Am I talking about having a relationship devoid of romance? Bite your tongue! It's just that Leos must learn the difference between love and romance. Love will hopefully stay constant, while romance fluctuates in a relationship because it's vulnerable to outside influences—midnight toothaches, wet diapers, and corporate downsizing, to name a few.

While Pisces will relate to Leo's need for romance and feed it on a banquet scale, practical Capricorn may leave Leo hungry for more. I urge every lover of Leo to *think* romantically. The minute Leos reach their "routine" threshold and their eyes glaze over, bring out the airplane tickets to palm trees and piña coladas. If you can't afford the luxury package, there are romantic walks on the beach, impromptu sex on the whatever, whenever.

At the same time, in your role as guru/lover you have to teach Leo a few lessons on surviving routine. Even the most romantic relationships must live through periods of more grays than crimson.

Now, with Aries as a partner, these two fire signs have a wild way of escaping routine. When things get dull, they just start a rip-roaring fight. You know, one of those classics that last for days with CDs flying, tears spilling, and a passionate making-up party.

It takes two

What do signs other than passionate Aries do? If they take my advice, they get the royal prince or princess to start contributing to their sex life. Often, Leos display more than a touch of arrogance. Instead of making an effort to bring variety to bed, they regally lie back and wait to be sexually served. Perhaps it's that star complex that makes the Lion lethargic about sexual innovation. After all, when you've been playing to packed houses, why change the performance?

If you're a Scorpio—and not about to pay homage at court on a nightly basis—you might talk to your lover about initiating sex once in a while. You might even share a few of your own sexual fantasies as incentive. As for Leo's preferences, both sexes love foreplay, while the Lion prefers oral sex when *he* is on the receiving end. (I wonder, do you have to feed him grapes at the same time?) Actually, the Lioness also loves oral sex, so with two lusty lions in bed, that spotlight may burn all night!

Now, back to the pull of romantic illusion on our less than grownup Lions (shall we call them cubs?). They may try to recapture what they call love, but what they *really* mean is the first intense, passionate throes of romance.

It's during those longings when flattery slithers in to seduce our less than mature Leo. While capricious Gemini may be tempted by someone's wit, or aesthetic Libra may fall for someone's good looks, it's blatant, shameless flattery that will stroke the Leo's tender ego.

Then, having convinced themselves they were being sorely taken for granted—and isn't this new audience member terrific and *flattering?*—they may exercise something else they consider their regal right: that old double standard.

On the prowl

Leos are notoriously possessive, and demand fidelity. Expect them to become crazed with jealousy if they suspect you're straying from the castle. Here are the rules: you'll be 100 percent faithful at all times, no ifs, ands, or butts. (No, that was not a misspelling.)

But what about *their* fidelity?

Leos who feel unappreciated are ripe for straying. Once again, they're entranced by romance—different background music; the scent of new skin; and those steamy, languid glances. They succumb. They blink. It's over. So poor, illusion-starved Leo has to hunt it down again . . . and again . . . and again.

If Leo is really less evolved (we're heading toward primate level here), you might find your lover lusting after *showier* specimens. The stereotype of the gorgeous blonde whose IQ hovers just above that of a radish is a favorite arm decoration. So what if you can hear the equipment rattle when she shakes her head; who's listening anyway? The Lioness may prefer the male equivalent: tall, dark, older, and preferably wealthy. This lady wants to be paid homage to with expensive presents and submissive adoration.

Yes, the shakier the ego, the more Leos need to have what they consider the perfect image (as conceived by Hollywood) by their side.

Let yourself go

Let yourself go in a relationship with Leo and it could be fatal. I am talking about letting yourself get out of shape. Lovers allow this to happen and then wonder why their partners stop lusting after them. This is a bigger problem for Leos because of their egos. Remember, with Leo (as with the demanding Aries ego) you're in a unique *ménage a trois* situation: You, your Leo, and your Leo's ego! Your lover cares what people think. A lot! Being so self-conscious, Leos are anxious to project just the right image.

In fact, you represent far more to your mate than just a partner—you're a reflection of his or her very worth. So, if you're half of this star package, you'd better believe that how you look is very important. Ironically, like that other fire sign Aries, Leos are not shy about telling their lovers just how much *they* have to shape up. (Is the unspoken threat "shape up or ship out"?)

Female mates of Leos should be prepared to meet with a dollop of chauvinism, too. The Lion will fully expect you to stay in sexy shape, while he (more likely than the Lioness) loosens the notches on his belt. Just another double standard courtesy of the house. If this happens, ask your lover if he would join you in the exercise program of his choice. Say that you would love his company because he makes things so much more fun (true), and he could use *just a little* tightening up (keep a straight face)! Now, if this doesn't work, don't wait longer than a hard swallow to talk about the weight problem. Nicely, gently, and with the same sensitivity that you would appreciate.

Let's get real

It's one thing that Leo wants you to look your best, it's another if Leo sees your best as decidedly worse as time goes by.

I'm not talking about people who drastically let themselves go. Those cases of neglect reflect a deep unhappiness. I'm talking about the rest of us who diet from time to time, work out, eat organically, dream orgasmically, but still watch little maps of Yugoslavia sneak in around our eyes. Time marches on. But we certainly don't want to live in fear that our lover might abandon us for a firmer thigh or a thicker hairline.

This is more of a hazard for mates of the Lion than for mates of the Lioness. I'm afraid we're still stuck with the "youth is beautiful and age had better be rich" syndrome in this country. While some Lionesses won't mind if looks are replaced with wealth (remember Onassis?), most immature Leos become decidedly unhappy once the bloom is off their Rosie.

If you even suspect that your Leo is that immature and superficial, then you might want to bring it out into the open. If a meaningful talk confirms your worst fears, pack up your Weight Watcher dinners and find someone with a better set of values.

Leo is never having to say you're sorry

Now back to more mature lovers who have conquered the need to form a coast-to-coast fan club. They love you, and you know how incredible it is to be on the receiving end of that fiery Leo love. However, you can't get away from the fact that your mate's flirting, and constant need for attention, pushes the envelope.

So, you talk about it and Leo tells you that you're hallucinating. Your lover gets angry and defensive. Unlike Taurus, the Bull who sulks and smolders, Leo's anger can erupt on a dime, with a great display of dramatics. However, if you're expecting gentle communication to ultimately make a difference, you're in for a pleasant surprise. You want an apology, too? Well, maybe a reality check is needed. Leo loves saying three little words and dreads having to say three others. "I love you" comes as easily as breathing. "I am sorry" is a little harder than undergoing an anal probe. It's that touch of arrogance again. Does royalty apologize? However, expect Leo to apologize in a dozen different ways: an impromptu dinner out, a gift for no reason, a kiss so long and passionate that your knees dissolve into Silly Putty.

Always remember that, being the performer he or she is, Leo's more than capable of growing into the most challenging of roles. As maturity evolves, you'll notice them expressing more of the positive traits of their opposite sign, Aquarius. These positive qualities are enough to inspire us all: unpossessive, non-materialistic, non-egotistical, sexually experimental, mentally inquisitive, liberated, socially and politically active, and Aquarius would no more treat someone as a sex object than vote Republican! However, make no mistake, this detached cerebral air sign also needs many of Leo's fiery and passionate qualities to fulfill its own potential.

So, if you love this larger-than-life, dramatic Leo, and if your existence seems to shrink when they're not around, forgive them their egos. If Eastern philosophers are right, and a humongous ego is just a red flag for insecurity, then Leo needs your tender loving therapy more than anyone.

Without sacrificing your own spirit or independence, make your lover feel adored, secure, important, needed, and respected. Do it 365 days a year and twice on birthdays. Then watch that famous ego shrink to a manageable size. Smaller, smaller—until one day your lover takes a giant step to the right and actually invites you into the spotlight.

If you can manage that you will have proven yourself to be a true miracle worker . . . or just someone very much in love.

Money and Leo

When it comes to money, Leo is the master (and mistress) of illusion. If Leos are in the money, they're incredibly generous—always ready to pick up the check or extend a loan to a friend (they don't have to be asked either). They give to charity and buy gifts like every day is Christmas. Then a catastrophe happens that you might not hear about on the eleven o'clock news, but it's earth-shattering nevertheless—Leo is broke.

Your lover's truly optimistic nature will help him or her get through a lot of blue Mondays. However, like most of us, Leos will sometimes suffer stress that outweighs optimism. It's then they weave their magic to create the illusion that everything is just fine!

Pride goeth before

It's their pride, of course. It just won't let Leos show how much they're hurting. Even though bills are piling up (including an eight-year-old demanding back allowance and threatening to sue)—our lover will foolishly look the other way and keep picking up restaurant checks. The really immature will get themselves seriously in debt, before reality cuts their charge cards in half.

A Leo client of mine admitted that despite terrible financial straits, he had just purchased a Mercedes. Why in the name of sanity did he do that?

"I have to maintain this lifestyle," he explained. "That way I'm forced to make the money to keep it up!"

So our Lion was too afraid to downsize, fearful that once there he'd never climb back out of the hole. If this masquerade continues for too long, proud Leo may follow the downhill path of other foolish Lions straight into bankruptcy (isn't it interesting they call a pack of lions a pride?). Too many become shells of their former confident selves. They don't want people to see them as less than they were. Less, in *their* minds, means less cash in their pocket and a lot less confidence. They begin avoiding people, rejecting friendships and even lovers . . . afraid of being rejected themselves.

Unfortunately, during their free-spending days, Leos acquire a lot of hangers-on, only to take advantage of their famous generosity. In return, they flatter Leo's ego. Of course, these fair-weather friends disappear when Leo's Sun dips behind a momentary monetary cloud. It's no wonder that when times are tough, Leos feel abandoned and worthless— they let themselves be taken in by pretty worthless people.

Taking money worries to heart

When it comes to a simple cold, the Lioness moans like Camille in the throes of consumption. When the Lion has a stomach ache, his roar can be heard in Milwaukee! However, when the malady is a really serious money problem, Leo pulls down the shades and suffers in silence.

Because this sign rules the heart, keeping all that stress inside is not a good idea—it can manifest in a heart-stopping array of problems. During these times your lover needs to communicate, to talk about it, angst over it, curse the Gods of Overdrawn. That frustration must get into the open.

Of course, we know that Leo's money is the least of why we love them. Money didn't create that fabulous humor, generosity, or the incredible way they have of turning the mundane into the magical! We have to tell Leos that truth, and convince them they're more than their designer labels. Stoke up that optimism and get them to renew their solar-powered energy. Leo's energy is what draws good luck to them, and once it's fully charged, there's little that can stop them.

When we're suffering from lack of funds, who do we want to blame first? Too often, it's the friend who reminds us we're being *challenged,* that our misfortune is just one of life's little tests. We don't want to hear it. We only want someone to commiserate with us.

But nevertheless it's true—we *are* being challenged. After all, doesn't it make sense that without a few road-blocks in our way, we'd never exercise the muscles in our brains, our street smarts, our ingenuity, our talents?

Now, when your lover's suffering money troubles and going crazy trying to find a way out, explain that finding a way out is good—going crazy is not. As a matter of fact, the less clear-headed your lover is, the less likely he or she will be able to see the way out.

Remember in the last chapter when I told you that you have to make Leos feel needed, admired, loved, and secure? Well, this is one of those days when a double heaping of everything is in order. To repeat the steps: Build up their confidence. Stoke that fire until their energy level rises. Then Leos will begin to draw good fortune to them as they have in the past.

Now, how do you accomplish this without a rabbit and mirrors?

Past performance

If your Leo is fairly mature, then sit down and remind him or her of better days. Take a stroll with your lover down memory lane. It's time to relive moments of triumph. Whether it's a minor moment, like when he or she wrote the book that actually got reviewed in *The Dental Hygiene Quarterly*—and wasn't it sheer poetry? Or a major moment, like when he or she flew to Oslo to collect the Pulitzer—remember every wondrous second.

Tell your lovers that you adore them not because they won recognition—but because they had the ingenuity and courage to go after it. They have to hear from you that there's *nothing* they cannot do—and naturally, if they fall on their face, you'll be there to dust them off. Add quickly that you *know* they'll succeed because there's no one quite as smart, gutsy, and fabulous. After this talk, Leo might realize the luckiest one is someone who is loved by you!

The crisis is over. The patient has decided life is worth living. Leo's even feeling ready to kick a little you-know-what again. This is the perfect scenario, right? This would all happen in a perfect world. But there are some cases that just cling to the critical care ward:

Leo: I'm sinking into some kind of hellish pit. Nothing's working out right.

You: [Cheerfully] The more positive energy you put out there, the more that won't happen! [Your mate studies your throat, judging what size noose you'll take.]

You: After all [you slyly add], it's like you were playing a part.

Leo: What do you mean?

You: Here you're starring in the role of unappreciated genius.

Leo: So what happens next?

You: I don't know, but I do know that whatever happens will be the result of the kind of energy you put out.

Leo: Will you stop talking about me like I'm a forty-watt bulb!

You: Sweetheart, you already have the energy. It was there when _____ [a brief review of past triumphs], it just has to be recharged. Now, in this movie of ours, with you in the leading part, what kind of ending would you write?

Leo: [Getting into it] I see the last scene, we're sitting on the beach at Monte Carlo, I'm ten pounds lighter, three inches taller, and there's a suitcase between us containing twenty million dollars. [Leo laughs] I'll also take two weeks in Miami and my old credit line.

You: Okay, we just have to figure out how to get to that scene.

Leo: How?

You: Starting now, pretend you're writing the screenplay of your life. What's the next act?

It's an interesting thought to imagine your life as a screenplay, isn't it? For Leo, the ultimate performer, that imagery is right on target.

Money talks

When your lover is solvent again, don't be blind to future warnings of trouble. Leo is a great party animal who knows how to enjoy money, spoiling the people he or she loves with costly toys. But watch when spending seems to get out of control. That could be a sure sign that something's wrong and money is being used as a very expensive Band-Aid.

Too many Lions feel that money is the great cure-all. If they're busy making it and spending it, it doesn't leave them a lot of time for introspection. That's just the way a truly discontented Leo might want it.

At a time like this, you can only try to get them to open up to you. Hopefully, you will have reached a point where Leo is sure of your love. Only then can the Lion or Lioness allow himself or herself to be vulnerable.

Whether or not they're spending money because they're unhappy or deliriously on top of the world, one thing is certain: the money is going to be spent. Virgo, you prefer to spend yours wisely, and that goes double for you too, Taurus. You love beautiful, costly things, but your purchases have sound investment value. When immature Leos splurge, they're only investing in a good time. Their metal is gold, and there's hardly a Leo on the planet who can resist 21k glitter when he or she needs a pick-me-up.

The trick, of course, is to get Leos to moderate their spending. Don't let it discourage you that even wealthy Onassis tried (and failed) to curb his famous Leo's spending sprees.

Happily, you have a lover who's a great self-promoter and tireless worker. Leos are blessed with courage and imagination. So, no matter how despondent they become when finances are stressed, remind them that their good fortune is very much like their ruler, the Sun—it will shine again!

Power and Leo

There's a French expression, *noblesse oblige,* which roughly translates as: generous behavior from someone of higher rank.

That perfectly expresses Leo's attitude toward the sharing of power in a relationship. When our lion or lioness is still an emotional cub, the best you can expect is a benevolent dictatorship. You'll be loved, cared for, pampered, and royally looked after. However, you'll always be made aware, by your mate's every action and nuance of tone, that it's only through his or her magnanimous generosity of heart, spirit, and bank book. Leo wields the power.

You see, your lover has a hard time sharing power. Leos even have difficulty delegating responsibility—just ask any frustrated employee of a Leo boss. Lions usually feel there's no one else around who can do it quite as well as themselves. They're not stupid, of course. They may allow someone to *feel* they're being given responsibility, but sooner than later, that person will realize that Leo is still gripping the controls. Now that's when they're relatively happy. When they are *unhappy*, Leos can become downright tyrannical.

Leo knows best

In some relationships, the power struggle begins immediately. Anger might be used to control the other person. Perhaps a frigid and haughty coldness (the lioness' favorite) will satisfactorily intimidate. We've learned how an immature Gemini holds control by keeping lovers emotionally off-balance. However, in your relationship with the lion or lioness, you'll find all they have to do to exercise control is to be themselves!

Just as Leos consider romance their royal birthright, they also take for granted that they were born to lead. Now it's true they're inspiring leaders, and if you're the type of lover who's more comfortable in the role of follower—who doesn't mind having to obtain the royal nod before deciding if the dental floss should be waxed or unwaxed—then this trait won't bother you at all.

Yet, ironically, the very passive, dependent types of lovers usually don't appeal to Leo. They're not enough of a challenge. Leo prefers very independent, assertive people who want their freedom. The result is an immediate clash of wills. But then, that's how life delivers those karmic lessons! If Leos were attracted to the marshmallows, they'd never get a chance to learn the painful lessons of compromise and humility.

So, with their best interests in mind, nature designed Leos to be attracted to the more spirited among us. People who'll challenge domineering Leo about five minutes into the romance.

That moment will arrive when you'll argue, and there will be times when you know that you're right, right? If your Leo is really a big baby cub, will you be afraid of saying that he or she is just plain wrong, afraid of a possible temper tantrum? Even the most freewheeling souls come to a screeching halt when confronted with Leo's roar.

Rip-roarin' Leo

My, what a big, loud, boisterous temper you have! Leos love to exercise their tempers because it draws them into the spotlight where they can overact to the hilt.

Remember when I talked to you about Leo's sign ruling the heart? Excess emotion can play havoc with it. While it's good for your mate to express anger, a temper tantrum isn't really an expression—it's an indulgence. A translation of a typical temper tantrum goes something like this: Pay attention to me, give me what I want, give it to me now or I may never love you again!

Happily, Leos don't hold grudges (especially when they know they were wrong!), but they desperately need to learn to discipline themselves, starting with their tempers. If they don't, the tantrums will continue until you let baby know—strongly—that you've had enough.

Get over it

Sooner or later Leos have to learn they're fallible just like regular mortals. That means they can be dead-on wrong! If that momentarily puts their ego into traction, they'll just have to get over it. It's one thing to feed Leo's ego with flattery that's based on truth, quite another to keep swallowing the truth in order to placate them.

The first obstacle you might encounter in trying to communicate is Leo's open mind—open about a quarter of an inch. This lover can be *very* opinionated. Actually, when Leos express their opinions, it's a bit like Moses coming down from the Mount. Example: "I heard your argument referring to my justified anger—as a *temper tantrum*—and I feel that you're being very disrespectful." No, Leos do not take themselves lightly! (Remind this lover that angels can fly because they take themselves lightly!)

To make matters worse, your lover can rival Taurus in stubbornness. So here you are, trying to communicate with someone who's quite convinced from the get-go that he or she is totally in the right. Then, even when they finally see your perspective, they have to fight their own stubbornness before admitting it.

For most baby cubs, it's a lot easier to throw temper tantrums than admit a mistake.

A lesson in humility

We've all been waited on by salespeople who project a very disdainful image. Their attitude says, "I'm only here because of a terrible mix-up in designing my life. I'm definitely too good to be waiting on you!"

Could that person be a prideful Leo who is learning a painful lesson in humility?

Well, your lover can echo that sort of attitude during communication with you—or lack of communication might be more like it. How often have you felt that a concession on his or her part was doomed because he or she viewed it as giving in or losing face?

We're back to that ego again. As long as your Leo's ego remains in shaky condition, any compromise will be seen as a defeat. As Leos grow stronger emotionally, they'll come to learn there's great strength and power in humility. Life won't be so much about "saving face" as facing life fully. At that point, your Leo will have taken a giant step toward adulthood.

Love is wanting to say you're sorry

Remember, I told you that Leos have a hard time apologizing. I have heard lovers of the Lion explaining, "Sending flowers was Roger's way of saying I'm sorry," or, "Jennifer knows that I know she's sorry, and that's enough."

I beg your pardon?

How in heaven's name is our Leo going to become a real grownup if he or she is not motivated to act like one? A partnership is ideally a fifty-fifty relationship built on respect. The kind of respect that doesn't take the other person's feelings lightly.

Leo: I do respect your feelings.

You: Then I'd like you to apologize.

Leo: That's silly. I already told you that you're right.

You: But you made me feel miserable for days!

Leo: Well . . .

You: Are you sorry?

Leo: Of course.

You: THEN SAY IT, BECAUSE YOU'RE DRIVING ME CRAZY!

Wait a minute, this dialogue got a little out of hand. We must stay calm and *come from love at all times*, so scratch that last line and substitute:

You: Well, darling, please say you're sorry and I'll tell my mother to untie you.

There, that was much nicer, wasn't it?

Compromise and humility

These are the two important lessons that you, as lover/teacher, are here to help Leo learn.

Interestingly, there are many in this sign that share a big secret: with all their talents, magnetism, generosity, courage, humor, and love of life, they don't really believe they're worthy of being loved.

These are the mates who are quick to reject you in an argument. Quick to walk out the door—slowly, of course—because they only want to hear you sob for them to come back. It's all because they fear rejection, and from that fear they reject the other person first.

Now of course, I am confident that all of you reading this book are amazing, loving, ultra-understanding people who can help their Leo lovers to really love themselves. Let's just review some of your own personality traits that may help or hinder. Aquarius, Leo is your polar opposite, and you might have to become a bit less detached and analytical in order to effectively communicate. Aries, if you can tone down your bluntness, then Leo just might listen to what you have to say. Gemini, remember Leos tends to take themselves seriously and so any advice you give is better received without jokes and drum rolls, please? Taurus, you will have to soften your very strong will and not (like your Leo lover!) always insist on having your own way. Sag, you have always stimulated and inspired Leo, so perhaps now your visionary thinking will give your lover an inspiring picture of what he or she can become.

Keep this as your goal: your lover will one day actually become the person he or she postures. So, when the curtain goes down on the day's performance, Leo will still be in character, no longer just a performer who dreads being alone.

People who truly like themselves are comfortable in their own skins. They know how to share power. They know how to compromise. They know there's strength in humility.

That's the person Leo deserves to be. It is the lover you deserve to have.

Decanates

Take two lovers born under the sign of Leo and they can be radically different. One is able to work for compromise in a relationship, the other is so self-involved that a try at communication ends up being a monologue. Why are they like day and night? Studying decanates can explain a lot of the differences.

You see, every sign in the zodiac is divided into three parts. Each sign spans sixty days, and each day represents one degree. The decanates encompass ten degrees each. While the first ten degrees reflect the nature of the sign itself, the other decanates have different planets as sub-rulers. So, while Leo is ruled by the Sun, people can also be sub-ruled by Jupiter and Mars, dependent on the date they were born.

Is your Leo a mirror-image of the sign? Is there a sub-ruler that will modify your lover's behavior? It's all right here . . .

July 23 to August 1

Your lover is a true Sun child, with a large appetite for life and equally large ego needs. These Leos are dreamers who have the ambition, imagination, and plethora of talents to turn dreams into reality. Play and work are the same. They love what they do and they love doing it around the clock. You try to get them to relax, but they're too busy concentrating on reaching their dreams . . . with a determination that will take your breath away.

This Leo ruled by the Sun is a born leader. Ambition is built in, and these Leos are willing to work for what they want. They seem to attract luck and success. Because they don't know the meaning of the word "failure," they'll need love to help cushion the blow if they ever collide with cruel reality. Don't worry though, this proud extrovert will be up and running in no time . . . hot on the heels of a new dream.

Your lover has great sincerity. These Leos mean what they say and say what they mean. Most important, always be aware of their great pride and dignity, and never step on either. Never embarrass Leo in public (or in private for that matter). As for ridicule—be merciful and slip them poison instead. Ridicule will definitely be fatal. They'll never recover and it will permanently damage your relationship.

August 2 to August 11

Here, the largesse of Jupiter blesses your lover with a giving, extroverted nature.

These Leos are sociable, friendly, and very likable. The planet Jupiter makes everything bigger than life—and Leo's big, beautiful, and bountiful optimism is contagious. When you're feeling down, this is the person you want to have around. Even better than their ability to make you laugh, their philosophical nature knows how to make you see beyond the moment.

This decanate is in love with new thoughts. If your lover is more mature, he or she will be intellectually active, interested in every conceivable subject from religion to literature, from politics to the occult. Discussing it all with you will be one of their joys: it's a lot like enrolling in college (night school, of course!). Be sure to give them the freedom they need in order to reach their potential. They'll definitely balk if they feel closed in. So don't panic if they want to go off by themselves every now and then. They need that time to recharge. Although they're dreamers like our Sun-ruled Leos, they know how to maintain balance between work and play, between ambition and just plain satisfying contentment in what life has given them.

August 12 to August 23

Your lover's sub-ruler is the fiery planet Mars, and you're probably already on mega-B vitamins just trying to keep up! This planet makes Leo ultra-assertive and ambitious. Your lover works for the love of it. They can be so productive that just watching them is exhausting. What they want, they wanted yesterday—and given their incredible drive, they'll probably nail it tomorrow!

Leos' egos demand that they be noticed, and few people are unaware of their impact. They exude a confidence that naturally takes center stage. Because they don't waste time hiding pleasure or pain, and their tact isn't always in use, many people are all too aware of Leo's rejection of them. Mundane conversation bores them silly—and less dynamic folk who can't make up their minds drive them crazy. They love the risk of life. Their courage, combined with an impulsive nature, leads them where only the heroic have gone before. It's more than necessary that your lover round out his or her maturity—because life can be dangerous for heroes who leap on a dare.

Learning the art of communication with this lover is vital. When their tempers start simmering it might already be too late—that pot is going to boil over! Mars definitely makes them combative, with a quick temper that can disrupt and destroy. It takes no prisoners.

The Leo Lover

July 23 to August 23

The Good

Romantic

Generous

Dramatic

Loyal

Assertive

The Bad

Impressionable

Impulsive

Vain

Demanding

Opinionated

The Ugly

Gullible

Spendthrift

Egotistical

Possessive

Know-it-all

"You have to dance as if no one is watching, and love like it's never going to hurt."
—Anonymous

Virgo

August 24 to September 23

Sex and Virgo

The symbol for this earth sign is the Virgin, and people usually misunderstand its meaning. It doesn't signify that your lover is shy or inhibited or any of the old, negative connotations associated with virginity. It reflects the Virgin in the best sense: pure in heart, unspoiled, and seeking the ideal of perfection in everything and everyone.

Astro-psychologists relate this sign to the developmental stage of nineteen to twenty years of age. We've left the baby and adolescent stages behind. We've entered the realm of the young adult. These people are beginning to explore the world by finding a job, developing their skills, and getting a feel for just how they can contribute their talents.

Ruled by Mercury, your lover is as articulate as that other Mercury-ruled sign, Gemini, but twice as grounded. No, make that three times as grounded. Where Gemini skims books (and often lovers), Virgo reads books and people from start to finish. Then they go back to read between the lines. Where Gemini loves to collect information, Virgo organizes it, categorizes it, and fits it into tidy little boxes in their minds. Is it sounding a bit anal retentive? Well, you know your Virgo!

Then again, perhaps you don't really know your Virgo all that well, especially if you're still in the honeymoon stage. So let's take a look at this vulnerable lover, this less than perfect human being who, nevertheless, fully expects to find perfection in you!

Nothing but the best

Let's backtrack a minute. You know by now that the theme of this book is mainly about not-yet-ready-for-prime-time lovers and the problems they present. I'm referring to emotional immaturity. It's quite possible to find someone incredibly brilliant who's still at the emotional level of a groupie. So please don't confuse brain power with being truly grown up. Actually, these can be the most dangerous lovers. They manipulate, seduce, and eventually leave track marks on your heart. Yes, it's emotional maturity, or lack of it, that can devastate a relationship.

So here we are with bright, often brilliant Virgo, who's highly discriminating and analytical. You love it when they dissect a movie or share their razor sharp insights on people. When Virgos apply their sense of discrimination in work, they can be as picky as a six-fingered banjo player.

"Isn't it wonderful," the boss purrs, "that new employee is such a perfectionist!"

However, what can be a strength in one situation may prove disastrous in another. What happens when your lover comes home, and in a foul mood, no less? The same talent for discrimination can reduce itself to being critical, and then sink even lower, to being picky without mercy.

They're critical about what you're wearing. Or, what you're wearing is okay, but definitely not how you're slumping. And don't you ever get tired of watching that imbecilic TV program? What Virgo seems to be saying is, "I left you this morning and you were far from perfect, and I return tonight and, dammit, you're still not perfect!"

The harshest critic

Much of your lover's dissatisfaction with you is really about your lover. If you think Virgo is too critical of you, then imagine how hard it is living inside their own skin. Both sexes are twice as critical of their imperfect selves.

After Virgos finish chipping away at their own egos, sometimes all that's left is the voice of an insecure, worrying neurotic. Then they make the mistake of listening to it:

"Well, you poor loser," the voice sneers, "how intelligent can anyone be if they love you?"

The answer goes straight for the jugular.

We all know psychology 101: we *must* love ourselves before being able to really love someone else. So, think about it: If your lover has a low self-image, how can your lover respect you for loving him or her? Critical Virgos are bound to see you (whether they consciously admit it or not) as some idiot who would attach themselves to anything with a pulse!

You deserve a lot more than that, don't you? The way to get it is to help repair your lover's self-image. The next time Virgo surpasses the "picking quota" for the week, probe gently into why. What made him or her so insecure?

Whatever they admit, don't say "that's ridiculous!" What's bothering your lover may seem trivial or even pure lunacy to you, but that's not an issue here. The best communication is listening without judgment. Virgos are embarrassed to admit less than logical emotions, but they'll respond to your questions if they feel your intent is pure. How quickly will they absorb your assurances of their worth? Trust me, they'll absorb them like a dry, dusty plant in a gas station on a hot Arizona highway drinking in a spring rain!

Fit to be tied

In a sexual relationship with Virgo, you must keep yourself in good shape. Unlike Leos, Virgos won't nag because they're worried about projecting the right image. They'll nag because they honestly think they know what's best for you!

In this case, Virgos think you should be smart enough to keep yourself healthy. After all, they get up an hour early to work out, they stopped smoking, they gave up eating anything that blinks. Please understand that when Virgos care about somebody, *really* care, they can never stand by and see their lover self-destruct.

If you don't take your Virgo/lover/fitness expert's advice, then be prepared to suffer the consequences. Virgo tells you once . . . Virgo tells you once an hour for six months . . . Virgo gives up on you and all that kindly advice turns to cutting sarcasm.

Virgo: Do you really need that candy bar?

You: I haven't had chocolate all week.

Virgo: I know that—you know that—but do your cheeks know that?

You: [Grabbing your face] What's wrong with my cheeks?

Virgo: [Icily] Not *those* cheeks.

Sarcasm, the eighth deadly sin! It's now that you must warn your Virgo to lose it or risk losing you. First of all, to be cleverly sarcastic is no big deal for Virgos—it's a built-in talent. Direct communication, however, is a lot harder and they're not always very good at it.

Begin communicating by attaching an invisible bell to their sleeve and ring it every time they indulge in sarcasm. Aries, point it out—don't yell it out. Cancer, be honest in letting Virgos know how sarcasm is shredding your ego. In time, if they really care about you, they'll stop.

When confronting your lover with his or her faults, use what seduced them in the first place . . . your mind. Let rational thinking, not emotions, impress them. Never forget that Virgos are practical and logical; they are *thinkers,* straining every bit of emotion through their intellects. (Keep reading because you'll soon discover how to get back some of that emotion needed for love and compassion!)

Of course, the fact remains that even if Virgo shapes up, *you* still haven't. The sarcasm goading you to physical fitness is gone, but your sex life is definitely suffering. I don't mean you must get into *Playboy* or *Playgirl* shape. But you must slim down, tone up, and . . . let's look at it this way: when was the last time Virgo reached for you with more enthusiasm than groping for a pork chop in the back of the fridge?

Unconditional love

Remember some of that needed emotion we talked about getting back? Well, it will interest Virgos to hear about their opposite sign, Pisces. At the same time, it will subtly, without intimidation, give them an idea of the qualities they're missing—qualities that would feed their hungry souls. Unlike Virgos, who filter every experience through their intellects, Pisces is a water sign who reacts to life and love on an *emotional level*. Instead of hiding emotions, Pisces pours out their feelings. There is no "I'll only love you if you do this or that"—only unconditional love that gives with both hands. Unlike critical Virgo who often stands apart in judgment, Pisces seems to merge with the feelings of their lovers, experiencing every pleasure or pain. The point is, discussing their opposite sign would be a wonderful way to engage your lover in a conversation about the *purity* of unconditional love. What intellectual topic could turn on a Virgo more? They'll be panting within minutes!

Down but never dirty

Sometimes the most ordinary elements can contribute to great sex. Here's one that might not immediately cross anyone's mind but a Virgo's. Cleanliness! Virgo is intense about cleanliness (the Virgin's search for purity, remember?). Too many lovers begin to skip showers, walk around in less-than-inspiring underwear and, in short, forget the sexiness of a clean, sweet-smelling body.

Hopefully you don't have the type of Virgo lover who resembles Felix in *The Odd Couple*, following you around with a crumb catcher. There are some Virgo females who carry cleanliness to extremes. They'll not only be ecstatic to shower before sex, but also after, and if possible, during. However, the normal Virgo simply requires a spotless stage (you) on which to perform.

Only . . . wait a minute, all is not settled yet. You still can't get the discipline to attack the love handles? Then perhaps you should ask yourself why. A little psychological excavation may be in order. One thing is for sure: if you don't find out the root cause, your dissecting Virgo lover will.

My lover, my fitness trainer, my shrink

Analysis is one hobby your lover finds totally fascinating. Virgos have more faith in their minds than in their emotions, so expect your every thought to be dissected. You can't stop eating chocolate? Virgo will probe: "Did your parents reward you with chocolate? What does chocolate remind you of? Does it turn you on sexually? C'mon, just close your eyes and think back."

To Virgo, nothing in life just happens, least of all bad sex.

Virgo: You didn't have an orgasm?

You: I was too tired.

Virgo: Is that all?

You: [Yawning] Darling, I was up at 6 a.m., skipped lunch, did a hundred pushups
   in the gym, worked overtime, and donated a kidney. I'm tired!

Virgo: [Rolls away and sighs deeply] Why don't you tell me what's *really* bothering you?

I forgot to mention your lover's second hobby—*worrying*. Not only do Virgos worry about what's completely out of their control (acid rain, Chinese relations, and the dangers of cloning), but they're positively artful at worrying about their personal lives. Remember that secret inferiority complex? Well, it doesn't matter how good looking, smart, and sexy Virgos are, they *still* worry that they'll eventually lose you. (Emotions have no rhyme and little reason). So I expect the Virgo in our scenario to thrash around half the night worrying about that missing orgasm.

Three hours later, Virgo will still be working on the diagnosis and you'll be pleading: "Honest, I hate orgasms—I never want another one—let me go to sleep!"

A gift of love

The advice your lover offers may be the product of his or her mind, but it comes straight from the heart. Advice from Virgo is like receiving a *gift of love,* and that's precisely how they see it. You might feel you don't have a closet big enough to store all those surprising gifts—but you can't exchange them, return them, or burn them. So what do you do with them? Simply listen, then tuck the gift in the back of your mind and let it collect dust. But never make your lover feel foolish for offering it.

As for that manic Virgo who's gone over the edge, who constantly lectures you in a holier-than-thou tone—on everything from the joys of tofu to improving your oral sex technique and rejuvenating your neck at the same time—don't be angry. Be gone!

Nude but never crude

You know by now that Virgos have an old-fashioned streak. They probably rarely tell a raunchy joke to strangers, and will only laugh politely if forced to hear one. If you've ever been foolish to stroke their thigh in public, the memory of your lover cringing is not a pleasant one. Virgos are not prudes, just very private, and their mates should never confuse how they act in public with what they fantasize in the bedroom.

That's precisely what's so confusing!

You see, with Virgo, what you see is not particularly what you get. It comes as a great surprise when their lover discovers the genteel sex they've been offering is leaving Virgo hungry for much, much more.

After all, your Virgo spent the first year of your relationship training you to be his or her idea of perfection. That means *taste* and *refinement*. Using a toothpick in public? A tomato stain on your jockey shorts? Flashy jewelry? All on the OUT list. You probably imagined that Virgo's keen sense of refinement extended to the bedroom. Well, it does—to the bedroom door!

Deep waters run wild

Virgos are loyal and faithful. The last thing they want to do is stray. However, many Virgo lovers repress their sexuality in early life and develop rich fantasy lives. They dream of earthy, uninhibited sex, light years away from their usual behavior.

These Virgos need a partner who will let them explore these facets of their sexuality. If they don't find that liberal lover, they may not look for sexual satisfaction outside the relationship—but they'll leave you in another way—receding into a private fantasy life you'll never share.

In the beginning of a sexual relationship, don't bother asking exactly what they like, or where they want to be touched. Your lover is basically shy, and what he or she wants is for *you* to lead the way. The more aggressive you are, the quicker Virgos will follow into uninhibited sex play. Once there, their vivid imaginations may leave you far behind. You just might find yourself staring in amazement at this lover, asking "Who are you?"

Scorpio, your sexual appetite can scare the pants off your lover, but hardly in the way you hoped! Remember that Virgo likes someone to lead the way, but not with a bullwhip. Cancer, you intuitively know that Virgo must trust you first and feel your respect. If you can be friends first, you will be better lovers. Leo, Virgo will be swept away by your high drama and exuberant sexual play. With your help, Virgo might even learn how to tone down his or her criticism and just communicate in body language.

Here's an exercise that might help all the signs with their Virgo mates. Its goal is to help them communicate what type of sexual play they like.

Treat Virgo to a wonderfully sensual back massage. There's only one rule: *you will not touch them without explicit instructions from them.* They must tell you where to massage them and exactly how. Starting from the bottom of your spine or from your shoulders down? Lightly or not? In long languid strokes?

Needless to say, once your Virgo's back has been massaged, there are other areas for intensive field work. Each time the object of the game will be made deliciously clear . . . the quicker your lover communicates, the quicker he or she will experience pleasure.

However, there are always the diehards—the Virgos who cling to their hangups. Years of sexual repression and feelings of guilt must be worked through. Warning: your lover's very reticence and shyness might in turn inhibit you. Don't let it! If you have a Virgo who seems to be there more in body than in spirit, there's only one way to proceed . . .

Just start without them!

It's a little like trying to teach someone to tango. The rhythm is strange, your lover feels shy and awkward. So you take your partner around the floor a few times, whispering sweet encouragement into his or her ear: "You really have natural rhythm," and so on, while he or she gains confidence.

Even if you and your sexually-inhibited Virgo have been together a long time, you might have given up on them ever becoming sexually free. Please don't stop trying. The trick is *no pressure,* just nice and easy lovemaking, with a lot of compliments one salacious step at a time. Should you open a bottle of wine or make available the inhibition loosener of your choice? Absolutely.

Then take the initiative, slowly, gently, but with the certainty that your partner will soon move to your rhythms. I promise that inside every Virgo soul is an incredible dancer . . . straining to hear the music.

Money and Virgo

Typical Virgos tend to finances with the care of cultivating a garden. They study the terrain; plant strong, healthy seeds; and watch them grow in abundance. All the while they fret, fret, and fret that an unnatural disaster is going to come along and wipe out the crops. In Virgos' nightmares, that would be losing their job and savings. It's akin to that dream we've all had of finding ourselves stark naked in downtown traffic. That's why Virgos are twice as productive on the job as anybody else, in order to make themselves indispensable.

Virgos' ability to do more work than a chain gang—combined with their acute intelligence, meticulous nature, and compulsion to worry over what never happens—usually guarantees success.

How do they spend their money? Well, with a lot less abandon than you might like. They've been known to splurge with all the spontaneity of an IRS auditor.

Actually, because the sign Libra rules their second house of finance, symbolizing balance, your mate is always searching for just the right balance between saving, splurging, enjoying, and being guilt-ridden when buying something he or she wants but doesn't necessarily need. The phrase "guilt trip" was coined the first time Virgo took a vacation instead of putting the money in the bank.

So let's face reality: Virgos will never spend money with the gusto of a Leo, the carelessness of an Aquarius, or the divine foolishness of a Gemini. They revel too much in the security money brings. In their worse moments of insecurity, convinced they're going to end up in the Home For Unloved Indigents, Virgos can even become penny pinching, and you know how sexy I think that trait is!

Can't see the forest for the trees
However, it's not mean-spiritedness that causes frugality, only fear. If your lover tends to clutch the purse strings too tightly, all you can do is attempt to cut through these fears of financial catastrophes. Also, remember my advice when talking to your cerebral earth sign: speak in his or her language—be logical at all times.

Perhaps if you write down the monthly income next to the monthly output, and show Virgo in black and white how far ahead you are, it might ease that knot in the back of their neck. Every time your lover voices a "what if . . ." tell him or her to concentrate on what *is*. Virgo must learn that only a fool hurries to meet problems that will arrive in their own good time. However, if you do the figures and find out that Virgo has every right to panic, then reduce your expenses, call Uncle Fred for a short-term loan, and put Virgo to bed with two aspirins, a glass of wine, and you.

Of course, your lover is realistic and absolutely right that money doesn't grow on trees. Even if it did, Taurus would probably own the forest, give logging rights to Capricorn, and hire Libra to work with the environmentalists!

Also, don't let an ill-timed Virgo criticism about your own liberal spending dampen your loving mood. This sign's worrying can be contagious and you might end up joining the enemy. In other words, don't let your mate's fears rub off on you.

A gift of giving
Have you noticed how your lover never quite feels good about life unless there's a sacrifice to be made? Well, actually, it's one of Virgo's most impressive characteristics—this need to give, to serve, to deny themselves willingly for a greater cause.

Here's how that noble quality might manifest in everyday life. Imagine that you want to take a vacation and your lover wants to buy a new car. Virgo insists on sacrificing the car for your tropical tan, and your first reaction is to feel both grateful and guilty. Should you feel guilty?

The author Ayn Rand thought all sacrifice is negative, and she gave this example, which I'm paraphrasing: If a mother buys a new hat and her baby needs milk, returning the hat isn't a sacrifice because the baby's need was more important. However, if the hat was really more important to the woman, then she did indeed make a sacrifice. In Ayn Rand's philosophy, any sacrifice you make is destructive because you usually end up feeling resentful about it.

So, when Virgo makes an apparent sacrifice for you—the light of their life, their *raison d'être* for putting on their shoes every morning—realize that nothing could make your lover happier, and perhaps it really wasn't a sacrifice in the first place.

Coming up short

Aries is the perfect visionary to start a project. Leo's the one who knows how to publicize it (and grab the glory), but it will be reliable Virgo who will do twice as much as anyone asked, finish the job down to the last detail, clean off the desk, and turn off the lights before going home.

Now, what could be wrong with a lover who works for the sheer joy of working? Someone who rarely feels too much is asked of them, but instead welcomes the chance to be of service? Who conscientiously saves their money? What is the weakness in this picture?

Although their often low self-esteem selves can be thrilled when receiving applause for their work, Virgos can often miss the cash prize. Libra could never fathom working as hard as Virgo (or as hard as anyone else for that matter), and if they do, you can be sure they'll expect to be amply rewarded. Even soft-spoken Pisces is never at the back of the line when bonuses are passed out. So when it comes to asking for a monetary translation of that thunderous applause, where's Virgo?

Use me, abuse me

You know where Virgo is, don't you? If your lover is less than a tower of emotional strength, he or she is right next to you—moaning and complaining about getting passed by, looked over, and dumped on so many times that he or she is beginning to feel like a landfill!

Poor Virgo. You feel sorry for him or her. You want to take your lover in your arms and make everything all better. But the longer your lover complains, the more frustrated you become. If you're a Capricorn, you really can't relate, because the last time someone tried to avoid giving you monetary recognition, that person ended up in the Guam field office.

You tell your lover to be more assertive. "Don't let them take advantage of you any longer," you urge. "You're too terrific at what you do. That place would collapse without you!" What you really want to do is yell, "Get a backbone, baby!"

Virgo swears that tomorrow he or she will march right in and demand that raise. What your lover won't admit is that underneath the bravado is that old inferiority complex nagging at him or her, whispering in your lover's ear that he or she is really not worth any more money.

Only because you're tuned into your lover do you begin to hear the doubts and fears. You start wondering if Virgo isn't caught in a downward, destructive spiral. You're absolutely right, of course, because the longer Virgos sell themselves short, the more inadequate they feel. The more inadequate they feel, the more afraid they become to demand compensation for what they do, the more afraid they become, and so on.

It's hard to believe that the most responsible, tireless workers in the zodiac can consistently undervalue themselves. That's why you must work even harder to strengthen your lover's self-image. After all, what's Virgo's is yours, isn't it? And visa versa. Excluded are the very rich and very selfish who keep their finances separate and protect every dollar with lengthy prenuptial agreements.

The point is, as a couple you won't reach your financial potential until Virgo becomes confident enough. Now, if your partner has a more aggressive chart, much of Virgo's usual timidity will disappear. For instance, a Virgo with a fiery Leo rising might do the trick. Then, if you put aggressive Mars in that first house of Leo, this lover probably won't only ask for a raise, he or she will demand a company car and four weeks vacation! As I have mentioned in this book, you have to have a personalized horoscope in order to get the whole astrological picture and truly understand the person you love.

So for now, don't anticipate that an astrological *possibility* will become a full-fledged problem. However, if it does manifest itself, at least you will know that in the long run, building up your Virgo's ego for all it's worth is the smartest way to go. Actually, it's as good as money in the bank.

Power and Virgo

In these pages, I've described the Virgos who seek perfection in their romantic relationships. Isn't that a little like seeking the Holy Grail in downtown Newark? I mean, what are the odds?

It's not easy being the mate of someone who's on a life-long quest for perfection. Virgo means well—and there's no sign with better intentions toward their lovers—but haven't you heard, *the road to hell is paved with good intentions?*

Less mature Virgos may still dream of perfection in a mate, but realize it's impossible to achieve. That won't frustrate them or drive them to drink, they'll simply get as close to their ideal as possible. That means they'll devote their talents to helping you realize your full potential. They'll do it quietly. They'll do it lovingly. They'll do it until you plead for mercy.

The cure that kills

The less perfect you are, the more our not-so-evolved Virgos feel the need for immediate therapy. They must mold you into their ideal and they attack the project with the same gusto with which they approach a treadmill. And so the "cure" for your less-than-perfect ways begins. Remember when I told you how those born under this sign love to analyze their lovers? Of course, there's long- and short-term therapy—but when Virgo is at the controls, it's like Woody Allen said of his psychoanalyst: "I was there so long, he put in a salad bar!"

If Virgos are after control, they won't get it unless you're a willing player. That means you must respond to the subliminal message Virgo is sending: You're not good enough! Not good enough for what? Well, to live with, and to love Virgo, of course. The less confident among you might start believing how horribly flawed you are. Then, will you look up to Virgo as being superior? If you do, then you'll have handed your lover the control that he or she was after.

If you have the temerity to question their in-depth psycho babble of you, really immature Virgos will fall back on yet another less-than-attractive trait: criticism. If you balk at this harsher treatment, the more mean-spirited the criticism can become.

Does this profile seem to fit your mate? Then start questioning what's going on. Is Virgo taking more pleasure in putting you down than raising your spirits? Definitely not a pleasant feeling. If you let it continue, the final stage is criticism of your personality in all its flawed facets, laced with heavy sarcasm. (Lucy, in the comic strip *Peanuts,* who drives Charlie Brown to screaming fits with her constant barrage of advice, is certainly a classic Virgo.)

So it all adds up to Virgo whittling away at your ego in order to control you. How mean is your lover for doing it? They're not mean at all, because nine times out of ten they're not even aware they're doing it. I told you that Virgo's constant advice is viewed by the giver as a gift of love. Well, Virgos totally rationalize their tough love approach to making you a better person. They actually believe it's helping you. They do love you, don't doubt it, it's just that their neurosis is holding their common sense hostage. The idea is to confront that neurosis quickly, hopefully painlessly, and to once and for all get rid of it.

If they were hard on you and took the easy path themselves, your anger might be justified, but Virgos are harder on themselves than on anybody else. Of course, in order for any lover to have real tolerance for your shortcomings, they must have the same tolerance for their own.

That's the problem.

If control in a relationship means power, as indeed it does, then Virgos' use of control begins with their intolerance of human weaknesses—including their own.

Accent on the negative

I have to admit feeling compassion for immature Virgos. They make such a fuss about a partner's shortcomings—but it's their very selves who walk around practically crippled from feelings of inferiority. If they ever did find someone they thought was perfect, they would go into psychological spasms, never believing the model of perfection would find them worth loving!

What happens when Virgos continue to view the world (and themselves) in a harsh and critical light? They fall into a negative morass that can be poisonous to their health and the health of their lovers. Virgos run the risk of narrowing their vision to such an extent that they can't see a shred of joy in life. They have to break the pattern of negativity, but how?

It's practically impossible for anyone to do it alone. You need to help your lover recognize his or her dark, destructive patterns, and show your lover how to consciously lighten up. For instance:

Virgo: You know those papers you helped me grade the other night?

You: Sure.

Virgo: Well, I found two mistakes.

You: Really? I'm sorry.

Virgo: Forget it. They were minor.

Well, c'mon, let's be honest here. Your lover doesn't want you to forget a thing. That's why it was mentioned in the first place. Perhaps you should have responded this way:

You: You know I stayed up till one in the morning doing those papers, and I was really tired.

Virgo: That's probably why you made the mistake.

You: But my point is, instead of telling me what I did wrong—something that I can't redo, and were minor mistakes to begin with—wouldn't it have been nicer if you had just thanked me for staying up late to do it?

Virgo: Didn't I?

You: No, you didn't. Actually, I've been wanting to talk to you about this tendency you're unaware of—being very critical.

Now, if your voice remains loving, this conversation could definitely bear fruit. But in order to change a negative pattern, it's necessary to control your thinking—and it's very difficult to control something you don't understand. You just might have to confront your own deeper levels of insecurity. Virgo is like layers of onions: peel away one layer of insecurity and there are five layers of cause and effect waiting to be discovered. Hmmm, I wonder if the fact that we cry when peeling onions is relevant here. Oh, well . . .

But just imagine how hard it is looking at that onion from the inside out—having to climb through layers of your psyche—struggling to free yourself before you can really love someone else. Your lover can use all the help and encouragement you can offer!

The choice is yours

Many Virgo arguments begin with comments on *procedure*. You know, "Why did you put the garbage in that can? I told you it doesn't belong there," or "How come you bought that toothpaste? I hate that flavor," or "You left the radio on, again, when you left the room. How many times do I have to tell you to turn it off?"

Ah yes, all the trivia that would mean nothing if we were just inwardly content. But when Virgos are discontent, garbage begins to symbolize everything that's wrong with their world. They begin to do what comes naturally—criticize. The easiest targets are the countless procedures that everyday life revolves on. When Virgos are at their best, they're discriminating wonders. At their worst, they're critical monsters, and you can be sure that something weightier than garbage is at fault.

Do you want to be right or do you want to be happy? Of course, the two are not mutually exclusive, except when you're in an infuriating argument with your critical Virgo lover. Then the choice is yours alone. Proving that you're right may bring momentary ego satisfaction and win the battle, but ending the interminable Virgo wars takes strategy. Let me explain.

Since you're only human, it's quite likely that when your lover begins analyzing and criticizing your faults (as though you invented them) you'll want to jump right into a verbal free-for-all. Don't do it. Fighting back with the same puerile weapon, tongue lashing at its lowest, isn't going to prove anything. It will only further poison the waters. It's certainly not going to make you happy, is it? Oh, yes, you might win a round or two, but the climax of this exercise will have you sleeping alone for weeks.

So don't fall into the trap and snap back, just ask your lover one question:

You: What's really bothering you?

Virgo: I told you, you were wrong to put the garbage in that can!

You: But . . .

Stop right there and don't worry about being right. I know you put the bloody garbage in the right can, and if you didn't, I forgive you! Get past the garbage issue, even if you have to fall on your knees and beg forgiveness from the garbage gods. Swear you'll never do it again. Is your lover happy now?

Just concentrate on the reality that you want to be happy, you want harmony without harping and criticism and shredded egos, and the only way to approach that destination is by keeping your eye on the bigger picture.

On the path

The path I'm referring to is the spiritual path through life that we all have to take. It represents the first lesson you have to teach Virgo.

Tell your lover that we're all at different stages of spiritual development. You may be behind or ahead of Virgo on the path, but one thing is certain—he or she must let you march down that path to the beat of your own drummer. Meaning you have to go at your own pace, learning your own lessons. Yes, it's nice, you tell your lover, to have him or her at your side for moral support. However, that strong push every now and then—which translates as "do it my way!"—doesn't help, it just trips you up!

It's the same experience we have with children. We know the lessons they have to learn, and we'd do anything to help cushion the blows. But we also know they have to learn by themselves, or it won't mean anything.

"It also doesn't help," you continue, "when you constantly put me down. I know you don't mean to hurt me, and that you love me, but we have to start building each other up. If we're not there for each other as true friends, who will be?"

Just ask that question and I promise that it will ignite the right brain cell in this lover. The response will be immediate introspection on his or her part, and the beginning of a meaningful change.

Accent the positive

Share this fascinating theory with your Virgo: we constantly put out positive energy or negative energy—and by doing that, we really help to create our own reality. Western medicine is just learning the power of positive thinking. For years we've all known that it's what we should take into a job interview along with our resumes, but now doctors are realizing it can be instrumental in curing ailments, mental and physical.

Take time out of the day to create really positive mental images. There's a variety of audio tapes on the market to help, where soothing voices guide you on a spiritual journey, until you become peaceful and at peace with yourself. Trust me, it will help keep discussions of garbage at a minimum.

Relationships, like spending and saving money, are a difficult balance for Virgos to achieve. But like any project, they're capable of considering it a challenge, if someone questions, "Do you think you can do it?" So do your lover a favor, and make that someone yourself. For the mind-focused Virgos of either sex, the challenge of understanding themselves is more challenging, and ultimately more satisfying, than a Rubik's Cube.

Decanates

Take two lovers born under the sign of Virgo and they can be radically different. One is able to work for compromise in a relationship, the other is so self-involved that a try at communication ends up being a monologue. Why are they like day and night? Studying decanates can explain a lot of the differences.

You see, every sign in the zodiac is divided into three parts. As each sign spans thirty days, each decanate is figured at approximately ten degrees. While the first ten degrees reflect the nature of the sign itself, the other periods have different planets as sub-rulers. So, while Virgo is generally ruled by Mercury, people can also be sub-ruled by either Saturn or Venus, dependent on the dates they were born.

Is your Virgo a mirror-image of the sign? Is there a sub-ruler that will modify your lover's behavior? It's all right here . . .

August 24 to September 2

Ruled by Mercury, your lover is sympathetic, caring, and the embodiment of discrimination. You feel that you have the litmus test of perfection to pass, and you spend half your time worrying about flunking. This Virgo's hobby of being highly critical doesn't exactly help your ego, either. Because your lover is so intelligent, you can't understand why he or she constantly sinks into worrying about trivia. Trust me, neither can they. These Virgos are high-strung, tireless workers, and need more praise than they'll ever have the courage to seek. If they're smart, they'll take time out to exercise and work off some of that internal combustion. It needs release in more than paperwork. Yoga would be a wonderful outlet for them, keeping them in the perfect physical shape that makes them feel so good— and calming their ever-worrying minds.

Yes, they need you to bring a light touch to their lives, to let them know that one failure does not make a disaster. So when they become entrenched in a problem, give your Virgo a healthy dose of optimism, and some badly needed perspective to show there is light at the end of his or her tunnel vision.

September 3 to September 12

Saturn rules over this decanate of Virgo, giving your lover even more discipline with which to cultivate his or her sharp mind. It also gives your lover a strong drive for success. These Virgos have their eyes on the top of the mountain, and (like that other earth sign, Capricorn, whose ruler is Saturn) it won't matter how long the climb, they intend to reach the summit. Along the way, they'll probably enjoy the financial fruits of it all—but if they're not careful, they can easily become boringly status conscious. It's possible money was an important part of their upbringing, either because their family had a lot of it or didn't have enough, and brain-washed them as to its necessity for happiness. Yes, it's possible to survive our childhoods! However, Saturn also makes Virgos aware of how to network their talents. Knowing the "right people" and being in the "right places" becomes a central part of their existence. In the end, that kind of shallow value system can weaken a Virgo's chance to raise his or her spiritual level.

Then, too, because Virgo is Virgo, they're not going to stop worrying even when the bank account is overflowing, so get your lover to concentrate on that half-full glass. Otherwise, he or she is going to waste a lot of time worrying . . . and it's a lot smarter to want what you already have!

September 13 to September 23

Ah, at last Venus! Just the tender touch our Virgo has needed all along. The planet of love lends more creativity to this lover, while giving him or her an outward, irresistible charm. Many of this decanate use their assets to their advantage as performers. Even if they don't use their talents professionally, it's very important that they use them in some way. Their artistic natures need an outlet before frustration sets in. This doesn't mean they have to professionally sing, dance, or do magic tricks; their creativity can blossom in the kitchen, or they can turn to woodworking. Anything that will take them away from that dark, lonely cerebral place they inhabit.

The trick for these lovers is to find the balance between their mind and emotions. They have to learn to let loose and let love permeate every pore of their bodies—without worrying about it or analyzing it out of existence. Your Virgo has to watch out not to become too selfish. Doesn't sound like our usual giving, altruistic Virgo, does it? Don't worry, it's Virgo all right. Venus might sidetrack Virgos into enjoying a narcissistic love affair with their own image, but they'll soon be whipping it to death with unrealistic standards of perfection. Yes, Virgos can be self-critical to a fault. So, if Venus does make them overly self-absorbed at times, it will probably be more of a sado-masochistic, self-love affair, if you can figure that one out. I'm still trying!

The Virgo Lover

August 24 to September 23

The Good

Intelligent

Discriminating

Analytical

Modest

Perfectionist

The Bad

Compulsive

Critical

Detached

Uptight

Demanding

The Ugly

Worrier

Picky

Superior

Repressed

Neurotic

Westley: Hear this now: I will always come for you.
Buttercup: But how can you be sure?
Westley: This is true love—do you think this happens every day?
—FROM THE MOVIE "THE PRINCESS BRIDE"

Libra

September 24 to October 23

Sex and Libra

Ruled by Venus, the planet of love, Libras are an inspiration. They instinctively know how to communicate, with an innate ability to balance logic and emotion. Even when quitting a relationship, they make the object of their non-desire smile to the end, simply by softening their honesty with gentle diplomacy. In short, the art of relationships is as natural to Libra as enjoying full sexual expression.

Unlike their opposite sign, Aries, whose weakness is often to be self-centered, Librans think only in terms of "we." That's what makes this the astrological sign of romance. Your lover will negotiate, compromise, and turn somersaults to make you happy. Since the gods usually bless Librans with a totally unfair amount of looks, intelligence, charm, and charisma, it's no hardship to love them back.

We're speaking, of course, of mature Libra lovers.

Now let's talk about their evil twin. You know, the one lying next to you in bed, noisily sucking on a variety of emotional pacifiers? The lover who goes around impersonating an adult and getting away with it? On the outside, this immature lover has that incredible Libra sense of style, sophistication, and class (exactly what dazzled you in the first place), but on the inside, he or she is a far cry from the nurturing mate you expected. It's like being served a filet-mignon that looks perfect on the outside, but you take a bite and discover it's raw. Put it back in the oven! (Apologies to my vegan friends.)

Of course, everyone has the potential to grow—it just might take more caring and divine patience on your part than you dreamed you possessed. So first, be honest and assess just how much love you have to give.

Is that all?!

Take another look, deeper inside yourself.

Good! I'm thrilled that the cupboard isn't as bare as you first thought. For the rest of you who want intimacy from a lover, but are afraid the price is higher than you want to pay, remember that true love emits an energy that can only boomerang. This power has been proven—what you give to love will come back to you tenfold.

Here's looking at you, kid

Ah yes, the lure of a pretty or handsome face. Librans, as I mentioned, are usually above average in looks. While some of the classic silver screen's sex goddesses were Librans

(Brigitte Bardot was a perfect example), many of history's seductive gigolo's were also Libra men.

This sign's acute sense of the aesthetic produces more than actors, artists, and designers—it also produces many impulsive relationships. Both sexes can be rendered helpless by a heart-stopping profile. If Libra's in love with you, then you're probably too attractive to have ever considered computer dating. However, does settling into a relationship guarantee that Libra will stop overheating when a new profile strolls by?

Immature Librans are all too easily seduced by physical charms, no matter how superficial. Like another air sign—their Gemini cousins—they're also addicted flirts. Of course, they want love to last forever after, but flirting is sort of like having long-term life insurance. If one lover doesn't turn out to be perfect, perhaps the next will . . . or the next after that?

Marriage mania

Astro-psychologists compare the developmental phase of Libra to that of a twenty-six to thirty-five year old. This is the time of life when a person becomes more social, trades those adolescent fraternity parties for sophisticated soirees, and may indeed get married.

Librans fall in love in a heartbeat, and too many skip down the aisle while still at the emotional crawling stage. That's why there are so many early marriages in this sign, as well as early divorces. Libra's motivation for marriage is always pure—if frequently premature. Remember, this sign thinks in terms of "we," and those born under it yearn to fulfill their karmic destiny and create the perfect union.

Poor Libras. Fate has placed an Olympic hurdle in their paths, designed to trip up the weakest. Yes, their destiny is to find their other half and complete their wholeness, *but* they must do it while learning to be independent. Actually, Libra personifies a lesson we all must learn: Before we can achieve the perfect "we," we must work on building the perfect "I"—or as perfect as we can get it.

It's your job to find out if your lover, and possible life companion, has already done his or her homework. To put it bluntly, is your lover as appealing as a triple-chocolate layer cake with all the substance of a puff pastry?

My puff pastry test

How often have you heard, "I value you as a friend," along with, "When I look at the back of your neck I get so turned on!"?

Yes, you deserve a lover smart enough to see beyond your looks. Someone who knows what to look for—humor, intelligence, integrity, kindness—the qualities that lift you out of life's trenches. I'm not ignoring the appeal of a delicious neck, but let's keep our priorities in order. After all, the one certainty about puff pastry is that sooner or later it's going to deflate. So, if you're in the beginning stages of a heady romance with scintillating, seductive Libra, beware of him or her falling in love with the curve of your lower lip. The last thing you need is someone seduced by an illusion that just happens to have your name on it!

Dreams of perfection

Libras go through life waiting to be dazzled into a fairy-tale romance. Don't bother them with rational thinking, just allow them to be overcome by the passion of the moment. They want their consciousness rocked by inner fireworks. All you need are magnetic eyes (color irrelevant), a body that doesn't stop (gender often irrelevant), and the ability to weave words into magical promises. Libra will be as mesmerized as the snake in the charmer's basket. In this superficial world, good looks promise romance—romance promises passion—and when Librans are consumed by passion, nothing else matters.

What Libra's doing is similar to a Virgo pattern of placing lovers on pedestals of illusion and self-delusion, then being devastated when they topple. Virgo, however, is seeking inner perfection while Libra concentrates more on outer packaging.

No matter how exciting the mating game, the bells eventually stop ringing. While the object of Libra's temporary affection is still listening to the chimes reverb, Libra has shaken off the cloud of plaster, stepped around the broken pedestal, and is off and running to the next conquest. What happened?

Could it have been that incredibly embarrassing *dip* you attempted on the dance floor? Was it that less-than-discreet belch you shared with the first three rows during *Swan Lake*? You probably sent Libra's social seismograph off the charts!

However, if you're socially flawless, even in Libra's demanding eyes, perhaps you simply introduced a demand or two yourself. How about: Please clean the kitchen? Take out the garbage? Ha! Surely you jest!

While any lucky Libran mate can expect frequent stage-settings of fresh flowers, dinners, candle-lit bedrooms, and perfumed pillows, it won't take long to figure out who gets to clean up in the morning. Librans are notoriously lazy when it comes to the unpleasant realities of life. (In this lover's view, romance and reality mix about as well as gin and 7-up).

So if you're serious about keeping your relationship, as well as keeping house, consider hiring someone to attack the bathroom once a week. At the least, offer to share the drudgery.

More than just a toy

We now know the standards Librans seek in their lovers, but what are the standards for themselves? As an air sign, mature Librans possess a formidable intellect. Their innate sense of justice (remember their symbol is the balance scales) makes them powerful lawyers; talents for compromise and communication create skilled diplomats. However, too often immature Librans coast along on their equally useful surface charms (this type becomes bored in elevators without mirrors!) and the deeper parts of them remain undeveloped. The results are very shallow waters.

"Well," a female Libra may protest, "I've achieved great success by being a so-called object of desire, do you have a problem with that?"

"I've got the looks and the class to write my own ticket, what more is needed?" the male Libra joins in.

Lovers of the intellect, such as Aquarius, will be too bored to answer. Sagittarius will be long gone! However, a sign like Taurus may be guilty of feeding Libra's vanity, surrounding them with expensive gifts, and enjoying the *illusion* they actually possess the creature they're spoiling.

But what about you? You're still in the relationship, and chances are you're not handcuffed to Ken or Barbie, but be honest, do you still miss the turn-on of a grownup, challenging mind? If the answer is a sheepish "yes," here's what to do:

1. Stop playing the adoring mirror for your Libra lover's narcissism.

2. Treat Libra like a grownup and expect him or her to do more than consume oxygen.

3. Let your Libra know that he or she has a mind with unlimited potential and it turns you on when it's turned on.

No pain, no gain

An interesting note: every horoscope shows *aspects*: these are the actual angles between the planets as they move through the heavens. Some aspects, such as the trine and sextile, ease our lives, while others, such as the square or opposition, create conflicts of energies. However, the harder aspects challenge us to grow mentally and spiritually. Often, people lacking tough challenges seem to float through life. We may envy how effortlessly life hands them the prize, but the truth is that they're only romping in cosmic kindergarten, where the lessons are easy and every day is play day. Astrology assures us there is justice in life—sooner or later, they too will have to graduate.

Libra's potential is to be a strong, well-rounded human being. Let's help them achieve it. Since this sign is all about balance, begin by understanding the qualities of Libra's opposite sign, Aries. Picture Librans with some of Aries' positive qualities: they have focused energy and ambition, direct communication (because they can survive very well if you disagree with them), and they don't look for an easy ride in life—in fact, they thirst for challenge.

Unless you challenge Librans to express some of the stronger Aries qualities (still dormant in their own nature), they may never grow up in this lifetime. But, while you express expectations, remember my mantra: *come from love*! Never attack, don't dwell on what's lacking in your lover. Instead, encourage, support, and bolster Libra's self-image. It's the difference between: "You never read books! What's the matter, are you brain dead?" versus, "I read this great book that I think you'll love. I can't wait to get your opinion of it."

As long as flattery remains legal, there's no crime in using a little, is there?

Watch out, though! Nothing's more powerful than a Libra who has all six cylinders working—looks, charm, talent, mind, emotions, and libido. This lover may just start handing you some expectations of his or her own!

Forever twenty

If Libra's career standards are often too low, their standards for their own looks are unrealistically high—that is, for any person without a full-time makeup man, personal fitness instructor, and live-in hair stylist. Unfortunately, our shallow, advertising-driven culture was created with immature Librans in mind. Perfect, air-brushed specimens smile at them from magazine racks when they buy dog food, keeping both sexes in a constant panic of insecurity. Unless they learn that age is inevitable, and there is beauty in every season, they'll live in genuine fear of their looks fading.

Having a flirtatious Gemini for a bedmate only reinforces Librans' lack of confidence. So they get their own extra-curricular lovers, hoping that yet another affair will transform grim reality into a Grimm's fairy-tale. When insecure Librans seek validation of their looks (and their worth) in a lover's eyes, the stage is set for a game of musical beds.

Getting the kinks out?

Cheating on a lover doesn't take a lot of imagination, but when Librans cheat, it definitely becomes creative. Sexual searchings may even lead them into bisexuality.

Yes, this sign has a bisexual tendency, which remains on snooze control until some emotional storm upsets their balance. Then, without harmony in their lives, they might start searching for it in unlikely places. It's a dangerous moment when their balance scale tips and they fall into the arms of very kinky lovers (we're talking more than Wesson oil here), who only further upset their emotional balance.

Please, let me please you

So great is their need for harmony that when anger throws Librans off balance, the whole foundation of their world is in jeopardy. Unlike Taurus, they never retreat behind silence. Most of the time, they rely on their famous talent for communication and compromise.

Well, maybe. Maybe not. Librans are great mediators when it comes to other people's arguments, but they hate confrontation so much they might never initiate one, even if it means swallowing their feelings. Remember, their mission in life is to *please*, so the last thing they want to risk is losing your love by hurting your feelings.

Even Rhett got tired of waiting

Scarlett O'Hara must have been a Libra, because she so often purred, "I'll think about it tomorrow. After all, tomorrow is another day!"

Yes, your lover is the great procrastinator of the zodiac. Librans may finally decide to talk about a problem, but they're expert in putting off the moment. First they have to think about it . . . for about a millennium. What we've got here is someone who hates voicing an unpopular thought. It might offend (translation: they might be less loved), remember? So they think and think and think . . . and think. Unfortunately, Israel and Syria will offer combined tourism packages before Libra reaches a decision.

Take the taste test

Before we talk about the best way to get Libra to communicate, let's run down a checklist of how well you communicate your love. Here's what's important to your Libra. See if you can answer yes to five out of five.

1. Libra, ruled by Venus, takes in every detail of your appearances. The sign is the epitome of elegance, and aesthetics matter a lot. Does the way you look communicate: "I understand this about you and so I took the time to please you"?

2. A silk designer shirt isn't going to mean anything to Libra if your fingernails are dirty. How fastidious are you about polishing *all* the equipment?

3. Libra loves foreplay and that means it should begin the minute you walk in the door. Mental stimulus is vital. Do you understand that verbal foreplay is just as important to your lover as touch?

4. When romance in the relationship dies, the relationship itself will soon follow. Do you keep that pulse beating with wonderfully corny, sentimental, and surprising ways to communicate romantically?

5. Libra hates having to tell lovers to be romantic, that's about as exciting as kissing their own knees. So, are you romantic without having to tape notes to your forehead to remember birthdays?

If you got five out of five, and you're still encountering a cold back every time you feel warm and friendly, it's time for the next level of communication. Even if that means risking your own hurt feelings.

Ouch, that hurt!

We know that it's sometimes easier to say, "C'mon, I want to know what's really bothering you," than to actually hear the truth. What we hear can be so unexpected as to rock our own self-confidence. Our first impulse is to defend ourselves. Or to hurt back.

Excuse the analogy, but some of us are better at training pets than we are at dealing with human relationships. We know that if we call a dog to us and then hit it, that animal isn't going to be enthusiastic about running to us again. Well, Libra won't risk telling you truths if you urge him or her to tell you everything and then erupt upon hearing the response.

So, think about your own thin skin and toughen it up before you try for true honesty. Remember, Virgo, the love your mate is showing you by trying to communicate should validate your self-worth, not cause you to doubt it.

When Librans actually overcome their own fear of rejection, they will finally be "coming from love." It makes just as much sense that you "accept in love." After you sort out your bruised feelings, you'll understand that your lover's finally growing up. More good news: if you've been told what's wrong, that means Libra actually believes you can fix it! What faith! What love! Don't disappoint him or her by not trying.

Libra has indeed given you the greatest gift: risking your anger and possible rejection to finally trust you with his or her deepest feelings.

Money and Libra

Imagine Libra and Taurus together in a passionate relationship. Two lovers ruled by the same planet, Venus. Is this a perfect union? Well, Taurus may be more physical when it comes to showing affection, while Libra likes to talk about feelings as part of foreplay. However, when it comes to money, both are seriously in lust. They may both desire expensive collectibles, but how they get them differs radically. Our earth child, Taurus, is far more practical, and content to wait for just the right time and the right price. Our air sign, Libra, wants immediate gratification.

Although status conscious, not even Capricorn can hold a candle to Libra when it comes to creating their image. Is it perfect? Too dated? Too overdone? Too understated? Their very shaky egos are not so easy to spot, because crafty Libra camouflages them in the latest European chic.

Yes, immature Librans obsess about what other people think. They go way out of their way to create just the right illusion. Perhaps a genius film director can create great illusion on a small budget, but your average Libra needs a healthy credit limit. Money is a necessary chess piece in the image game.

A secret strategy

So, you've tried to explore your lover's financial picture, but all you get is a blank screen with a secret password on it? Your lover keeps a deadbolt on his or her wallet? By now you're beginning to realize that your mate is very secretive about finances. What's more, Libra is not going to be flattered if you begin prying into private territory.

In the zodiac, Librans have the sign of Scorpio in their second house, which rules possessions. Enigmatic Scorpio (who's coming up in the next chapter) is famous for being secretive.

"But we're married, and it's my business too!" you strongly protest to the mirror in the bathroom. I agree (please excuse me for following you into the bathroom), but suggest that you protest in the right arena—to your lover.

About that Swiss bank account

You might think that I'm going to urge a no-holds barred confrontation on this point. Not exactly. A wise astrologer doesn't fool around with Scorpio, and with this sign on the cusp of Libra's second house, ruling finances . . . well, a *gentle* confrontation is preferred. Remember at all times that you are not in a war, you're in a discussion!

This last point is vital because Librans, regardless of their smooth-as-silk exteriors, have hard metal where it counts. Even the female Libra is often a soft, tender flower resting demurely on a cast-iron stalk! There is a militant streak in Librans that accounts for many famous military men (Eisenhower heading the list) being born under this sign. What triggers their tempers is not only perceived injustice, but any attempt to invade their territory—like someone digging into their finances. That might be enough for them to call out the troops.

An interesting note: While Libra and Taurus share the same ruling planet, Venus, the sign of Taurus also rules the eighth house in Libra's horoscope. The eighth house has to do with other people's money—how you share it, inherit it, control it, invest it, and so on. And wherever Taurus is found in the horoscope, one thing is certain, the person risks getting stuck in materialism.

Caring is sharing

When it comes to money—especially joint finances—Libra must learn the true meaning of sharing. As far as I'm concerned, that's generosity and openness from the heart. However, with possessive Taurus on the cusp of this eighth house, it makes the lesson a lot harder to grasp.

Please understand that I don't expect your lover to become a radically different person overnight. Libra isn't going to clear out the savings account and face the unpredictable future with the raw nerve of a Gemini! That isn't going to happen, and there's no reason why it should. Saving is fine. Being less open about finances is something else.

Enter a new phase of communication with your lover by telling him or her that you feel shut out:

Libra: [Astonished] Shut out of what?

You: Out of an important part of your life.

This will come as a shock to someone who dreams only of how to bond more closely. Then explain how you feel about his or her secrecy with money, without making any demands. Remember three important facts are on your side:

1. Your lover's quite capable of thinking a problem through—as opposed to immediately reacting with emotion. You don't have to spell it out for him or her either. If Librans know that you feel financially frozen out of their life, they'll know exactly what they should do.

2. Librans desire harmony above all else, and this instinct on their part is your greatest ally.

3. They have an innate understanding of the art of compromise.

So, sit down and reach out to your lover. Remember, Leo, that you deeply love this person, you just don't happen to like the trait of financial secrecy. Pisces, don't get all emotional and confuse the trait with the lover. Both of you need to call on your reserve of patience. Remember that you can change the trait, and you may never find another lover with Libra's irresistible charm.

Finally, keep your eye on the objective at all times: to create the harmony that Libra craves and that you want to give. Don't expect Librans to give up old habits without a struggle, but in the end, their talent for compromise will win, and so will you.

An age-old problem

So, now that you've managed to convince Libra to open the vault, what you've found might surprise you both. Deep inside is another cause for your lover's tightfistedness—one he or she might never have confronted: the secret fear of reaching old age without financial resources. Librans might want to slam that vault shut! But don't let them.

You've hit on something very important here. If Librans haven't developed their abilities and inner emotional resources, that fear may be justified. With only waning looks and old love letters to keep them warm, it's going to get pretty chilly after the age of sixty-five. That's why this sign usually puts a lot of finances between them and the insecurity of old age. In the end, many a Libra who never took the time to become a whole person will substitute money for the security their charms once guaranteed.

It all leads us back to where we started—strong insecurity makes it doubly difficult for Librans to part with their money or possessions.

A new security blanket

Librans know how many assets they have in the bank, but you'd be surprised at how unaware they are of their own worth. Some really immature lovers—hiding their insecurities behind designer sunglasses—are downright bankrupt!

When someone knows they have talents, intelligence, and confidence to offer, they're not frightened of the future. Becoming all they can be (no, this is not a recruitment for the army!) will be a lot easier if you're around to shout encouragement from the sidelines.

It's an old maxim—the best lovers are also friends who help each other to explore and to grow. So, when was the last time (and hopefully there was a *first* time) when you gave your lover's potential some thought? Is your Libra everything he or she can be? Is there a part of him or her that's unfulfilled? Frustrated? Do you know what it is? Has it been too long since you shared that kind of closeness?

Too often we think that we completely know our lovers inside and out. It's then we stop asking question about dreams, hopes, and fears—and worse, sometimes we even stop listening.

What does all this have to do with Libra and money? Well, did you realize that Librans fear ending up in a soup line behind someone who's better dressed? They urgently need to develop more faith in their ability to handle the future. The only way to do that is by assessing their inner resources. That's where you come in:

You: Remember you used to talk about starting that business?

Libra: That was years ago.

You: What ever happened to that dream?

Libra: Are you serious?

You: Well, I was thinking about you last night, and how much talent you've got that you're not using.

Libra: [Smiling] I was using *all* of my talents last night.

You: I think you ought to dust off that old dream. Let's talk about it.

Libra: You *are* serious!

Now, that's a probable beginning, but you have to write your own dialogue. Maybe your lover's a Libra male who always wanted to be a writer, but he stopped using his cerebral resources because his charm and looks easily opened doors. Can you both work something out to give him more free time to write? Or perhaps your Libra lady has always dreamed of being an interior designer, but she fell into *Libranosis*, that state of total indecision. There are schools where she can go part-time, and there are books on the market that give advice and lead the way. Where there's that proverbial will, Libra can find a way. Just be there to help strengthen that will. Make Librans know—in their minds and down to their shoes—that they can do it!

Now, I'm not saying that you have to stop complimenting your Libran partners on their physical charms, but it will help to refer to their mental abilities and talents once in a while. Get them used to thinking of themselves as productive people who are able to turn dreams into realities. Then when they go to the shrine (the bathroom mirror), they'll see a lot more than just a good looking face. They'll see real honest-to-goodness substance that has been worked for and won all by themselves. They'll also see you standing next to them—a reflection of pure pride.

Power and Libra

Remember the unpleasant truth that I told you about Librans? That they cannot tell an unpleasant truth? This harmony-loving sign simply doesn't want to risk your anger by telling you something potentially upsetting. Librans believe that as long as they flash that charming smile and pretend everything is just fine (manipulation equals control . . .) you will continue to hopelessly adore them (. . . equals power). It simply doesn't occur to Librans that you might love them even more if they trusted you with their real feelings.

Now, you might not consider an attempt to keep you happy the same as manipulation. Cancer, no doubt this tranquil "let's avoid messy problems" relationship sounds like heaven! If you're a Libra as well, you and your lover are probably walking around in simultaneous backbends, just trying to please and keep the harmony flowing. "What's wrong with that?" our Libran lovers ask, their heads dangling above the floor.

The answer: "Everything." In order to keep control of their relationships, Librans begin to manipulate even themselves. At this stage in fledgling maturity, they have no idea how dangerous that is. Eventually, their unspoken motto "peace at any price" will become too expensive for either lover to pay.

After the pattern is well established, Librans discover they're trapped. Even if they honestly want to talk, they literally cannot communicate what's bothering them. There's too much of an inner struggle going on—a fight to the death between honesty and possibly losing the security of your love. Poor Libra will simply throw in the towel and lie by omission. If the problem is sexual, then a headache, toothache, you-name-it-ache around bedtime becomes an easy out. When you ask why your lover has turned down sex four nights in a row, and you hear, "My eyelashes are killing me," you know things have gone too far.

Prescription for trouble

Repressed emotions linger, grow, and fester. It's what keeps the pill people in business! As I've noted before, anger turned in on itself becomes depression. Isn't it bizarre how willing we are to take nearly lethal doses of pills to ease depression, when simply talking about the root of our anger could work like a miracle drug? Unfortunately, a lot of unhappy people don't have anyone there to listen. It's sad, but oh, so true. How lucky for your lover that he or she has you!

Creative Librans can devise a number of ways to avoid facing unpleasant feelings. They might go dancing and drinking with a friend, they might watch *Casablanca* five times in a row, or if things get really bad, they might just visit the friendly pill people.

"I'm just a little down today," they explain with a serene smile, while they clutch their bottle of pharmaceuticals.

Channeling their repressed feelings into safer outlets is another Libran area of expertise. Is your lover nagging you about something totally unimportant? Does he or she become extremely angry when dealing with a minor problem? Is Libra inexplicably depressed over some trivia on television? "Why am I crying?!" Libra asks, incredulously. "This adorable spelling bee champion just screwed up 'osmosis,' that's why!!"

Oh, my aching back!

The game of manipulation is as dangerous as Russian roulette. Repressed emotions can surface anywhere—and a favorite spot is in Libra's body. Think about it—where do Librans store all that repressed emotion? Often in their suddenly aching back. Libra rules the lower back and also the kidneys, so make sure that your lover drinks a lot of bottled water!

Don't forget that each astrological sign rules different parts of the body. Does that Taurus with the rasping voice have an unspoken truth stuck in his throat? Does Virgo, with that sensitive stomach, have a few truths to digest? Are Leos, the sign that rules the spine, taking pain killers because they're aching to tell someone "Get off my back!"? Stress will always manifest physically, and most people never make the connection between their painful emotions and hurting bodies.

Sometimes we even exhibit physical complaints from the part of the body ruled by our opposite sign. For instance, Libra's opposite sign is Aries, which rules the head. If you find your lover complaining of migraine headaches, then perhaps something is on his or her mind, building up pressure and threatening to explode.

Soul food

Yes, Libra can be complex, but then so can all the other signs in the zodiac. What about Gemini's terror of being tied down in a relationship—even when it's good? Cancer's nightmare of financial collapse—even when stocks are soaring? We all have our peculiar fears and foibles. Being in love doesn't only mean "never having to say you're sorry." It often means having to yell, "Help!"

So help is what I am offering in understanding this complex creature you have chosen to love. Librans, more than any other sign, believe in "true love"—love that was destined to be. And yet their totally unrealistic expectations can ruin everything. Your lover needs to learn the meaning of the term "soul mate." Few people really comprehend its depth. It definitely doesn't mean someone who is more miracle worker than lover, someone who is a cure-all for everything that's wrong with your life.

For Libra, the initial thrill of finding a seemingly perfect lover surpasses the adrenaline rush of winning the *Wheel of Fortune* jackpot. But then theres, "Oh, you're kidding! I have to pay taxes on the winnings?" That's right, there's no free lunch. Especially when it comes to relationships.

Communicate to your lover that if you're truly soul mates—a karmic relationship in which you have both known and loved each other in other lifetimes—chances are you've met again specifically to keep working out your problems. What a gift you've been given! The whole cosmic game plan is for you to help each other grow spiritually, learning to love in spite of—and because of—life's problems. I believe that what you don't come to terms with in this lifetime, you'll meet again in another lifetime. How many times have you felt that unbelievable feeling of familiarity with someone. You're instantly and totally comfortable with them. "Have we met before?" you ask. You can bet you have!

Time and time again

One of my older Libra clients told me that she was contacted by a Gemini male she had loved some thirty-five years earlier. Once she had dreamed of a commitment from this lover, who at that time (in true Gemini fashion) was busy sampling the honey from all the flowers. Although their relationship had broken up long ago, there was still a lot of deep feeling between them.

"Well," he sadly admitted, "I had my chance for happiness with you and I blew it. I will always regret it."

Libra tried to lighten his mood by saying, "Perhaps we'll do better in the next life."

"Are you so sure that we'll meet again?" Gemini asked, instantly brightening.

"Oh, I think we will. There's still a lot between us to be worked out."

"Then I'm happy I messed up," her old lover said, with that fascinating Gemini logic, "because now I know that I'll see you again."

A need to be needed

Astrology is fascinating because it holds the key to so many of life's mysteries. For instance, how did our immature, repressed lover get to be that way? Why do some Librans only think they're worth something if somebody needs them? That's how Librans see love—that's why they often search for self-worth in their lovers' eyes.

In the zodiac, the sign of Libra has a difficult square aspect to Cancer (symbolizing the mother) and also to Capricorn (symbolizing the father). Remember, I told you that a square is an aspect that requires more work in life, but at the same time, it teaches us a lot along the way.

For many Librans, this aspect indicates that they were in early conflict with their parents. They found it difficult to have their needs met without upsetting the harmony. Instead, they might have been in the position of having to satisfy a parent's desire first. Only when the parental need was met, was Libra considered a *good* child.

You can see the pattern, can't you? Perhaps in some extreme cases, the parent even withheld love if Libra didn't perform correctly. Whatever the scenario, many a Libra learned early in life that pleasing others was the way to happiness. They learned how to repress their own needs, in order to win someone else's approval . . . to be of value.

Have you ever really discussed what your lover's childhood was like? Do you see any of the above description in your mate's treatment of his or her own children? And if you're just beginning this long amorous trip, wouldn't it be wise to know what your lover thinks about these things before children come along?

So ask Librans what life was like way back when . . . when they didn't please Mom or Dad. If they turn white and clench their knuckles, it might be the beginning of some very interesting revelations.

Putting last things first

In this case, the "last thing" I'm referring to is your Libra lover—the person who must now begin putting himself or herself first. Your Libra has worried about offending people for too long, and has attempted to run a twenty-four-hour-a-day, seven-days-a-week popularity contest. In order to do that, Libra has swallowed truths, bitten off his or her tongue rather than voice displeasure, and compromised his or her true feelings. It's time Libra pushed his or her needs to the head of the line!

Help your lover by getting him or her to stop hiding behind manipulation. Do it by using Libra's need to be needed in its most positive way. Wait for a quite moment, like after dinner, and tell him or her that you *need* something, and without this "something" you're going to be absolutely miserable.

Now you have your Libra's attention. Take his or her hand, look deeply into those brilliant eyes, and tell your lover that that *something* is honesty.

This conversation might not take as long as you think. Remember, Librans like to solve problems. What's more, Librans are wonderful listeners, and will give you their full attention.

Between the two of you, you should be able to devise a way for Libra to express what's on his or her mind, before you both suffer from another marathon migraine.

You: Honesty will bring us closer together, not farther apart.

Libra: I hope so. [Your lover is obviously unconvinced.]

You: Let's start with why you went to bed early the other night with a headache? What caused it?

Libra: I don't want to upset you. [Libra is looking more uncomfortable by the second.]

You: Sweetheart, the only thing that upsets me is not knowing what's really going on in your mind. I need you—

Libra: I need you too!

You: . . . to tell me the truth.

Libra: Oh.

Not only will you appeal to Libra's need to be needed, but by explaining that it's just not *fair* to shut you out of his or her thoughts, you'll be appealing to that famous Libran sense of justice! The balance scales have got to swing in your favor.

Even if it takes much longer, and many more conversations, it will be worth your time and effort. Look at it this way, communication is so much cheaper than having to pay an eyelash specialist!

Decanates

Take two lovers born under the sign of Libra and they can be radically different. One is able to work for compromise in a relationship, the other is so self-involved that a try at communication ends up being a monologue. Why are they like day and night? Studying decanates can explain a lot of the differences.

You see, every sign in the zodiac is divided into three parts. Each sign spans thirty days, every day equaling one degree. Each decanate represents approximately ten degrees. While the first ten degrees reflect the nature of the signs itself, the other decanates have different planets as sub-rulers. So, while Libra is generally ruled by Venus, people can also be sub-ruled by Uranus and Mercury, dependent on the dates they were born.

Is your Libra a mirror-image of the sign? Is there a sub-ruler that will modify your lover's behavior? It's all right here . . .

September 24 to October 3

Your lover's Sun falls in the Venus decanate of Libra. Here are the true Librans in all their glory: artistic, more than a little vain, falling head over heels in love with love, and then wondering why ugly reality has to ruin everything! Reality, of course, being the simple demands of any grownup union. However, this Libra, when not yet a full adult, is a classic romantic—whose feet are firmly planted in the clouds. They fall in love, but should they make a firm commitment? Libra will equivocate the question out of existence. Handle responsibility? Not if they can avoid it. That's why many are involved in more than a few hit and run romances.

So take your time with these Librans. Make sure they've outgrown their fickleness. If they're really ready for you, then you can expect someone who will always try to see your point of view, who detests arguments, and who strives to bring harmony and beauty into your life. If you can have all that, then handle this Libra with the best kid gloves, because you have indeed found the perfect lover.

October 4 to October 13

Uranus is the sub-ruler of this decanate, and combined with Venus, it's a very exciting combination!

While many are involved in the arts (a multitude of actors are born under this decanate), Uranus also bestows a strong humanitarian streak. These lovers not only want to bring beauty into their own lives, but they yearn to bring it into everyone else's too. Not all of us respond to the higher vibrations of Uranus, but those who do have a strong social conscience. They will look for ways to improve society and make a difference.

There's also an influence of the planet Saturn, which means that unlike those born under the first decanate, who might need more time for commitment, these lovers take their relationships very seriously. Responsibility doesn't frighten them in the least. If anything, they may assume too much responsibility toward a loved one. It's not that they become overly possessive, it's just that all-consuming caring on a twenty-four-hour basis can suck the oxygen out of any room. The cure is to let them know when you simply need more space.

Also, help these lovers develop their natural sense of humor toward life and toward themselves. Sometimes they become too gloomy, too insecure. They need you to make them believe they can move mountains. Once they feel your faith, not even the Himalayas will be safe!

October 14 to October 23

Sub-ruled by Mercury, you'll need running shoes to keep up with these lovers. Mercury sharpens their minds and their tongues. They have a driving need to communicate. So not only may your lover speak four languages, but he or she may show a natural bent for writing.

Now, take Libra's innate sense of justice, combine it with Mercury's articulate talents, and you could fall in love with a future Supreme Court justice!

This articulate Libra is usually very popular, and the competition will be stiff. So, if you're in love, keep your eye on the brass ring. If you want to win in the end, then be there when Libra's blue Mondays run into Saturday nights. Yes, this sign can get irritable and many a regretted remark will fly off their tongues. If you can love these Librans enough to help them restore their much-needed balance, the love you get back will sustain and nourish you. It will make you the envy of all those who were shortsighted enough to let that brass ring slip through their fingers.

The Libra Lover

September 24 to October 23

The Good

Seductive

Diplomatic

Artistic

Discerning

Popular

The Bad

Vain

Manipulative

Pretentious

Indecisive

Image-conscious

The Ugly

Narcissistic

Dishonest

Lazy

Procrastinating

Superficial

"When people care for you and cry for you, they can straighten out your soul."
—LANGSTON HUGHES

Scorpio

October 24 to November 22

Sex and Scorpio

They love intensely. They hate intensely. They live in the passion of the moment. Scorpios use their formidable intellects to focus completely on sensations at hand, and their favorite sensations consist of sexual pleasures that are all-seductive and all-consuming.

Ruled by both fiery Mars and the dark planet Pluto, this water sign is linked to the eighth house of sex, and so it makes perfect sense that it also rules the sex organs. Many Scorpios are devoted to this part of the body with a passion that's akin to a religious calling. However, you probably won't find either sex in the gym boasting about their sexual conquests. Scorpio considers boasting strictly for amateurs.

The eyes have it

There's an air of mystery about Scorpios that hints at their inner depths. Indeed, they seem to be born with a innate knowledge of erotic love. Perhaps it's their fascination with the undercurrents of life, including sexual taboos that are deep, dark, and seductive. However, most Scorpios (who are usually very secretive) don't have to say a word about their love of erotica. It's all in their eyes.

Oh, those eyes! So hypnotic that you find yourself drowning in their depths. Once you're the focus of their intent gaze, it's impossible to escape the magnetic energy. What their mesmerizing stare is telling you is this:

"I want to own you, body and soul. I want to penetrate the most secret part of you. However, I myself am afraid of losing control and having to deal with my deepest feelings."

Oops!

Now, if your Scorpio lover actually said those words to you, would you take two steps back and reconsider? Probably not. You see, Scorpio's sexual allure is so hypnotic, so total, that like Ulysses, you would feel compelled to continue—answering the siren's call, being swept closer and closer to danger but incapable of turning back. Only, what if the voice added:

"I just want to warn you that because I don't want to be penetrated (emotionally speaking), I can become self-protective, suspicious, and distrustful."

Well, the sad truth is that you might be smart enough to cancel dinner, but you would probably still convince yourself that Scorpio either has a wild sense of humor, or is experiencing temporary insanity and it will all be over by midnight! The truth is that Scorpios seek partners who can help them to better understand their complex souls. They have a primal need to merge with a lover, to experience a union with someone on a deep physical and spiritual level. That's why Scorpio represents the sex drive—because it's a means to this end of surrender and transformation. Only there's a hitch. While Scorpios desire this with all their being, they still fear letting a lover get too close to them, and becoming too vulnerable.

Wild, wicked, and wonderful

Both male and female Scorpios are experimental in love. Although this is one of the most heterosexual signs in the zodiac, there's nothing they don't want to explore, and the more socially forbidden, the better. There's also little they won't indulge in when it comes to sexual stimulation. The more graphic, the better. Reading Keats to a Virgo lover might be magical, but if you're going to read to your Scorpio lover, try an earthy chapter of *Sexus* by Henry Miller. Naughty videos, magazines, and toys (especially those that require AA batteries) are all Scorpio favorites. Hopefully, if you're in love with a Scorpio, he or she is a bit older, because then they might have worked out a kink or two in their infamously kinky natures.

When Scorpios are younger they really don't know how to recognize love and often mistake passion for the real thing. "Oh, my gosh," the young, horny Scorpio cries, "I've had three orgasms in a row—let's elope!"

However, most immature Scorpios will shy away from commitment like wild horses, and might even prefer to go it alone rather than be saddled with the responsibility of a relationship. But when they do commit themselves, it is permanent and, you guessed it, *intense.* Remember the Scorpio whose eyes silently told you, "I want to own you body and soul and penetrate the most secret part of you"? Well, be prepared for the kind of all-consuming passion that made Elizabeth Taylor marry Scorpio Richard Burton, twice. When a male or female Scorpio makes love to you, they will feel your orgasm in the marrow of their bones. When you cry, they will taste the salt of your tears. Their intent is to totally merge with you (physically, psychically, spiritually) and therefore, their sex drive is powerful.

But wait! What about that deep down fear of losing control and really sharing their hidden feelings?

Let's pause for the realities of life. Having wild, wicked and way out sex has nothing to do with Scorpios baring their soul. Both males and females are lusty animals, and if they're fortunate enough to find a lover who will pay oral homage to the part of the body their sign rules . . . they'll be divinely happy. But they can also be private to the point of paranoia. If they as much as suspect that you're trying to control them, or if you probe too deeply into their private realms (not to be confused with their private parts!) they'll smell danger, and the immature will become very afraid. Yes, they desperately want an idealistic physical and spiritual union, yet, as I told you, they still fear what they might have to sacrifice in order to get it.

So what happens? If you frighten a passionate but immature Scorpio lover, he or she might react by trying to seek control over what frightens him or her—namely, you! This can be done by giving you so many orgasms that you'll be semi-unconscious until Christmas. If that doesn't happen, you might get a taste of other control tactics, such as Scorpio's talent for intimidation and dictatorial behavior. If you want a relationship that's going to hum along smoothly with a lover who doesn't sit in the front seat of an emotional roller coaster ride, then Scorpio is definitely not for you. When immature, these lovers are volatile. They have tempestuous tempers and a mega talent for overt jealousy. If given truth serum, they would admit to feeling miserable before they admit to not feeling anything at all. Oh no, embarking on a relationship with Scorpio recalls Margo Channing's famous line in the classic film *All About Eve*: "Fasten your seatbelts, it's going to be a bumpy night!"

Possessive to a fault

With insecurity comes the devil of crazy, green-eyed jealousy—and he never travels without a full arsenal of possessiveness. An immature Scorpio often makes the mistake of confusing closeness for ownership. In *Erotic Astrology*, I told you that Scorpios may not actually brand their initials on the inside of a lover's thigh, but it isn't because they don't fantasize about it!

Possessiveness is a quality that a sign like Pisces loves because it makes them feel wanted and secure. However, an independent lover like Leo will hate the ownership tendency of Scorpio, because they simply refuse to be dominated. Even "live and let live" Aquarius loves freedom too much to stick around the house in order to keep Scorpio's paranoia at a low. Because Taurus can out-opinion and out-possess any Scorpio, clashes between these two signs are definitely possible, so keep the first-aid kit handy!

You do not have the right to remain silent

Knowledge is power, and Scorpio wants to know everything about you. Just try looking into those eyes and lying—it's impossible. It won't be long before you realize that your lover would make an excellent detective, because he or she is that perceptive. The hidden mysteries of life fascinate Scorpios (death and sex are at the top of these fascinations), and their tactical maneuvers to get to the truth have been honed to an art form. Hmmm, I just thought of something interesting. Perhaps there's a stronger tie between sex and death than we realize. After all, the French (who know a lot about these things) do call the orgasm *le petit mort*, the little death. That moment when time is suspended and we are in blissful cosmic limbo. In the same way, the orgasm is what Scorpios desire for exactly the same reason—to transcend reality and experience a death of the ego. It's that sublime sensation they seek in the arms of their lovers.

Anyway, back to our Scorpio investigative abilities. Trust me, and don't try to hide your age, weight, tax bracket, or how many lovers you have enjoyed—with Scorpio, you don't stand a chance!

Bitter revenge

Lovers of a Scorpio who harbor a death wish will make sure they go out of their way to make Scorpio feel rejected, or worse, betrayed.

A very good reason to never play the usual lover's game (flirting and trying to make the other person jealous) is that a less than mature Scorpio has a wicked vengeful streak. You might be playing around fairly innocently, but, believe me, you are playing with fire.

The deep, dark waters of Scorpio's psyche will immediately begin to churn. They will imagine scenarios far worse than any reality. Obsession will set in and they will chew, rechew, and never swallow your tearful and truthful explanation. Finally, they will seek revenge and when it gets to that point, they show no mercy. As a matter of fact, like the scorpions, whose deadly sting kills them as well as their enemy, the sting of the Scorpio lover is only used when they are totally threatened. Then their pain is enough to make them lash out and to hell with the consequences.

Now, that doesn't mean your lover simply will telephone you or dramatically mail you the ashes of your burned love letters. Oh no, Scorpio is master and mistress of psychological manipulation. Along with knowing the most sensitive parts of your body to stroke and caress, Scorpios are intimately familiar with your tender Achilles heel. You know, that vulnerable spot in your psyche that you thought you had so artfully disguised? Be prepared to have your lover plot, plan, and take his or her delicious time. Then, when you least expect it, Scorpio will go right for that Achilles heel with a vengeance. You may recover from this psychological attack in time to tell your great-great grandchildren how you survived, but you will still bear the emotional bruises. It's much smarter to understand this lover and avoid all that volcanic spewing in the first place. The strategy is simple: just never threaten Scorpio's sexual insecurities—anyhow, anytime, anywhere, with anybody. Any questions?

Feeling a little hungry?

One of my clients told me a chilling tale of revenge by her Scorpio ex-lover. He didn't use sarcasm or inflict any painful embarrassments. You see, this Scorpio was beautifully subtle and diabolical: his punishment was that he simply withheld sex. Knowing how much Scorpio loves sex, it's safe to assume that this lover must have been really, really angry! Of course, he never admitted what he was doing and she was much too proud to accuse him of it. It just happened night after night and their union *unhappened* soon after.

Come to think of it, she always claimed that sex wasn't that important to her. But with her Mars in Scorpio, I suspected the astrological truth: this lady has a very healthy appetite for sex. Interesting note: in a woman's chart, the sign in which Mars is found tells you her sexual preference in men, and in a man's chart it tells you a lot about his own sexuality. Well, with Mars in Scorpio, this lady was a passionate sexual creature and her lover knew it only too well. Being expert at discovering just what punishment was going to hurt the most, and knowing that sex fed her soul, Scorpio put her on a starvation diet.

Of course, before it gets to the extreme behavior noted above, if you know that Scorpio is brewing a dark concoction of fear, jealousy, and revenge in his or her mind, try to talk to your lover at the outset. If you've messed up, then say you're sorry and let Scorpio delight a bit in your groveling. This show of humility won't hurt you at all, only don't overdo it, bleeding knees are not necessary. However, if you are innocent, then talk it out and show Scorpio where his or her thinking has hit a blind spot. Remember that the minds of Scorpios come with X-ray vision, and they will know when you are speaking the truth. If they know (and you know they know), but they still continue to torture you, then suggest therapy, immediately if not sooner.

Power of the Phoenix

So, who exactly is this private, passionate person you've lost your libido to? Astro-psychologists equate Scorpio with the developmental phase of people between the ages of thirty-six to forty-five, when suddenly we become aware that we're not going to live forever and the light at the end of the tunnel becomes definitely otherworldly. It's also a time when we come into our own powers, and the powers of Scorpio, both physical and intellectual, are legendary.

As Scorpios mature, you will probably notice many qualities of their opposite sign, Taurus, coming to light. This earth sign's qualities will begin to keep Scorpio grounded, their tendency to be swept away by emotions will be modified, and relationship stability will rear its glorious head. Once developed, the innate loyalty of Scorpio can even surpass the famous loyalty of the Taurean Bull. Passion will begin to be tempered with gentleness and your lover will do all that's necessary to make your relationship work.

However, on the way to this ideal maturity, Scorpios will go to extremes, and more than once you'll fear they have managed to self-destruct. But no matter how far they fall, unless it's because of lunacy or 'ludes, Scorpios can always find their way back to the light.

They simply have an incredible power to regenerate themselves. Example: the scorpion who loses its tail and promptly grows another one.

Remember that inhabitant of a styrofoam house on the corner of Broadway and 26th Street? The one who had sunk so low his nose was scraping the pavement? That could well have been a Scorpio whose passions had gotten out of control until, like the scorpion, he began stinging himself to death. Sadly, drugs and alcohol can be a favorite escape route for Scorpios on the run from themselves. But remember how that Broadway resident one day miraculously pulled himself together and found a whole new purpose for being alive? That was another of this sign's amazing strengths and symbols—the phoenix rising from the ashes, the head bloody but unbowed.

So never give up on Scorpios, because their intelligence and strength are monumental. Just when you think all hope is lost, they will re-empower and reinvent themselves. If you are truly in love—and if you truly love—then give Scorpio the support and inspiration he or she needs. It's the foundation for all miracles!

Money and Scorpio

You might think that Scorpio's desire for control extends to a tight grip on finances. Not true. Although your lover may salivate while watching a bank balance grow, and know how to stick to a budget, Scorpios can be very generous when it comes to sharing money in a relationship. Can they be as materialistic as their opposite sign, Taurus? Of course not, that's why it's their polar *opposite*, remember? Yes, Scorpios like to travel first class, but they're strongly spiritual and not as overly concerned with material goodies like Taurus, the Bull. Scorpios are not interested in working for money alone. These are all or nothing people, and they must be engrossed in what they're doing or they simply don't want to do it. That doesn't mean they don't like money (remember, this sign rules the unholy trinity: sex, death, and money), it just means they require work that makes demands on their intellect, on their investigative abilities to research, and on their formidable talent for long-range strategy.

Reaching for the brass ring

You can be sure, however, that once Scorpio gets bitten by the competitive bug, he or she will be in that corner office before the competition can cry "Thief!" They do it with a magical sleight of hand: playing their aces close to the chest and never letting their strategy be known. Male and female Scorpios are both formidable opponents. Even in hard times, these people are never found in the fetal position with a thumb in their mouth and a forefinger stroking their eyelashes. Oh no, remember that one of Scopio's symbols is the phoenix rising from the ashes. They have the power to regenerate themselves because they're true warriors with the bravest of hearts, and you should never, never count them out.

When Scorpios do find a professional niche that fascinates them, then money becomes important not only as a reward for talent, but because it brings what every Scorpio lusts after even more than your fabulous body—control.

Love me, love my private parts . . .

Note: Some extreme Scorpios want to keep secret what kind of cereal they had for breakfast. Mix that extremism with a heavy dose of money control—and you might expect a few problems.

You: You got a telephone call today from a Robert Jones at the Pacific Bank.

Scorpio: Oh yeah, I'll have to call him back.

You: [Puzzled] But both our accounts are at the First Bank.

Scorpio: Honey, I have a separate account. It doesn't touch any of the money in either our checking or savings.

You: [Strange lights dancing before your eyes] You do?

Scorpio: [Smiling] Yes. Don't you have one?

You: No, I don't have one! *I didn't know you had one.*

Okay, now you know, and the first thing racing through your mind after, "Who is this stranger I suddenly don't know?" is, "How much money is in that personal, private account anyway?"

Would it shock you to consider that it's none of your business?

The truth is that you fell in love with a Scorpio, and this is someone who treasures privacy. Yes, sometimes Scorpio can seem a little paranoid. Well, sometimes he or she *is* a little paranoid, but you have to respect your lover's wishes. Scorpio isn't shutting you out of his or her life simply because there's a bank account you didn't know about. And if you know that your partner isn't a second-story man, or a lady who shoplifts fine jewelry, then you can pretty much guess the amount in that bank account won't pay for a world cruise. Chances are it's just enough money to let your Scorpio feel independent. If you're living well above poverty level and you're not scrambling for every penny, what's wrong with that?

What could be wrong with it is that in our society, reflected in films and in every fairytale we read as kids, we're supposed to get married, live happily ever after, share every waking thought, and let our spouses know how much money we have—down to the penny—at all times.

Tipping the balance scales

So, this is the moment of truth. Are you secure enough in your relationship to know that your lover has a separate bank account without having to know the balance? Do you love your Scorpio enough to want him or her to have enough privacy to feel comfortable? Even if that makes you feel a lot less comfortable?

Aquarius, your motto is "live and let live." If you're happy enough with the money you both make and save together, you probably won't mind at all knowing that your lover has a separate bank account. You might even like someone who wants that kind of freedom, because it allows you to have freedom of your own. Taurus, this might be more of a problem for you, because you might see this independence as betrayal. Don't steam behind a wall of silence. Instead, sit down and talk about your feelings with your lover. Hopefully, your Scorpio is at a maturity level that will put your mind at ease.

Capricorn, you might even admire a partner who chooses to be independent with a separate bank account. Chances are you probably already have your own. Cancer and Pisces, work on your self-esteem! Understand that a separate bank account does not mean that your lover loves you less. No matter what your sign, there's a good possibility that Scorpio has helped to manage your money. You see, Scorpio rules the eighth house in a horoscope, and that includes other people's finances.

Now, how do you deal with someone who might be helping you out with your finances, but at the same time isn't telling you everything about theirs? You do it the way I have taught you, of course: gently, patiently, quietly, calmly, with total love, and no weapons!

It's about the money, honey

It's well within reason to explain to your lover what a sensible idea it is to let each other know what financial holdings exist. Ask where a private bank account might be, but—and this is the hard part—not necessarily how much is in it. Say that it's possible something could happen to one of you and that means that both of you should know how to get in touch with the other's finances. Again, *don't* ask for the balance. You can bet that your partner will be anticipating the third degree. Waiting to be asked just how much money is in that account . . . and why didn't you ever mention it . . . and what happened to sharing our lives . . . and what happened to love . . . and . . . this kind of guilt trip is not headed for the bedroom and wonderful sex, it's headed for separation! So fool Scorpio and don't ask for how much money has been put away. As I told you, it probably can't buy bars of gold, only a feeling of independence. But to a Scorpio, you can believe that feeling of privacy is worth its weight in gold.

Of course, if you say that you don't care how much is in the separate account, Scorpio will immediately turn on the famous X-ray vision he or she uses to see through people and know that that isn't true. It's far better to say: "Honey, I think we should at least know where each other's finances are, and if you prefer that I don't know the exact amount, that's all right." Wonderful! You haven't gagged, you haven't stuttered, and your bottom lip is only slightly bleeding. I am proud of you.

Now, perhaps just that act of faith on your part will let Scorpio relax and do what's so difficult for this complicated sign to do—trust! The more you trust your lover, the more trust you will receive in return. That's a truism for every mate, no matter what his or her sign. In the end, it will be his or her love for you—and appreciation of you—that Scorpio will be absolutely unable to hide.

Power and Scorpio

As you know by now, a lover seeks control because it gives him or her a sense of power. The irony is that thirst for power is usually most severe when a person feels powerless. Have you ever noticed that when people are really confident of their powers they don't have to rule others with an iron hand? So, if you're having problems of power with your Scorpio mate, it's a good bet that a lot of pain has made him or her feel powerless, and that pain has gone unspoken. Astrologers have referred to this sign as "the wounded healer." It refers to Scorpios' tremendous potential for healing both themselves and others. Yet they must first venture into the dark areas of their soul, find those buried resentments, those emotions that have been turned inward and frozen in fear, expose them, and be transformed. It sounds a lot more serious than "take two aspirin and call me in the morning," and yet the incredible power of your caring, trust, and love can help to make it happen.

Look at it this way, you fell in love with the most complicated being in the zodiac, someone whose passions can thrill you in parts of your body and soul you never knew existed. That kind of intensity merits helping Scorpio to become a healthy, whole person—doesn't it? Also consider this point: once your lover's energies are freed from self-destructive patterns, there will be even more of that fabulous, intense sexual energy for you! I offer that perk to get you through the overtime that lies ahead!

Hide and seek

Until Scorpios' hidden fears come to the surface, the repression can show itself in many disturbing ways. For starters, they can *overreact* emotionally when you push their "vulnerability" buttons, even if you have put your finger on it just by chance. Perhaps you made an off-handed remark about something that you hardly suspected was bothering them.

Instead of responding like a fairly healthy, mature adult, chances are you met with a temper bordering on violence. Or an icy shoulder that sent chills to your heart. How do you turn those tempestuous tides?

Well, let's recap: you know that your lover gets uptight when you get near to discovering his or her true self. The question is, "Why?" If your lover's honest feelings are kept under lock and key, what would happen if they got out? What exactly is he or she afraid of?

Those of us who have played the game of trying not to think about something—whether it's an old grudge, an unflattering remark, something hurtful our parents did to us at puberty, or whatever—know the power of repression. We know what a burden it is to carry around resentments and how often they come to the surface in headaches and heartaches. There's an expression that holds a lot of wisdom: "You are only as healthy as the secrets you keep."

It's just one of those things

It's interesting to think about what really frightens us, because we never consider how much power it has over us. Who gave it all that power? We did! Year after year, as we build up our defenses against it, hiding, ducking, avoiding, and evading it—sometimes even trying to deny its existence—the *thing* grows stronger and stronger until we either have to confront it or be overwhelmed by it. Think a moment. It make sense that as we come to confront what frightens us, the power it has over us diminishes – the light goes on in the darkened room—and lo and behold, one day it no longer paralyzes us and we are a whole person again. That's the goal, my friends. It doesn't happen overnight. But it's worth every bit of our energies on this life's journey. It makes the difference between not only being comfortable in our own skins, but being able to offer the love of our lives a real honest-to-goodness healthy adult.

How many people have you known who wait and dream about finding that fabulous once-in-a-lifetime love, and then when they find it, they're not adult enough to handle the relationship? Probably the statistics would outdo the number of kids with wet pants in kindergarten!

A few more words about "the wounded healer" that is hidden in Scorpio. I told you that it's necessary Scorpios treat their own emotional wound first—the killer wound that has terminated more than one promising relationship; the wound that has encroached upon their own self-confidence, and is sucking dry the balm they need to feel good about themselves; the wound that has all the power over them!

Now, always keep in mind that we're talking about a *less* mature lover, because more grownup Scorpios might go through the fires of emotional hell—as steel is forged in fire—

and these warriors walk out of it stronger than ever. Your less wise lover can do the same, he or she just needs a loving hand to hold when the trip gets too hot for comfort. But be prepared during this meltdown for your lover to not always show the appreciation you deserve. Don't forget how easy it is to fear or resent people who bring our deepest insecurities to light. We tend to lash out when someone touches that very sensitive wound. Growing a thicker skin during this time might not be a bad idea at all!

Beware of pressure points

Most important, begin communication by treading lightly. Scorpios are *very* private people and they have to know their lovers for quite some time before they let their guard down (you *are* in this for a longer haul than just the weekend, aren't you?)

Trust is essential with this sign, so don't pressure because Scorpio will only back away. Most importantly, how is your own trust level? It's only common sense that you have to show Scorpios trust in them before they will trust you. Those are the rules of the game. However, with their trust, the walls of self-protection will eventually come tumbling down. With the battlements down, communication will come. With communication, the dark monsters that have been lurking underground for so long will come to light. And eventually, with the light will come the transformation Scorpio has been seeking.

It might be a good idea to review the astrological symbols of this lover: the scorpion, who can kill itself with its own deadly sting. That's the part that needs to be transformed. The eagle that soars above everything else—that's the highest energy of Scorpio. And the phoenix, the bird that rises from the ashes of its old self and is totally transformed and regenerated—that's our goal.

Solving the mystery

The best news is that your lover is someone who has great courage. Scorpio will need it now to go into that dark room of his or her psyche and turn on the light! On your side is Scorpio's innate love of the unknown and the thrill of uncovering it. There is no mystery this sign is unwilling to investigate. When trust has made communication between you possible, why not offer that suggestion to your lover? Suggest that old hurts and resentments are causing unhappiness. Does your lover have the courage to investigate the biggest mystery of all—himself or herself?

Remember, this is a challenge that must come from love and respect, and not echo your own resentment or frustration. Your Scorpio will know the difference.

Every sign is the same when it comes to the struggle of realizing personal potential. There's healing to be done, whether it's Capricorn's hangup with stature, Taurus' hangup with material comfort, or Scorpio's hangup with buried resentments. All our signs share the need for a rare medicine: the love of partners who are patient to a very generous fault, and who are willing to really commit themselves to a relationship, giving it the time and energy it really needs to grow.

So, keep your eye on the goal: helping Scorpio to heal old wounds and to see your lover transform from the Scorpion into the Eagle. When therapy is completed, I promise that you will be delighting in the most incredible and intense sensuality that you can possibly fantasize. Just like the eagle, my dear, you are going to fly!

Decanates

Take two lovers born under the sign of Scorpio and they can be radically different. One is able to work for compromise in a relationship, the other is so self-involved that a try at communication ends up being a monologue. Why are they like day and night? Studying decanates can explain a lot of the differences.

You see, every sign in the zodiac is divided into three parts. Each sign spans thirty days, each day equals one degree, and each decanate encompasses approximately ten degrees. While the first ten degrees reflect the nature of the sign itself, the other decanates have different planets as sub-rulers. So, while Scorpio is generally ruled by Mars and Pluto, people can also be sub-ruled by either Neptune or the Moon, dependent on the date they were born.

Is your Scorpio a mirror-image of the sign? Is there a sub-ruler that will modify your lover's behavior? It's all right here . . .

October 24 to November 2

Ruled by Mars, your partner's personality is a compelling paradox. On the outside, he or she seems to be cool, calm, and collected, but look a little deeper and you will find seething emotions behind those intense Scorpio eyes. These people tend to be extremists; there is little black and white in their thinking, and hardly any middle ground in their compromises. Yes, Mars-ruled Scorpios have the potential to be either a sinner or saint, and one must take the whole chart into consideration before passing judgment. However, one thing is certain: if they respond more to their darker side in this lifetime, they will be self-destructive with a vengeance, and their jealousy and temper can cause themselves (and their lovers) more than one sleepless night. But if they respond to their higher selves, there is no other sign in the zodiac who can compete with them for sheer will and dedication to ideals. The choice is theirs.

Of course, the choice to commit yourself to this relationship is yours alone. So, take your time and take a good look at which direction you lover is headed . . . up or down!

November 3 to November 12

Remember that Neptune can be the planet of both illusion and delusion, so again, it's the maturity of your lover that indicates which planetary vibration is the strongest.

In the advanced type of partner, Scorpio's formidable self-discipline (after having conquered his or her own nature) is now turned outward to sacrifice for a higher purpose. So you may have found a lover who, thanks to Neptune, is inspired to lofty ideals, and thanks to the energy and fire of the planet Mars, you can share the excitement of seeing it all become a reality. In doing so, these higher-evolved Scorpios can make a tremendous difference for the good of society.

However, if your lover is still possessed by the emotion of the moment, then he or she can succumb to pleasures of the moment—and all too often that includes the well-known escape routes: sex, alcohol, or even drugs. If there was a little too much experimentation in their youth, hopefully they are now ready for more important matters—namely, growing up and realizing their potential. Never forget Scorpios' ability to transform themselves . . . your love and faith can be the impetus to make it happen.

November 13 to November 22

Just in time comes the Moon! If your lover has a sub-ruler of the intuitive, sensitive Moon, you can expect far more sympathy in his or her nature. There is also the potential to be very psychically sensitive. Ever wonder how they seem to know just what you're thinking? It's the ability of Moon Children to tune into someone else's psyche. That doesn't mean that your lover will lose a bit of Scorpio's passion and intensity—if anything, it just intensifies it! However, expect their volatile feelings to be tempered with more softness, warmth, and the ability to put themselves in your shoes.

You'll appreciate this latter quality when you find yourself in a disagreement with your lover. Before it turns to an all-out war, this Scorpio, who is swayed by the qualities of the Moon, will be far more ready to communicate—and his or her famous X-ray vision into your shortcomings will be tempered with empathy and kindness. These qualities are definitely the ingredients for long-term happiness.

The Scorpio Lover

October 24 to November 22

The Good

Erotic

Intriguing

Powerful

Passionate

Healing

The Bad

Deviant

Manipulative

Violent

Jealous

Suspicious

The Ugly

Devouring

Underhanded

Destructive

Vindictive

Paranoid

"Love is an irresistible desire to be irresistibly desired."

—ROBERT FROST

Sagittarius

November 23 to December 21

Sex and Sagittarius

When it comes to sex, this fire sign, ruled by abundant Jupiter, brings a banquet to the table. Your lover approaches sex with the same passion that he or she exhibits when exchanging ideas—and your lover does both magnificently under the sheets. A Sagittarius favorite is the foreplay of verbal gymnastics. If you haven't experienced some scintillating discourse with your intercourse, then you have yet to know the mental and physical seduction of a Sagittarius lover.

How fitting that the symbol for this sign is the Archer—half-beast, half-human, shooting arrows of insatiable curiosity into the air and aiming for the highest truth. That knowledge includes an in-depth study of sex; however, Sag (that's their popular nickname, with a soft "g") isn't interested in buying a manual on the subject. Both sexes want to experience every facet of love, from anticipation to orgasm. In the same way they thirst for adventure, nothing excites Sag more than the terrain of a newly seduced body.

It's all in the eyes

If you're lucky enough have encountered a real grownup Sag lover, then you know that sex can be a meaningful and spiritual experience. However, if your lover is still stumbling on the rocky road to maturity, then problems can arise. Let's say that your relationship is fairly new, and even though Sag swears that he or she is "crazy about you," your lover's eyes still drift away when some *body* new enters the party. It's not too late to cash in your chips and quit while you're ahead. Okay, you protest, Sag's eyes are focused solely on you, wonderful! Nothing can go wrong . . . or can it?

After the seduction and falling in love (not always in that order), most people settle into the comfort and security of their relationships. Hold everything! That's exactly what can scare the pants on a Sag lover. (No, that was *not* a misprint!) You see, those born under this sign love their independence and freedom. They need space. Lots of it. Acres of it!

A suggestion from me: before you become Sag's lover, it's smart to become his or her friend. Let Sag get to know you before *really* knowing you, if you know what I mean! If it's too late and you've already given your heart and beautiful body to an immature Sag who finds one-night stands too lengthy, you might want to reevaluate your commitment. However, if your lover is further along the road to being mature, and just seems to be fonder of his or her freedom than of you, perhaps some nonverbal communication can help. (I will explain later.)

Getting to know you

Before we plan our strategy, let's take a look at exactly how much of a banquet you're bringing to the table. Hopefully it isn't crackers and Velveeta! You see, after seduction, this lover wants a real partner. Not only will you be required to be a "buddy" in the sense of sharing Sag's love of the outdoors, but you will be expected to be as intellectually alive as your lover. Do you know what's going on in the world or do you limit your news to a quick briefing at prime time? Do you have a thirst for knowledge? Your Sag does. Do you love to travel? Are you curious about different cultures? Your Sag always is. Do you need time to be alone or does spending time with yourself feel like a bad blind date? Sag needs time to go off and find himself or herself again. And again. And again. They need a lover and companion who understands that and doesn't feel threatened by it.

Aries, you can probably match this sign's love of adventure, and your appreciation of physical sports is a big plus. However, Cancer, your tendency to cling could spell disaster. As for you, Pisces, Sag's idea of freedom being next to Nirvana is your idea of being next to nothing. Aquarius, you could make this relationship work because you are not possessive and you have your own independent and restless nature. Your love of the unconventional and Sag's love of the unknown could end with sex under a Guatemalan volcano. It doesn't get hotter than that!

What's your rush?

Of course, when we fall in love, most of us want a commitment. The Sag lover is no different, but it usually happens much later, so have patience. Whatever you do, do not make demands until you have become an important part of this lover's life. Until that happens, demands will only send them packing, and they'll run off with your radical Aquarius friend and you'll get a postcard from Guatemala!

Another motivation to have a strong relationship before you expect a strong commitment is this sign's desire to please. Frankly, an immature but always enthusiastic Sag can tell you what you want to hear—and make promises they can't keep. Yes, they mean it at the moment, but moments only last sixty seconds, and that might be all right for a memorable Saturday night, but not for a lifetime.

It's important to repeat an old truth: No matter what your sign, you have to study your own personal horoscope (and your lover's) in order to understand just how compatible you might be. For instance, if you're a Cancer, you might have four or more planets in Leo (a big Sag turn-on, by the way) changing the whole tone of your chart. So use what I tell you as guidelines now and get to know your personal self in-depth later. It's interesting to note that a tradition in India is to match horoscopes for compatibility *before* marriage. That's very wise insurance the West has yet to understand.

Now you have learned how astro-psychologists view all the signs, and Sag is another fascinating study. They equate this lover with the ages of thirty-six to forty-five. That's right, the time of midlife crisis, but it's also a time when, if we've done our homework, we're ready to deepen our talents, heal our wounds, and claim our real power. Considering that, it might sound confusing that Sag shares (enjoys?) a quality with its polar opposite, Gemini. Both love to flirt. I am not going to lie to you: even if Sag worships you, but is at the emotional level of a hip-hop groupie, he or she will be tempted to do a lot more than flirt. Yes, the ultimate goal of this sign is to discriminate and weigh cause and effect. Someday even an immature Sag might understand that if you play around, you risk a very important relationship—namely yours. But for now, if your lover still wants to taste every dish at the banquet, there will be times you will suffer the acid reflux!

Playing for keeps

A very smart way to curb the urge to play is to be the main play partner. "Let's go hiking this weekend!" your lover exclaims enthusiastically. "Oh no," you think, "I just want to hang out at home, do the *New York Times* crossword puzzle, and molt!" Well, keep that crossword puzzle warm, but don't let it stand in the way of you taking off with your lover or he or she will find someone who doesn't have to plan to be spontaneous.

Here's a variation on the problem:

Sag: Honey, I really want to take off and do a little hiking this weekend.

You: [Dreaming of a lazy Sunday, but sacrificing it all] Okay, that sounds great. When do we leave?

Sag: To tell you the truth, I was planning to go alone this time. [A pause that seems to last until Easter.]

You: You . . . don't . . . want . . . me . . . to . . . come?

Sag: Just this weekend, okay?

Of course, this is the crucial moment. Go in the jealousy direction and you will say something like:

You: Who are you *really* going hiking with?

If you go in the anger direction:

> *You:* That's just great—you're going to take off and have fun while I sit at home all by myself. That's just great, dammit!

If you go in the hurt feelings direction:

> *You:* I really don't believe this. I was going to give up everything I had planned for this weekend just to be with you, but you don't even want to be with me. I don't believe it!

Do you really want to go down any of those roads? Trust me, they all lead to dead ends. Wouldn't it be better, smarter, and more mature to realize that all lovers need their space? Your Sag just needs a little more of it. I mean, it's fine to be "joined at the hip" when you're having unforgettable sex, but walking around like Siamese twins all the time can definitely trip you up.

> *You:* Okay sweetheart, I understand. Go off and enjoy yourself. [Oh, the wonderful, mature lover that you are! How about adding just one more thing.]
>
> *You:* I would love to go hiking with you, though—how about planning it together on _____ [name the weekend of your choice].

Remember that nonverbal communication I told you about? Not everything has to be articulated and some actions do speak a lot louder than words. Now's the time to buy the two of you a great gift, like the sexiest tent in the sporting goods department. Don't just tag along on a hiking trip, be a part of it. Buying that tent, or hiking boots, or compass, or whatever, will communicate to your lover that you want to be up front and center in his or her life. Whatever your lover's passion, get passionate about it. Obviously, Sag will become even more passionate about you.

Once inside that tent, light a candle and heat up some warm oil. Then massage the parts of the body ruled by Sag: the hips and thighs. Take your precious time. I promise you won't waste a minute thinking about a five-letter word for "sap sucker" in the *New York Times* crossword puzzle.

Money and Sagittarius

The ruling planet of Sag is Jupiter, the largest planet in our solar system, and it likes to do things in a big way. You probably know by now that your lover intends to travel through life first class. Combine that with your lover's love of adventure, and if he or she has the money, then a seat next to your lover on the Concorde heading for Paris won't only be in *your* imagination.

Jupiter inspires Sagittarians to be ultra-generous with their friends (money is always just a means to an end for them), and there's one kind of friend that Sag definitely will not have: a friend in need. Are you looking for a loan? Wow, you have a fabulous opportunity to import whale blubber for the gourmet market? Your sister needs liposuction? How much do you need? If Sag has the money, so will his or her friends.

However, Jupiter is also the main reason Sagittarians are apt to overextend themselves. Now mature Archers can make wonders happen with their ability to weigh all factors, apply seasoned judgment, and predict right-on outcomes. The problem with immature Sagittarians is that they often bite off more than they can chew, and when money is involved, that can cause serious indigestion.

The dream machine

You have found a lover who is seduced by the possible. He or she dreams big dreams and wants you to share his or her vision. That's why it's so important for you to help your lover fulfill his or her adult potential—because then, believe me, anything and everything is possible.

Until that time, Sagittarians' blind optimism can lead them into pitfalls. When they're "feeling lucky" they might indulge their love of gambling. If they haven't the discipline to know when to stop, they'll find themselves so far in debt they won't even be able to afford to dream. That lack of discipline can also make Sagittarians overextend and overpromise. What makes it all the harder is their contagious enthusiasm. Nobody believes in the idea—or in themselves—with such spirit. They have the chance of a lifetime to make a dream come true, they tell you, and they project that dream with the all the enthusiasm Dr. Salk put into his first vaccine.

As mentioned before, to Sagittarians, money is a means to an end, and the older they grow the more spiritual that end becomes. They have a profound sense of the world's problems and they dream big dreams to fix them. Really evolved Archers can envision better ways to create conservation areas for animals, progressive school programs, international relief work, and so on. If Sag can get his or her idea off the ground, it's possible that hundreds or thousands (heck, let's dream as big as Sag and say *millions*) will someday benefit from his or her philanthropic spirit and vision.

If a Sag hasn't reached that spiritual level, and is just plain folk like the rest of us, he or she is probably dreaming and scheming of less lofty ideals. It's rare for Sagittarians not to love horses, and one of their fantasies is to buy their very own and indulge their passion. Whatever it is, you may suspect after a while that although the dream is fabulous, the plan to get it has more holes in it than the *Titanic*. Experience has taught you that when your lover is really excited about something, he or she has a tendency to exaggerate, and right now your lover is so excited about a current dream that it might sound something like this:

"I've been working this idea out for months now *(probably since last week)* and it can definitely be done *(with a miracle from Lourdes)* and all I need to do is to finalize a few things *(like figuring out how to do it!)*.

All the time that you're listening, the smile on your face is becoming frozen and your sixth sense is warning you that when this bubble bursts, both of you are going to need an umbrella!

Don't tell it like it is

Like Aries, that other dynamic fire sign, Sag is known for being frank. The less evolved types can be downright blunt. There's a good chance that you've already learned to avoid questioning them if you're not geared for a truthful, and blunt, response. The answer to "How do I look in these pants?" probably put your ego into traction. Now that you've been introduced to Sag's specialty of raw truth, you know how much it hurts to be told something in an insensitive manner, so don't make the same mistake.

That's right, Aries, you have to tone down your own tendency toward bluntness. Sagittarians will appreciate your honesty, but they will swallow it easier when coated with just a teaspoon of honey. Leo, you're another fire sign who knows how to spotlight a good idea and turn it into a spectacular. You might be just the partner Sag needs. Virgo, Sag's big dreams and impulsive nature will probably give you a spastic colon. Frugal Capricorn, Sag's tendency to spend freely and pay later will upset you so much that you'll be envying Virgo's colon! Once again, I give high points to the air sign Aquarius to fan the flames of fiery Sag. Their shared love of adventure, combined with their humanitarian ideals, should be perfect. Now, if Sag can get that Capricorn to forgive everything and contribute some sound financial advice, they've got it made.

Listen up!

Let's ask the question again. What do you say about Sag's bubble floating over your head and threatening to burst? First of all, you say nothing. Keep this goal in mind at all times: you do not want to be the one to burst your lover's bubble. He or she might forgive and forget, but why chance it? Instead, listen intently because the basic idea may be really sound and it's just Sag's lack of experience that's taking it in the wrong direction. Question what you think is off balance. Listen to the answer. Have a dialogue instead of an argument. Trust that your lover is smart enough to hear your concerns and to discuss them. If he or she isn't smart enough, there's no time like the present to find that out and to deal with it.

Start communication in a really positive way. Such as:

You: Sweetheart, I think that idea you told me about last night is really brilliant. [Pause while your lover basks in the compliment.]

You: I had some questions that I need your help on. Could you explain a few things to me?

Now ask the meat and potato questions that usually begin with, "Where are you planning to get the money?" Actually, if you've been in a serious relationship with Sag for some time, then be really smart and phrase it this way: "Where are *we* getting the money?"

Now, I wouldn't be really forthcoming without warning you of the hazards around the next curve: your lover prefers to do things on impulse, spontaneously, and he or she isn't going to be crazy about you putting on the brakes. "Hey babe, I'm ready to go!" Sag's body language tells you, "Why are you holding up the show?" Trust me, in the end Sag will thank you for caring enough. Nothing inspires appreciation like helping your lover to head off disaster, specifically from people who lend big Sag money based on big promises and threaten big lawsuits when you don't deliver.

It's also a fact of life that no lesson takes hold as quickly as the one we learn for ourselves. Sag's optimism and vision might have to be pulled back to earth every now and then, but this sign is a very quick study. Ask the hard questions and let your lover see the solutions. Or lack of them. Be there to help come up with the answers if you can, and if the only answers point to an idea whose time has definitely not come . . . let Sag discover the reality.

Most importantly, through the good times, the bad times, and all the times in-between, be that person who shares your lover's dreams and works with him or her to make it all happen. With Sag, the excitement is in the planning of the adventure, and getting there is always all the fun!

Power and Sagittarius

You might have already discovered that your Sag is athletic, finds making love in the outdoors a definite turn-on, and has a fabulous sense of humor. Now you know that he or she also has a profound sense of justice. That's why an evolved Sag cares so deeply about the wrongs in the world and wants to right them. Very rarely will you meet someone of this sign who lives by a double standard, and knowingly takes advantage of anyone, especially someone they love, in anything resembling an unethical or immoral way.

Of course, the key word here is "knowingly"! In a relationship, what causes most of our problems are unconscious patterns that we keep repeating. After all, they're just as comfortable as a second skin to us, right? Why should we change them? Well, there are some patterns that need immediate interior decorating, because they are destructive. Often it's our lovers who tell us the shocking truth, and then depending on how flexible we are, we either decide to change the pattern or change the lover!

So a Sag at his or her peak performance is righteous in the most positive sense. When less mature, this can turn into self-righteousness and a holier than thou attitude, which will have you researching poisoned mushrooms on the Internet! When caught in the "I know best" syndrome, your lover can be dogmatic, and when you have problems, instead of communicating with you, Sag can become judgmental and turn to lecturing, punctuated with deep sighs at your slowness in grasping their lofty thoughts. Being paranoid is usually unsettling, and the person who is doing the preaching assumes the control. The result: You are stripped of your share of power in the relationship, and it's all downhill from there.

Now, people who like being talked down to have a self-esteem problem, and we will assume that is not you. Like any lover who has been talked to as though he or she were still in Pampers, you become hurt. If you're a sensitive Cancer, it might be enough to cut off communication permanently. Or you become angry. Leo can't stand being patronized by a lover and will roar disapproval. Or maybe you don't express your feelings and just smolder in the corner. Taurus, you know a lot about smoldering. So what's the best thing to do? Well, obviously, this book is about communication and that's precisely what's urgently needed now. What's important is choosing the wisest words to say.

Let's start off with what words *not* to say. Opening with, "You're going to get a nosebleed if you don't get off your high horse" is probably not a great idea. Instead of these exact words, let's discuss the feeling you want to convey. Mainly it's the way your lover expresses things—too black and white, too right or wrong, too often!

One way to start is to remember your acting talents, because you can show Sag just how annoying, debilitating, and infuriating it can be to be talked down to. Ready?

You: Sweetheart, were you always a Democrat? [Or Republican, Independent, or whatever.]

Sag: Why do you ask?

You: I just wonder if you gave the two-party system the amount of analysis it really requires.

Sag: What?

You: I've been doing a lot of reading about politics and I can see where you have just more or less gone with the crowd. [Pause for total shock.]

Sag: What in the hell are you talking about?

You: Obviously, I'm talking about the benefits of a three-party system. [Sigh] Have I lost you?

Sag: [Sputter, sputter, sputter]

You: Oh, I'm sorry. Did my tone offend you?

Now, depending on how sadistic you are, you can let your lover stew a little longer, or gently say . . .

You: Actually, I was trying to give you an idea of how frustrating it is when you talk to me that way.

Sag: [Sincerely confused] What way?

You: As though I have a brain that's a little weightier than an egg shell! [Pause for eye contact] Honey, it really makes me feel terrible.

Okay, that should get things going, and it's now up to you to call on those friends you invited along: love, tact, intelligence, and patience. Don't lose your cool or you'll lose the argument. On second thought, let's make that the *discussion*. Just remember how fair and smart Sagittarians are, and once you give them the example of the time when they made you feel as intelligent as Barbie or Ken, they'll begin to see your point of view.

But what is immensely important is that whether you choose to give your lover a taste of being on the receiving end, or if you just want to communicate your unhappiness simply and clearly, you must—repeat *must*—focus on the problem and not on your partner's personality. Also, if it's only happened a few times, then you don't have to dramatize it (Leo, are you listening?) by saying "You always do this!" Just be honest with the facts and with your feelings.

If you opt for the simple approach, without the acting debut, I would like to suggest this as a way to begin:

"You usually speak to me with respect and sensitivity, and for some reason you've changed. I think we have to talk about it, because, to tell you the truth, I'm having a real problem dealing with it."

Simple, nonthreatening, and to the point. You might even want to tell your lover that it's something he or she probably doesn't even realize he or she is doing. Yes, you can afford to show some generosity. Giving your lover the benefit of the doubt is smoothing the way for some healing communication.

What's important is that you use your astrological strengths and not your weaknesses to get the message across: Virgo, your ruler Mercury lets you be persuasive and articulate. As for the sarcasm that comes so easily, as Archie Bunker used to say: *Stifle!* Cancer, use your great sense of empathy to communicate with your lover. Resist playing the victim because once you let Sag know how badly you have felt, you'll get all the love and TLC that you need. Aquarius, although anyone who talks down to you will soon find themselves talking to the wall, you do love Sag's intelligence enough to reach out and communicate. Try not to detach from your feelings, and you'll be surprised at how good it will feel to be totally honest with a lover who is worth the effort.

Immature Sagittarians may not know it, but with your help they're on the path to discovering one of the best qualities of their polar opposite, Gemini: the ability to resist becoming rigid in their beliefs. With Gemini's inspiration—and your help—they will realize there is not just one road to a truth, but a myriad of fascinating paths that lead to the same revelation.

So don't become discouraged. One day, instead of going into cardiac arrest when you disagree with his or her views, your Sag will have grown into a far more flexible human being—someone who realizes that different ways of thinking, including those of his or her lover, deserve to be respected. In today's vernacular, it's called giving someone enough *space* in which to be an individual. The wonderful thing about space is the more you give to someone, the closer it brings you together.

Decanates

Take two lovers born under the sign of Sagittarius and they can be radically different. One is able to work for compromise in a relationship, the other is so self-involved that a try at communication ends up being a monologue. Why are they like day and night? Studying decanates can explain a lot of the differences.

You see, every sign in the zodiac is divided into three parts. Each sign spans thirty days, and each day represents one degree. The decanates encompass ten degrees each. While the first ten degrees reflect the nature of the sign itself, the other decanates have different planets as sub-rulers. So, while Sag is ruled by Jupiter, people can also be sub-ruled by Mars or the Sun, dependent on the date they were born.

Is your Sag a mirror-image of the sign? Is there a sub-ruler that will modify your lover's behavior? It's all right here . . .

November 23 to December 2

With ultra-powerful Jupiter, your lover is the perfect example of this sign: generous, extroverted, and the person everyone wants to invite to the party. You have found someone who loves to talk about everything and everyone (gossip is a weakness), travel to places known in his or her vivid imagination, and explore all of life's and love's possibilities.

These are the dreamers and doers of the zodiac. Their adrenaline is always moving at 120 mph, and you've got to have energy to keep up with them. Expect life with these lovers never to be dull, and I promise that you'll never be disappointed. However, there might be times you wish there was an anchor attached to your Sag's right ankle, just to ground him or her a bit. Hopefully, your Sag's chart will show a strong Saturn placement, which will add more seriousness and depth to your lover's nature.

As I explained in the previous pages, be prepared to be swept away by your lover's dreams (both sexes are the ultimate salespeople), but keep your own objectivity so that you can play Saturn's role: thoughtfulness and thoroughness, helping them to overcome the flaws in their fantasies.

You're lucky to have this lover, because his or her positive thinking is as healing as sunshine. When you're feeling down, a conversation with your Sag, who is the eternal optimist, is just what your spirit needs. There will be a lot of ups and downs as Sag chases those elusive dreams. However, the glass—no matter whether finances have filled it with champagne or cola—will always be brimming to the top.

December 3 to December 12

Mars turns up the fire under your lover's already sizzling nature. If he or she doesn't like the status quo—and Sagittarians usually do not—they simply refuse to put up with it. Instead, they opt to be pioneers, the ones who might teach radical trends in everything from philosophy to religion. When do they want to see these innovative changes take place? Yesterday, of course! This is the type of progressive thinker who needs a partner with an active mind and imagination to keep them interested. If they don't find the right person, they'd rather go it alone rather than forego a minute of adventure.

It won't surprise you that your Sag refuses to be hemmed in by the conventional anything! This is not the nine-to-five variety of lover, so don't even try. This Sag is extremely independent, and it's important that you be mature enough—and, hopefully, confident enough—to let your lover indulge in his or her taste for adventure—with (and often without) you! Don't take it personally, Sagittarians just need to be alone from time to time to replenish their spirit. Like the other fire sign, Aries, also ruled by dynamic Mars, your partner can be very courageous. However, he or she can also be foolish about taking risks, so be prepared to apply Band-Aids for bruises and TLC for wounded egos. It doesn't matter, though. Your Sag will happy to suffer a few falls or a fractured ego, just to have the adventure. They are determined that when they're ninety years old, they will never look into your eyes and, with a voice full of regrets, say: "Darling, if only I had . . ."

December 13 to December 21

Your lover's sub-ruler is the life-giving Sun, and it's blessings will also light up your life! You have found a lover who personifies the best qualities of the Sag sign. He or she has the potential to be kindhearted, generous, philosophical, and inspirational. Unless your lover has some emotional hangups (check for bitten fingernails), then the energy of the Sun can lift his or her thinking out of the mundane and into the magical.

These Archers have a definite inspirational quality—and their thinking extends far beyond the well-being of just the two of you. Yes, your lover will inspire you to reach your own goals, but if he or she is really evolved, they'll want to help other people to improve their lives. With the right finances, it can manifest in acts that are philanthropical on a large scale. However, even without money, you'll find Sagittarians going out of their way to help others out, to make a real difference.

Naturally, there is no Sun without a shadow or two. So, depending on the aspects in your lover's chart, and if he or she still has some growing up to do, you might find these wonderful qualities hampered by a certain amount of vanity and extravagance. These are two very unattractive traits that you can do without, but when your Sag grows into his or her powerful potential, these traits will dissipate.

The Sagittarius Lover

November 23 to December 21

The Good

Optimistic

Generous

Adventurous

Spiritual

Independent

The Bad

Naïve

Extravagant

Restless

Dogmatic

Judgmental

The Ugly

Gullible

Irresponsible

Philandering

Zealous

Intolerant

"Love is not love, without a violin-playing goat."
—Julia Roberts

---------------------->

Capricorn

December 22 to January 20

Sex and Capricorn

What makes the aforementioned quote by Julia Roberts so delicious is that the symbol for our earth sign Capricorn is indeed the goat. Was the *Pretty Woman* in love with a Capricorn? Did she just like the imagery of a goat playing the fiddle? We'll never know, but we can imagine that, as a passionate Scorpio, Julia might well have grazed with a few celebrity Goats in her time.

Nowhere to go but up

Since we're talking about Hollywood stars, two Capricorns come to mind who really personify the attributes of this Saturn-ruled sign: Cary Grant and Faye Dunaway. They seem to be the essence of people in control. Not a hair out of place. Not a move that isn't calculated to charm. Their eyes clearly focused on the top of the mountain, and with the sure-footedness and stubborn determination of the goat, they arrived at their destination in style. Yes, Capricorns know where they're going, and they're very choosy about who they invite along for the climb.

I mentioned that Capricorns can project (whether real or not) the essence of control because, unlike signs who might try for control in a relationship with passive-aggressive behavior, or anger, or word games, or jealousy, or you-name-it in the list of immature behavior, our Capricorn males and females simply assume control as their natural birthright.

Astro-psychologists equate Capricorns with the developmental phase of ages fifty-six to sixty-eight. This is the time when the last rung on the ladder to success is within sight. When they're at the height of their powers and tasting the sweet success of achievement. Of course, if they don't taste success, then life can turn sour and depression takes over. That's a Capricorn downfall that we will discuss later—and it can send them tumbling down the side of the mountain.

Sex and the status seeker

The mature Capricorn male or female is great "marriage material." They know how to assume responsibility, commit themselves for the long haul, and realize that a mixture of sex and love is the most potent aphrodisiac. However, in the less than mature Goat (male or female *kids*), their desire for success, authority, and control can translate into being very status conscious about their bedmates. In his younger years, even the social climbing Cary romanced and married a few socialites—including Barbara Hutton, the world-famous heiress to the Woolworth fortune. "You can love a rich girl as well as a poor girl" was probably coined by a Capricorn mama.

Capricorn females on their way up the social ladder often put a strong importance on how much money a potential mate has, or just how much he can help advance her career, or just how much he or she will impress others, or . . . well, you get the idea and it can be summed up in two words: how much?

A friend of mine, in love with a Capricorn female, is aware of *how much* pleasure his lover takes in bragging about his accomplishments to her friends. The only problem is the titles he earned were a long time ago. He wants her to be proud of him for the person he is now, not for the mover and shaker he was, but his lover is still too insecure to do that. You see, some baby Capricorns *need* to bask in the reflection of their mates, whether that reflection glows because of a Woolworth type of fortune, business status, great looks, and so on. The message is: somebody outstanding is in love with me, and that makes me *somebody*.

What's the hurry?

Once they fall in love, both sexes are very cautious. They're not about to rush into anything and they take the time making sure it's *the real thing*. You date. You fall in love. He or she loves you back. You date some more. You want a commitment. Capricorn wants more time. You begin to worry that you'll be serving Geritol cocktails at your engagement party. Have faith, because one day (around the age of maturity) your cautious Capricorn will realize that love doesn't come with a guarantee. He or she will be ready to commit to you, body and soul.

Seriously now

Then will Capricorns relax? Oh no, they care what other people think too much. It's that drive for perfection they have in common with the other earth sign, Virgo. Combine that with some of Leo's status-hungry concern for how they're impressing other people and you get: "Are you really thinking of wearing *that* to dinner?" and "Do you think this table setting is absolutely perfect?" Yes, this sign can become obsessed with achieving perfection in everything they do, and the result is they take themselves *very* seriously. Aquarius, you could care less about status, so if something you've said has gotten your Goat's goat—like blurting out in exasperation, "Will you get over yourself!"—Capricorn probably won't even raise his or her voice . . . just a look will do. The power of the Capricorn's will is that strong, and many lovers just crumble under it.

A female client (a Moon Child) remembers how the Capricorn love of her life wouldn't hesitate to skinny dip off the side of his boat when they were alone, but got very uptight when they were strolling along the water's edge and, wanting to keep her jeans dry and explaining that her T-shirt came down to her knees, she began to take them off. She was stopped mid-thigh. He gave her the *look*.

Saying the "L" word

Yes, this practical earth sign can be very conservative and reserved. Since caution dictates Capricorns' next move, it often accounts for how tightly they clutch their emotions. There are some insecure Goats who have a real problem expressing their love. They just can't risk losing a bit of that hard-won control. They prefer to say "I love you" with expensive gifts, but the words themselves come a lot harder. You still want to hear them? You actually expect the Goat to appear vulnerable? To put their feelings out there and risk rejection? Well, then hopefully you're in the beginning of this relationship because the time to start communicating your desire to hear the "L" word was yesterday! Remember that Capricorns are very structured people, and you can't afford to let this particular structure get set in cement. If you turn away from the problem, your Capricorn lover will only grow rigid and be too proud later on to accept help. A scenario comes to mind related by a female Pisces client.

You had to be there

Our sensitive Pisces found communication with her workaholic Capricorn mate was almost nil. He was so focused on climbing to the top of the mountain that he didn't realize what a vast distance had grown between them. After five years of marriage, his emotional unavailability had become cruel and usual punishment. Because Capricorns are pragmatists who rely on factual information to succeed in life, they tend to doubt their own intuition and feelings. In extreme cases, they can be pretty insensitive to their lover's feelings as well. When Pisces revved up her courage to express her real feelings, Capricorn just interpreted her vulnerability as weakness. (I hope you're smart enough to realize that being open in your feelings isn't being weak —it's simply being committed to making your relationship work!)

Now, this particular Goat usually ended attempts at communication by simply walking out (leaving the scene of the crime, perhaps?). Pisces—a sign that loves to rescue lost causes—finally convinced him to take some time from his empire building to see a therapist. This is what happened, and trust me, Mel Brooks did not write this scene:

Music: [Cue the goat with the violin]

Therapist: I want you to look into each other's eyes and say the first thing that comes to your mind.

Pisces: [Looking adoringly at her Capricorn mate] You have beautiful eyes, darling. [Long pause while Capricorn struggles to reciprocate.]

Capricorn: You know, you should pluck your eyebrows sometime. [Sound effect: Pisces' self-esteem deflating like a punctured balloon.]

Therapist: [Stunned] Did you hear what you just did to her?!

Capricorn: [Walks out]

Now, do you understand why I told you to start communication right away? The problem with Pisces was that she let herself be intimidated by her lover's emotional coolness for too long. By the time they went to a therapist, it was a glacier that would take ages to melt.

So, begin by telling your lover that although you know how much he or she cares about you, you also love to hear the words. When Capricorn understands that simply saying the words and articulating feelings brings you so much happiness, he or she will try. It might be slightly awkward at first, as the rusty gates of communication swing open, but it will become easier, and eventually these words will become second nature.

If this heartfelt communication doesn't work, and your lover still treats his or her emotions like a relative asking for a loan—it may be necessary to seek professional help. Only don't go to the therapist who counseled Capricorn to look deeply into Pisces' eyes and say whatever came into his mind. She's still on tranquilizers.

Mountain climbing, anyone?

So, do you think you have what it takes to enjoy the view from the top with this lover? Sag, in the same way that you're too much of a spontaneous gambler and fun-lover to enjoy conservative Capricorn, Taurus (another earth sign) will find much in common with the Goat, starting with their shared respect for money (and tendency to hang on to it!). Now both might find exposing their emotions a little easier than passing a kidney stone, but the great sex that they'll enjoy will be an inspiration to bare bodies and souls.

Aries, your strong will is more than a match for Capricorn, but if you're not getting the words you need to hear, remember you can't order them on demand. Tread softly and don't try to whip the Goat into action. Cancer, like the trauma victim in the scenario, you might find yourself enlisted in Capricorn's domestic army (meaning taking orders while he or she takes control), but you know that you need the poetry of intimacy expressed in words. We all have to know what we need and have the courage to go after it. So, Pisces, don't be afraid to communicate your needs to the sergeant at arms!

What about Leo? Well, the Lion, who is ultra-generous with words, money, and emotions, may find that Capricorn is too uptight to tango. But then there is always healing Virgo waiting in the wings. Virgo loves Capricorn's solid nature and earthy sensuality, and is willing to help the Goat learn the fine art of communication. What about this sign's polar opposite, the Moon Child? Well, they say that opposites attract, but as Gerald O'Hara told his daughter Scarlett in *Gone With The Wind*: "Katy Scarlett, never forget that like marries like." His words ring true in the case of Cancer, who is much too tender for the Goat's demanding and domineering nature.

However, remember astrology 101: even though your Sun signs may not be wonderfully compatible, once you know your horoscopes, you might see that many planetary aspects change the whole cosmic picture.

Start without them

Now that you know your Capricorn lover has problems letting go and feeling vulnerable, it would help if you were courageous enough to let him or her know just how much you care. This may be harder for female lovers of the Goat than for males, because we females are so conditioned to wait for signals (preferably diamond ones) from our lovers before baring our own emotions. Yes, I understand that all lovers prefer to hear those words of commitment first, but in Capricorn's case, you would be smart not to wait. Just think of it as jump-starting the engine. Your words will give your cautious lover the ego boost and self-confidence that he or she needs to risk his or her vulnerability. Translation: to take a chance on losing control and being rejected. You know by now that metaphors are my weakness, so getting back to jump-starting the engine . . . realize that you are already in the driver's seat. Oh, you don't know your own power? Well, consider this truth: Capricorns crave perfection and, therefore, just wanting you in their arms is a very meaningful compliment. Now, don't you feel better knowing that you are Capricorn's idea of a perfect creature? Don't you think with that kind of leverage you can afford to be ultra-generous and speak first?

Scorpio, you're one of the few signs whose own sexuality may speak louder than words. Your legendary sexual intensity will not only have the Goat purring like a kitten, but he or she will understand that your possessiveness is just an expression of your love—and (remember love is stranger than fiction) that may just give your lover more of the confidence needed to express his or her deepest feelings.

Better than social security

Since Capricorn can be an intimidating sign because of its tendency to equate vulnerability with a contagious disease, those of you who have read this far must be very much in love or, at least, very much in lust. In order to inspire you to keep working on your Goat's potential—to grow strong by becoming more vulnerable—I have saved the best incentive for last.

Your lover may have hangups about articulating love, but never confuse that with his or her ability to speak very eloquently through sex. If you treat them to licking/kissing the back of their knees (the part of the body ruled by this sign), trust me, they will never stop "talking!" Although Capricorns are usually late bloomers, they seem to become younger and sexier as they grow older. When they hit their stride, they are notoriously very sexual people. (Didn't Cary Grant have a child at the tender age of sixty-three?) So when most older folks swing only on the golf course, your Capricorn lover will still be ready and more than able. Where do you think the phrase "horny old goat" originated? Not only can both sexes go from zero to incredible in sixty seconds, but their stamina is so incredible, you'll begin to suspect they're running on batteries! Of course, that rapid acceleration also accounts for their ability to do away with foreplay (and often afterplay) and just focus on the job at hand.

Oops, you cringed at me describing a night of fabulous sex as a "job"—but please know that your lover is very task-oriented. He or she strives for efficiency. However, if you're in bed with someone who keeps glancing at his or her watch, and you have the distinct feeling that your orgasm is three minutes overdo, you may be in trouble.

So along with communicating your need for the "L" word, include your need for foreplay and afterplay, with talk and tenderness. Again, I stress that you must communicate these needs in the beginning of your relationship, while your lover is still crazily in love and wants to please you. Hopefully, he or she will still be in love twenty-five years down the line, but let's just say that it's easier to sculpt the perfect relationship while the clay is still soft.

Once you have established an easy flow of communication, just lie back and enjoy the many positive traits of this sign, including awesome will power, sexual energy, and drive to succeed. You'll never know (or care!) what strategy for success your Capricorn uses to keep you in sexual nirvana, but Capricorn will definitely work his or her little Goat tail off to accomplish it.

Be patient, be loving, be courageous. Be the first one to assure your lover that your feelings are there to stay . . . then, chances are, your Capricorn will be too.

Money and Capricorn

You might admire Capricorns because of their determination to succeed in life, be impressed with their tenacity, and really proud of what they intend to accomplish, but you may have no idea of the cost.

All or nothing

You see, when Goats are mature, their determination and discipline help them climb ladders to more spiritual goals. (Remember that very famous Capricorn whose birthday is December 25?) Now, we don't expect our Goats to forego the pleasures of the material world, but we can help them strive for balance. The problem is that when Capricorns are less mature, their craving for status can produce values that are a bit lopsided, and making their mark in the world becomes everything. What's wrong with that? Well, think about it: nobody gets *everything* by concentrating on the goal only between 9 a.m. to 5 p.m. (not even with skipping lunch!). That kind of consuming desire is a full-time job and easily becomes an obsession. Everything else, including the needs of lovers and family, can recede into the background.

Perhaps if Capricorns didn't have what it takes to succeed, they might not miss out on life's many other pleasures (such as more playtime with you!). However, they were born with the deck stacked in their favor. Capricorns have the ability to use a laser-like focus on what they want, manage their resources to get it, produce like nobody else, and accumulate admiration and a number of Swiss bank accounts. Ah, it sounds like the American dream, doesn't it? But unfortunately, usually later than sooner, Capricorns and their lovers are presented with the hefty "American Excess" bill.

The rating game

Remember when I told you that depression can have the Goat tumbling down the side of the mountain? Well, "the blue period" (not to be confused with that of the artist Picasso) begins with the struggle to get to the top and assume control. It's a drive for perfection that consumes Capricorn and anything less is decidedly second rate. Unfortunately, that can also include themselves! Since their goals are admirable, but far from realistic. Capricorns can easily end up feeling as though they're not good enough—just second rate.

Poor Capricorns, nobody ever told them they're just human after all, like the rest of us mortals. So when they don't turn the planet upside down and fail to make Donald Trump and Martha Stewart look like lazy shirkers, they feel powerless. Now, hopefully, more mature Capricorns will realize that it's the perfect time to be their own best friend, and take themselves out for a drink and spend some quality time alone. The less mature Goats react to failure by turning on themselves with anger and self-criticism. "You idiot," their despondent half tells them, "How could you be such a loser?" That rhetorical question is followed by waves of negativity, and when the tide pulls out, they're left in a profound depression.

So if you're in love with a Capricorn female, you might want to watch for a compulsive drive on her part to groom you for the corner office. Does she just mention her desire to see you succeed, or are there graphs over your bed monitoring your progress? Both Capricorn males and females can become more workaholics and less emotionally available lovers. If you see red flags signaling there's a problem ahead, it's time to communicate and talk about priorities.

Life is short. The night is long. Let's start.

Setting the stage

Capricorns usually have a few thousand things on their minds after a long day. So, unwind with your favorite whatever and do what only you know how to do to relax the Goat.

Note: I recently read a book negating the need for verbal communication between lovers, because it said: "Nobody likes to be attacked." Well, the author missed the point, because that is precisely what I advise *never* to do when trying to communicate. No matter what the sign—fire, air, earth, or water—nobody likes to be approached in an aggressive manner. So, begin by putting yourself in a giving, non-victimized state of mind, where you can truly come from love. Then try this for an opener:

You: You know, I've been feeling guilty lately.

Capricorn: Why?

You: Because I've been unhappy and I haven't talked to you about it.

Capricorn: What's wrong?

You: Well, I think we're a little off balance. I mean, we spend a lot of time working for goals and that's terrific, but I think we're missing out by not spending more time together and with the family.

Capricorn: [On the defensive] You're saying *we* but you really mean *me*, right?

You: I think of us as partners. If what we're doing doesn't work for one of us, well then, it seems pretty obvious that both of us are going to suffer.

Capricorn: So what are you saying? You want me to pull back and let my work suffer?

You: I don't want your work to suffer, I just want us to think about priorities and what's really important. [A slightly chilled silence.]

You: [Lovingly] You're what's most important to me.

> *Capricorn:* If that was true, then you'd realize how much time I need to devote to my work.
>
> *You:* [Gently] But is your work more important than us? [If Capricorn's eyes glaze over and the pause lasts more than a minute, you may be in trouble.]
>
> *Capricorn:* Of course not.
>
> *You:* Then let's compromise so that your work doesn't suffer and our relationship will stay in balance. Okay?

Since how you say something is always far more important than the words you use, keep sincerity and gentleness not only in your mind but in your voice as well. It makes sense that a lover wants to spend more time with a warm and compassionate "partner" than with one who reminds him or her of a scary fifth grade math teacher. Also, don't forget that referring to both of you as "partners" is a reference that goal-oriented Capricorn can really appreciate.

When I speak of being warm and compassionate, please don't confuse that (as Capricorn might) with weakness. You can convey these wonderful attributes along with strength at the same time. After all, you're in love with someone who doesn't tolerate their own weaknesses very well (translation: human frailties), and they don't do much better tolerating weaknesses or failure in others. So, yes, come from love, but don't forget your backbone! Let your Capricorn know that you also know who you are, what you deserve, and nothing but a real fifty-fifty partnership is going to make you happy.

It's about money, honey

Remember that Capricorn is ruled by Saturn. This planet is known to constrict whatever it touches, and so you may find that you're in a partnership with someone who is too often tight with money.

Capricorns, who are usually sensibly frugal, can become miserly due to their chronic pessimism. No matter how sunny their financial picture looks, they always have their palms out to test for rain. It doesn't make this trait any easier to live with, but at least you can understand why they might feel safer with a disaster relief fund. However, living with a tight-fisted lover usually spells more disaster than relief, and the most powerful antidote is to be as independent as possible.

For instance, a female Goat will probably want her own bank account, and that will avoid a lot of problems. However, for another less independent female sign who gets to pull the purse string only at Christmas, then something's gotta change. Hopefully it will be her dependence, followed by the resolve to put away her own money and flex her financial muscles.

If your lover has yet to learn that stingy isn't sexy, it might be just the time for a silent lesson in the art of generosity.

The next time your male Goat says that dining out at your favorite restaurant just isn't in the budget, communicate by example. Tell him that you want to treat for dinner and then take him out for a fabulous meal. Chances are that your partner knows very well that you don't have that much money (compared to him, anyway) and your generosity will be very impressive. When the bill comes, don't weaken and look helpless, or (heaven forbid) ask for him to pay it. You invited him, and you illustrated your generosity with your credit card and your desire to make him happy—the lesson will not go unnoticed.

There are a few fire signs out there (Aries, Leo, and Sag, specifically) who find a tight-fisted lover as sexy as support hose. Cancer and Pisces, be sure to mix your deep understanding and empathy with the strength and determination that I mentioned earlier. Aquarius, Capricorn's conservative approach to finances may be a total turn-off, but since one man's poison is another's aphrodisiac, Taurus, you will definitely warm to the shrewd money-saving ways of Capricorn. Virgo, even if you don't get as hot as Taurus, in this relationship, expect a definite sizzle.

As easy as a, b, see!

You may not realize it, but you're really halfway home. You already have someone who not only appreciates the value of a dollar, but has the will, determination and know-how to make lots of them. What your lover may not have is a true partner. Yes, I mean you. After all, it's meaningless to use the term "partner" if you don't back it up with real support.

Try being as pragmatic as Capricorn, and you'll understand that the more supportive you are—and the more you work with your lover to realize goals—the more success he or she will enjoy. The more success they enjoy, the more control they're able to wield in their world. The more control they wield, the more confident they become. The more confident they become, the less fears they have. The less fears they have, the less pessimistic they are. The result: Capricorn will stop holding on to every dollar as though it were their oxygen supply.

With your sublime wisdom and help, your Capricorn lover will find that the balance in his or her life is even more precious than the one in his or her checkbook.

Power and Capricorn

Esoteric Astrology teaches that not only does Capricorn rule the knees, but its deeper significance is that they must learn how to bend. The lesson is one of humility.

You might have heard the observation that all comparison is dangerous because it makes you feel either inferior or superior. Well, Goats often gloat when their obsession with perfection starts paying big dividends. It becomes easy for them to feel superior to lesser mortals. If they lose perspective (and how many obsessive people have any?) they can go through life with their noses high above the crowd and their knees tightly locked. It's a position guaranteed to throw them off balance.

The power trip

You've already learned that your Capricorn loves achievement and the status it brings, and is willing to work for it. The danger comes when Goats feel they've let themselves down and they become depressed. In order to distance themselves from their gloomy feelings, they throw themselves into more work.

Until Capricorns get in touch with their feelings and are willing to share them (translation: willing to risk appearing imperfect), their power trip is headed for the dead end of any relationship. Now you might calm yourself by thinking, "Well, as soon as my lover makes it, there will be more time for the both of us." Wrong. The downside of Capricorns devoting all their energies to climbing to the top, is that someone risks being left below. As the expanse widens between you, contact becomes more and more difficult, until the relationship suffers terminal altitude sickness.

It's lonely at the top

If Capricorns reach the top and taste the sweet victory of success, it isn't long before they feel a chill. Brrrr! It's cold up here. They feel lonely. Only they can't come to grips with their feelings because they've been out of touch with them for so long. The Goats may not be happy; in fact, they may be quite miserable, but they've become so rigid that they can only continue on their power trip. With their insecure feelings tightly locked away, they are also wielding a perverse power over their relationships. After all, haven't they intimidated you with their emotional detachment? Don't you bend over backward for a smile? Haven't you secretly wondered that maybe it's all because of something you've done?

Opposites attract

I advise lovers of Capricorns to show them a new potential—that of their polar opposite sign, Cancer. Just imagine your lover with some qualities of this sensitive water sign. Cancers know all about feelings and how to trust their intuition. They're not ashamed to be vulnerable, to wear their hearts on their sleeves and verbalize a need for love and support. While Cancers are always in danger of becoming too dependent in a relationship, Capricorns are in danger of shutting themselves off from their emotions. They can get so good at it that eventually they easily shut themselves off from your emotions as well.

Lover du jour

Let's imagine that we're concocting the perfect lover from these polar opposites. We take just the right amount of Cancerian emotion and mix with an equal part of Capricorn ambition, stir lightly, and voilà! We have the ideal, well-balanced lover. Of course, he or she still has strong ambition and a drive for perfection, but now it is tenderized and humanized. Because these lovers relate in a whole new way and share their feelings, they're able to empathize with your feelings as well. The result is that instead of being so emotionally isolated that they leave you at the bottom of the mountain, they now use their formidable gifts of patience and discipline to lift you up as well. This is the balanced lover you deserve, someone who knows that the view from the top is nothing if you're not at his or her side to share it.

Oh, did I mention that this gourmet recipe would be served with generous portions of Capricorn's sexual stamina followed by Cancer's cuddling? Delicious!

From the blues into the pink

It's time to introduce your lover to some of the Cancer pastimes of his or her better half. Remember when I suggested that you become a real partner to your lover, because the more success he or she celebrates, the happier you both will be? That doesn't mean you have to join Capricorn's workaholic schedule. If you do, then not only will you have one ultra-stressed lover in the relationship, you will have two. Capricorns use sex to unwind, and I don't want to deprive anyone of that pleasure, but there are other ways for them to de-stress and get in touch feelings other than those created from an orgasm.

Don't wait for the next time your lover gets stressed to the max, and anxiety turns into depression. Change that pattern now.

Because Capricorns take life and love so seriously, it's time to bring the silly, ridiculous, funny, and hilarious into their reality. Capricorns may not like practical jokes (dumb) or being teased (cruel), but they have a great sense of humor when they can schedule time to enjoy it.

Do you go to movies together? Try switching from moody Ingmar Bergman to a revival of the Marx Brothers. Go to the beach and kick up some waves (if you're acting older than fifteen, you're not doing it right). Sit on a bench in the park and listen to children laughing. Capricorn loves tradition, so spend a lazy Sunday licking ice cream cones and browsing around antique shows. Lie on your backs under the stars and if one of you talks about business, the other can bestow the diabolical punishment of their choice.

Finally, bring this earth sign back to his or her roots with a weekend walk in the woods. Breathe in the perfume of the pines (make that sage if you're in the desert), and watch your lover magically de-stress. It's the perfect setting to talk about feelings. No, not what your Capricorn knows, but what he or she *feels* about something—what does your Capricorn's intuition tell him or her? Ask a few gentle questions. Ask about what he or she loves, and why. If Capricorn has been wanting something (name an item they fantasize about), is it because of its status potential, its investment quality, or because it really speaks to them? What is it saying? Let your lover *hear* what he or she is saying and *feel* its meaning.

Remember, this is not an interrogation. Be warm, loving, and gentle. In time, you can bring more expression of feeling into your lover's world and into his or her heart.

Getting to know us

Tonight, after your Capricorn has enjoyed his or her favorite de-stresser (and we're not talking about a walk in the woods), talk about this book. Oh, the title makes your lover smile and he or she shows a little interest? Then read a page or two about your sign and your polar opposite. (Go to the index in this book to locate your opposite sign. Get to know its character traits and you will get to know a lot more about yourself and your potential.) Does your lover think you would benefit from any qualities of your opposite sign? Chances are he or she will be very ready to tell you. Then read to your lover about the Cancer-Capricorn polarity. Does he or she recognize any missing traits in these portraits?

Afterward, when you look into each other's eyes and assure each other that you are both totally perfect, flawless, and amazing examples of the best of both your signs, then, trust me, you're either wonderful liars or very much in love.

Decanates

Take two lovers born under the sign of Capricorn and they can be radically different. One is able to work for compromise in a relationship, the other is so self-involved that a try at communication ends up being a monologue. Why are they like day and night? Studying decanates can explain a lot of the differences.

You see, every sign in the zodiac is divided into three parts. Each sign spans thirty days, and each day represents one degree. The decanates encompass ten degrees each. While the first ten degrees reflect the nature of the sign itself, the other decanates have different planets as sub-rulers. So, while Capricorn is ruled by Saturn, people can also be sub-ruled by Venus or Mercury, dependent on the date they were born.

Is your Capricorn a mirror-image of the sign? Is there a sub-ruler that will modify your lover's behavior? It's all right here . . .

December 22 to December 31

Saturn rules your lover with an iron hand. He or she is more serious more of the time than you might like. These Capricorns have the drive and ambition to move mountains (after climbing them, of course), and they are extremely shrewd. If really obsessed with power, they won't hesitate to use other people to further their goals. You might want to get a few values straight before committing yourself to this lover.

To begin, talk about how much of his or her time will be spent pursuing personal ambitions. About sixteen hours a day? Does that leave just an occasional weekend and evenings for time together? Don't be shy about discussing what's really of value to both of you. Yes, you can be this powerful Capricorn's partner in life, but that doesn't mean you have to be a "silent" partner!

To help this lover maintain balance, try bringing more of life's lighter side into your relationship. Stop and smell the roses together. Enjoy nature, laugh a lot, and love even more. Get your lover to spend lots of time away from charts and graphs, plotting and planning to rule the world. It's all about helping your lover enjoy the more emotional and human side of himself or herself. Actually, since this Saturn-ruled lover has the perseverance to accomplish just about anything, present the goal of maintaining a "balance" in life as a challenge. Does Capricorn think he or she can do it? It's like asking Tom Cruise if he can play a hero. Even if Capricorns reach their goal a little later than expected, they'll arrive with their values intact—and never regret the time spent enjoying life along the way.

January 1 to January 10

Soothed by the gentle presence of Venus, these Capricorns are more in tune with their artistic nature. Your lover may demonstrate a talent for music or dance, or simply show a love for these expressive mediums. Now imagine mixing that aesthetic sensibility with the determination and drive of Capricorn. Boggles the mind, doesn't it? Talent and drive are formidable partners, and so by all means, try to provide all the encouragement and inspiration you can.

Venus and Saturn together could create works of art or simply create the forum in which these works could perform. Whether on the business or performing end, your lover shows great potential to contribute to the arts. Again, what's very important is for these Capricorns to become more in tune with their intuition and feelings. Venus lays the fertile groundwork for this to happen, and the more vulnerable they become, the more their sensitivity and talents will flourish. One of the failings of these Capricorns is to be a bit stubborn at times. However, they will compensate for this human frailty by being one of the most loyal lovers in the zodiac. They are in your relationship for the long run, and hopefully, you can both make it a work of art.

January 11 to January 20

Your lover's sub-ruler is Mercury, lending an intellectual bent to Capricorn's determination to succeed. The influence of this planet may take your lover into research, or science, or professions that are mentally demanding. Since Mercury is the planet of communication, these Capricorns may be drawn into the fields of journalism, radio, and television. Whatever they do, they will now be doubly armed: they will have Saturn's formidable tenacity and Mercury's ability to express themselves. However, I always caution that every strength can manifest as a weakness in a different arena. For instance, Mercury lends a discriminating talent that can be very impressive at work—but in a personal relationship, the same influence can make your lover all too critical and demanding.

If you find that your partner is too quick to criticize you, with a mouth that should be registered as a lethal weapon, suggest that your lover put his or her feelings down on paper rather than perching dangerously on the tip of his or her tongue. Capricorns with Mercury's influence (ruling communication) will enjoy expressing themselves this way. Plus, the act of seeing their feelings in black and white and taking the time to read and think—and hopefully to edit—will avoid many arguments. Just to be on the safe side, make their next birthday gift a case of white-out.

The Capricorn Lover

December 22 to January 20

The Good

Ambitious

Dedicated

Productive

Realistic

Frugal

The Bad

Driven

Perfectionist

Methodical

Conservative

Materialistic

The Ugly

Obsessive

Depressed

Mechanical

Cautious

Miserly

"There is always some madness in love. But there is also always some reason in madness."
—FRIEDRICH NIETZSCHE

Aquarius

January 21 to February 19

Sex and Aquarius

Upon discovering that Aquarius has double planetary rulers, Saturn and Uranus, you might wonder whether this signifies a split personality. However, it only means that there are two types of Aquarians and they are light years apart. Which planet has the most influence over your partner? Since Saturn rules Capricorn, just read the previous chapter and you might recognize the person on the pillow next to you—someone who is far more at home in a conservative and structured world (President Ronald Reagan typified this Aquarian). However, if he or she responds to the magnetic force of Uranus, you have found someone who is among the world's progressive spirits and who is marching, skipping, and dancing through life to the beat of his or her own drummer.

One of a kind

You have to be an independent spirit to even consider the possibility of entering into a relationship with an eclectic Aquarian. When Aquarians fall in love with you, it will be because they want you rather than need you. They don't *need* anybody for most of the reasons other lovers do: ego enhancement, steady sex, fear of being alone, being fed chicken soup when sick, finding a soul mate, etc. Well, perhaps that last item might have Aquarius daydreaming its possibilities, but they know only too well how difficult it is to find someone as individualistic as they are.

The symbol for this air sign is the water bearer, a man balancing an upturned urn on his shoulder, depicting the Aquarian role as a vessel for higher consciousness that flows from heaven to earth. Translation: These people have the potential to be visionaries who are attuned to higher realms, tapping into new dimensions of creativity and thinking.

Rebel with a cause

However, all too often Aquarius is plagued by "divine discontent" and frustration with the status quo. While Sagittarians may accept the reality of crime, evil, and corruption, seeing it all in a philosophical context, Uranus-ruled Aquarians never accept it. They're reformers who want to tear it down, destroy the tyrants who created it, and start again with a clean slate. They may do it with anarchy or by working within the system, but either way, unlike most of us who don't "walk the talk," they will put their minds where their message is.

Their arena might be political or social. They may join causes or lead them. Whatever they do, they will advocate radical changes. Their strategy will be unconventional. They will be as unpredictable as they are in bed.

Love it or leave it

Aquarius is open to knowing all kinds of people. The more out of the ordinary the better, because this sign never runs with run-of-the-mill people. They revel in *differences* and can party as easily wearing a black tie on Park Avenue or tie-dye at a Woodstock reunion. However, when it comes to choosing a steady sexual partner, the field narrows. Since they don't seek approval from the opposite sex and, unlike Leo, can't be seduced with flattery, they're less sexually driven. In fact, their sex drive may become sporadic and, if occupied with other mental pursuits, they can abstain from sex for long periods.

However, once you have awakened your lover's sexual desires, you will find Aquarius an incredibly exciting lover. Although this sign rules the ankles, keeping an Aquarian's circulation in good shape is essential for his or her health, and what can do the job better than a few hours of incredible sex? Just understand that seduction must begin with massaging the most erotic organ in the Aquarian body . . . *the mind.* Yes, you have to be a mental turn-on, and only then can you lie back and watch the energy move down from their brain to their chest, to their stomach, into their thighs, and . . . home at last!

Now, I purposely said this sign has the *potential* to tune into higher frequencies and be a channel for enlightened thinking. However, all of us spend our lives trying to realize our potential and the rest of the time discovering the profound meaning of dumb. Nobody can be more off-the-wall, stubborn, eccentric, erratic, and often wacky, than an immature Aquarius. Of course, this makes bedtime just a little less exciting than skinny dipping with your lover in the Pacific at midnight on the Fourth of July wearing only sparklers, but it comes close.

A wild child

When this lover asks if you're in the mood to try something different, be assured that it won't be a wasabi sour cream sauce. Well, on second thought, it might be . . . but it won't be on your swordfish! Aquarius wants to experiment with new positions, new aphrodisiacs, and new sexual toys (Uranus rules electricity, and their affinity for gadgets with batteries is guaranteed to stand your hair, and many other things, on end). Also, please remember that what might seem like kinky and exotic play to you might be standard fare by Aquarian standards. If you're the type who feels like you need a map once you leave the missionary position, this is not the lover for you. Not only are their minds wide open to accept the original—and often bizarre—but their bodies are as well.

I told you that Aquarius is fascinated by differences in people, and what could be more *different* in our society's sexual mores than bisexuality and homosexuality, or group sex? These will be areas of intellectual interest, even if the waters are never tested. Now, you don't have to try everything on the menu, but hopefully, you are a lover with the courage to experiment sexually. However, the more you gasp at their non-conforming ways, the more you will earn a special place in their hearts (if not in their beds), because Aquarians love to shock.

Aries, you have the adventuresome spirit to try that wasabi sour cream sauce, but your tendency to dominate might upset Aquarius, who refuses to be controlled. While Cancer is too much the homebody, Pisces too mystical, Capricorn too cautious, Scorpio too possessive, and Taurus too traditional for Aquarius, the other air signs—Gemini and Libra— will find that an Aquarius lover fits like a glove. Gemini, if you can put the mind games into storage, then you offer the intellectual playfulness and sexual curiosity that excites the Aquarian imagination; and Libra, your love of the arts will stimulate Aquarius almost as much as your love of erotica. Sorry, Virgo, read on . . .

To have to or have not to

Never tell this lover "you simply have to do this" or he or she will rebel on general principles. Jot that item down, and here are two more: Aquarius is an air sign and they will be gasping for more of it if (1) they suspect you are trying to control them, and (2) if you try to criticize them, even if it's offered with love. See what I mean, Virgo?

I have two clients who learned about Aquarian stubbornness the hard way. The woman, a fashion-conscious Libra, tells how her husband wore a shocking lime-green tie that he loved. She tried everything, from buying him designer ties to hiding the great offender. He'd always find it. Finally, she gave him the big ultimatum: "You *have got to* stop wearing that hideous tie!"

Ten years later they celebrated their anniversary in a very sophisticated Manhattan restaurant. She wore black Armani, and he wore a tuxedo, a big smile, and a lime-green tie.

The other client is a Leo male who is currently resisting his Aquarius lover's attempt to drag him off to remote Zion National Park for a vacation. (This sign often feels the most free in barren and isolated places.) "This is not my idea of romantic," he says, "and I'm putting my foot down and telling her that she just *has to* come along with me on this cruise to Mexico. It's luxurious. It's safe. What's not to love?"

Well, if he knew the essence of his lover better, he'd know the answer to that. But he's destined to learn about his Aquarian's individualism the hard way—alone on a dock in Mazatlan having totally missed the boat.

Great expectations

It spells disaster to base any relationship on thinking that you're going to change a lover, and this is especially true for Aquarius. They just gotta be who they gotta be. I told you that Aquarians want and need their space. Now, you might need lots of space yourself—or you might not. In the beginning of a relationship, the last thing most lovers want is lots of space. They want to crawl inside the other person's skin and set up housekeeping!

Just how much space do you need? Will you expect Aquarians to automatically change their needs because you need more of them? What is it that you expect in this relationship anyhow? Depending upon your expectations—and how realistic they are—you may unconsciously be setting the stage to be fulfilled or just filled with frustration.

So all you lovers out there—think about your expectations. Do you believe that with enough encouragement (or nagging) a Virgo is going to want to keep you company at the corner bar every night for happy hour? Do you expect Libra to suddenly see the romance in a steady diet of six packs and take-outs from the Colonel? And that Gemini you're so crazy about, do you really expect them to sit patiently listening to your problems without looking as if they're having a fingernail extracted? Well, if you're basing your future happiness on these kind of unrealistic expectations, please understand that you're setting yourself up for a major letdown.

Mea culpa?

Very often our lover may be loving us the best way he or she knows how, and it's not good enough because we're married to our expectations. When they're not met, we can react emotionally and not that wisely. We begin to feel it's our fault.

Question: Am I simply not lovable enough to get them to change?

Answer: [What we don't want to hear] It has nothing to do with your being lovable—it has everything to do with your unrealistic expectations!

Question: I feel depressed. Where did I go wrong?

Answer: [What we don't want to hear] Well, perhaps you took a wrong turn way back when you fell in love with the person you *expected* your lover to become.

Question: All I want is a simple change, is that too much to expect?

Answer: Let me tell you a story about a lime-green tie . . .

Getting to know you

To keep your expectations in the realm of reality, it makes sense to find out more about your Aquarius lover. What can you expect may change over time as he or she evolves and matures? What qualities are already set in cement? Equally important, what are your lover's expectations of you?

For instance, you know by now that this sign never resists the fun of breaking a sexual taboo. If they have dreams about an "open marriage" where more than two are invited, or feel (compliments of Woody Allen again) that bisexuality is just doubling their chances for a date on Saturday night, then you might want to find out about their fantasies before settling in for the winter.

Light that fire

In time, with your encouragement and inspiration, you might even awaken more of Leo's fiery qualities in your lover. Their polar opposite, Leo, exudes warmth and passion, seeking ego-nourishment and hungry for a lover's every word and touch (Aquarians don't need their egos stroked in order to feel their worth). Leos are generous with their time, gifts, and expressions of their love (Aquarians live so much in their minds that they can seem undemonstrative and aloof). Leo loves from the heart (Aquarians must learn to listen to their minds less and to their hearts more).

Unfortunately, even though Aquarians can be intellectually advanced, they're not mind readers. And wouldn't you know that lack of telepathic powers is a common limitation of every sign? So if you need more outward Leo-like expressions of your partner's feelings, don't just let your frustrations simmer until they boil over in an argument, ask for what you need. I fervently believe that love does work wonders. With your three allies—honesty, respect, and a lot of real caring— Aquarians will not only understand what they can do to make you even happier, but they will try. Only don't expect it to happen overnight or ever. You can hope for it. You can go to Lourdes and light candles. *But you can't expect it.*

For Aquarians, more than any other sign, the greatest gift you can give them is to let them be themselves. In the final analysis, we all may try to change our ways a bit to keep our mates happy, but we *want to be loved for who we are.* So while you're trying to open up their minds to other ways of living and loving, you have to be happy with the basic no-frills package, then anything else you get will be strictly wonder-full.

It always comes down to the bottom line: communication. Understand who it is you love, and whether or not your expectations are so high they will take you only to the bedroom door, or realistic enough to carry you all the way to a commitment of heart and soul.

Money and Aquarius

While Saturn-ruled Aquarius displays the same drive and determination to succeed that's so evident in Capricorn, our Uranus-ruled lover can also achieve material success, but many times it's in spite of them, rather than because of them.

For the uncommon good

Aquarians can be found in a variety of professions as eclectic as their nature: scientific research in progressed methods of healing, on the cutting edge of technology, or discovering new ways to perform miracles with microchips. They're drawn to astronomy, and because Uranus rules astrology, many with this planet strongly placed in their horoscopes either practice the art of astrology, or are simply fascinated by it. There's a strong humanitarian streak in most mature Aquarians, and on an advanced level, there are those who are seriously devoted to improving our world, committed to fighting social injustice. These reformers seek out humanitarian groups and often create their own. They even become their country's president. Franklin D. Roosevelt and Abraham Lincoln typified the humanitarian's vision of Uranus-ruled Aquarius.

It might go without saying, but just to be on the safe side, let me emphasize that these people are a rare breed with a different set of values: *what they do* is more important to them then how much they're paid to do it. So they can be ambitious, but not in a materialistic sense. They're purists who won't conform to anybody's value system except their own. They won't be bought. They won't sell out. They'll tell everyone from secretaries to senators what's wrong with our system and they won't be politically correct about it.

Yes, Uranus-ruled Aquarians have potential to touch the stars. But those stars are light years away, and so most of this sign—like most of us—have a long, long way to go.

However, even though the average Aquarians may not be motivated solely by money, once they are turned on by a challenge they will rise to the occasion with 100 percent dedication. It's that total commitment that often brings them recognition, power, and the financial benefits that go along with it.

The freedom trail

Whatever they do, both sexes will feel more comfortable in a work environment that gives them plenty of freedom without anyone looking over their shoulder (their dislike of authority is built into their DNA). In recent years their prayers for more freedom have been answered. Thanks to laptop computers and new technology, they can now work from their homes. It's the next best thing to being self-employed and not having to answer to authority. Well, of course, they still have to report to a boss, but at least they have the "space" they need so much—and in this case it's cyberspace. Speaking of authority, how your lover reacts to it might present a few problems and, in turn, impact your financial partnership.

For starters, his or her unpredictable nature can get them into trouble at work with those in positions of authority. Only, your partner might not consider it "trouble" at all. They might just view it as an opportunity to break free. Even the most understanding of bosses, who value Aquarians for the visionaries they are and the radical, often brilliant ideas they originate, may not be prepared for the anarchist they can become when morally outraged.

Example: the boss announces he is against the employees forming a union. Or he refuses to pay a better than minimum wage. Or anything else that would get "Norma Rae" up on a soapbox. Even if your lover is sitting in a corner office making a six-figure income, if an underdog is treated unfairly your lover will rise to defend that person. So what do you do when you return home that evening and find your lover opening a bottle of champagne. "What's the celebration?" you ask. "I quit!" Aquarius announces with a big grin.

How are you going to handle that? Probably a lot better if you have more money in the bank than utility bills on the kitchen table.

Capricorn, since you meticulously plan your every business move and strategy, this kind of impulsive behavior will totally bewilder and exasperate you. Pisces, if you start an emotional monologue beginning with "How could you?" and ending with "Please go back and apologize, for me!" then I forecast disaster. You'll think Aquarius doesn't love you enough if they don't do it, and Aquarius will believe that if you really loved them, you'd never ask!

Talking points

If your Aquarius fits the pattern of someone who refuses to fit a pattern—someone who can be unpredictable and radical—it might be a good idea to have a discussion at the beginning of your relationship. Aside from talking about separate checking accounts (take it for granted that the Aquarius female, just as independent as her male counterpart, will prefer to have her own bank account), you should also make an agreement, if at all possible, to discuss major career moves before acting on emotion. Translation: "Sweetheart, walk out, storm out, do whatever you want, just don't say 'I quit!' until we discuss it. Perhaps there's a better way to handle the situation."

Of course, if your lover's sense of ethics, morality, dignity, or a host of other worthy items are at stake, and your lover did reign in his or her temper long enough to try to negotiate a compromise—and failed—you'll understand why your lover would have to quit, won't you? Oops, Taurus, if you hesitated for more than five seconds in answering, perhaps you have some thinking to do before living with an idealistic and impulsive Aquarius.

Even you, Virgo, may lose patience when your special brand of intellectual reasoning falls flat with an impassioned Aquarius. When your own moral outrage is sparked, you opt for the patient politics of the Geneva Convention. Aquarius wants the Boston Tea Party!

Remember that your fighter for social justice doesn't leave his or her ideals, integrity, temper, or outspokenness in the workplace. One of the pet hobbies of Aquarians is knocking down the pretensions of other people, and they just love to deflate those who are full of themselves.

For instance: Your status-conscious brother sold his soul to buy a twelve-bedroom replica of Versailles on Long Island, and his wife is suddenly speaking with a French accent. You might not want to invite your lover to the house warming. Well, at least wait until after they solder their 24k gold family crest onto the barbeque!

Taurus, either working or living with an Aquarius promises to give you a memorable case of hives. You're too comfortable with the status quo and this sign delights in turning it upside down. Libra, although your intellect is perfectly attuned to that of Aquarius, this lover's "let the chips fall where they may" outspoken attitude might upset your balance. However, if anyone has the diplomacy and tact to tone down Aquarius, it's you.

Dreamers, Inc.

Of course, on the path to maturity there are many varieties of Aquarius. Some are so mature and evolved they will blow your mind. Other will just boggle it.

One of the latter varieties might be an immature lover who belongs to the wanna-be class of Aquarius. These people's ideals are so lofty they can't get their feet planted on the ground long enough to accomplish anything. They're all dreams and no action. All theory and no practice.

Some people say that intellectuals are often absent-minded because they're focused on more important thoughts. Perhaps that's true. However, when the less disciplined Aquarians are absent-minded and disorganized, it can permanently keep them a lifetime member of Dreamers, Inc. They plan to "get it together" and spend the morning making important phone calls. The inner dialogue goes something like, "Where the heck is that piece of paper with the telephone numbers? Well, I'll do this paper work first, but wait a minute . . . there's something that's even more important, but I can't for the life of me remember what it is . . . I'm just going to have to write this stuff down . . . and what the heck did I do with those damn telephone numbers?" And on and on. By five in the afternoon, they probably feel like a mosaic, with pieces of their good intention scattered all over the floor.

If you decide that you love this Aquarius enough to try and put those pieces together, a motivated lover can accomplish wonders. Please, Gemini, stop looking around the room for a candidate—we're talking about you! If you browse in your favorite bookstore, you might come up with *Take Your Mind to Work, A File System for Dummies,* or anything else that will get your lover started. Then, if you take time to be still and really listen to your lover's dream, your marketing ability will meet Aquarian's vision and the electricity could light up the room.

Since nothing comes with a guarantee, perhaps we should think of Plan B. So what do you do if six months down the road your lover has read the books and is still putting bank deposits in the file cabinet and leaving the key to the file cabinet in the refrigerator? Well, just because you couldn't help one Aquarius is no reason to let a good idea go to waste. How about incorporating Dreamers, Inc., getting a logo, making yourself president, and charging dues for membership? Just don't let your lover keep the books!

In the final analysis, life with your Aquarius lover will be many things, but "dull" will not be one of them. Whether your Aquarius is someone mature enough to work toward a dream or someone who is still a "work in progress," he or she has the potential to make a real difference in the world. Just think of how much better your world has become since you met.

Power and Aquarius

Astro-psychologists equate the development phase of Aquarius with ages sixty-eight to eighty. This is the period when they're free at last! They're no longer dependent on money, career, and other status symbols for ego gratification. They know who they are. That knowledge also frees them from caring what other people think about them. Janis Joplin sang, "Freedom's just another word for nothing left to lose" . . . and at this stage of the cosmic/evolutionary spectrum, the potential for greatness has never been greater. The future is wide open to the outer reaches of possibility.

Note: This higher state of consciousness is something we are all "on the path" trying to reach. But don't forget, sometimes it's just when our eyes are focused on the horizon—intent on our goal—that human frailties manage to trip us up.

A balancing act

Before Aquarians really understand the need for balance in a relationship, they tend to live more in their minds than in their feelings. Quite unknowingly (let's give them the benefit of the doubt), they become so involved in their work that they begin to keep their lovers at an emotional distance. At its worst, when you gently, compassionately, and intelligently (I know that you're perfect) bring this behavior to their attention, they become annoyed. You get the distinct feeling that your lover resents having his or her energy diverted from their work. What's worse, you begin to worry that perhaps they just don't consider it (translation: you!) that important. Their whole attitude speaks volumes, starting with, "Hey, it's just an emotional issue, so how important can it be?" Aquarians, who filter everything through their intellect, feel that emotions are messy (that's why they always come with Kleenex!), they're energy draining, and simply confuse pure logical thinking, right?

In your lover's mind, all they're doing is simply being preoccupied with other *important* things. It's not going to last forever, so why are you making such a fuss about it? Somehow they've lost track that they were "preoccupied" before Yugoslavia became Serbia and Montenegro. It's been a while!

When you complain about it, you just might become emotional. By doing so, you just might trigger three of their less lovable traits, which just might drive you crazy: resistance, digging in their heels, and getting really stubborn.

Different means to the same end

You already know that both Saturn and Uranus rule Aquarius, and that your lover will respond more to the energies of one planet than the other. Aquarians can be more Saturnian and go after success with a structured, military-like strategy, spending their waking hours trying to trump The Donald. Or they can strive for success in the individualistic Uranian way, working around the clock to help avert a humanitarian crisis in the Sudan. It doesn't matter which they do because once dedication becomes obsession, the result will be the same—your relationship will suffer. Aquarius will take away your share of power in the relationship through his or her aloof, emotional detachment.

I suggest that if you're truly in love with an emotionally unavailable Aquarius, you have to remind him or her how to get in touch with those emotions. In the chapter on Capricorn I gave suggestions on how to bring this Saturn-ruled sign more in touch with their feelings. The same advice is appropriate for Aquarians, whether Saturn or Uranus is dominant in their horoscopes, because they're all people who have to begin living more in their hearts than in their heads.

That low-down feeling

So, you've been with this emotionally detached Aquarius for a while now and you're beginning to feel as necessary in his or her life as fly paper, but that may not be true. Too often they're giving you the left-handed compliment of being so comfortable in your love that they can take it for granted. Of course, the first lesson for every lover of every sign in every country around the globe is *take nothing for granted*!

If you're lucky enough to have a lover with a fairly strong ego, then he or she will be more flexible. Since this is someone who hates mind games and the feeling of being manipulated, be sure to be totally honest—they're mature enough to handle it. However, if your lover's ego is being supported by a splint, and your Aquarius is paranoid about feeling "managed," then he or she will strongly resist.

Interestingly, Aquarians who want to change the world are very often too frightened to change themselves. It's that old control issue again. Change takes courage because in the transition we have to give up the security of our negative ways. Not everyone is strong enough to do it. Aquarians are afraid that giving up control means they might have to give up their *individuality*, and you know that's their very lifeline.

If your lover expresses this fear to you, then you will be able to assure him or her that the last thing you want to change is what makes them so unique, what makes them the person you fell in love with. However, even if this unspoken fear isn't rational and has no basis in reality, it's real to Aquarius and it can make him or her impossible to budge. If that happens, here is another strategy. It's sly and sneaky and one of my favorites.

Shock value

I have cautioned you not to demand anything from independent Aquarians, or to even suggest that you're telling Aquarius what to do. But what about *asking* them to do something?

Aquarians, as you well know, love to shock people into awareness. It's his or her *specialité de la maison*! So why not feed your Aquarius a little of his or her own recipe?

You: I'm just stuck on something—maybe you can help me.

Aquarius: What's happening?

You: Well, I had lunch with _____ [someone your lover knows well], and she's having trouble with her husband. He's just become emotionally unavailable.

Aquarius: What does that mean? Is he out of town?

You: No, he's right here, but he's become so involved with his work that he doesn't seem to know how to be intimate anymore.

Aquarius: The sex is bad, huh?

You: No, I mean intimate in a close and nurturing way. Sex is fine; it's the before and after and all the other times that are empty. [Pause while Aquarius ponders.]

You: She's tried to talk to him and it doesn't work. How can she shock him into awareness? What can she do to open his eyes? Do you have any ideas?

Aquarius: [Flippantly] Send him divorce papers.

You: [With all your heart] Honey, I would never want to do that to you.

Aquarius: We're not talking about me.

You: [Gently] Yes, we are.

Now, how's that for shock therapy? The dialogue can change, and perhaps it's the male partner with the problem, but the intent remains the same—to shock your Aquarius into opening his or her eyes, and to really think about what you're trying to communicate.

Of course, we all realize this can be interpreted as the dreaded manipulation Aquarius hates. Counteract that with a huge dose of pure, undiluted honesty. Explain to your mate that you were driven to asking advice because you had tried to communicate in other ways for so long without success. Explain that living with someone who is so individualistic calls for something more radical than writing to Ann Landers—it begs for inventive measures. If you have true love behind your words and in your eyes, Aquarius will know it, and might even be flattered!

Have a serious conversation about what advice Aquarius would have given this frustrated lover. How would he or she have shocked the person into a state of enlightenment? Chances are that by the end of the conversation, you will have done exactly that.

Coming of age

As Aquarians evolve and grow into maturity, they will mirror more and more of the qualities yet to be realized in the Age of Aquarius. Now, for those few among you who may not realize it, this refers to far more than just a hit song in the Broadway musical *Hair*. It's all part of a phenomenon known as the Precession of the Equinoxes. The earth moves slowly through the universe in a counterclockwise movement, and when a new constellation rises on the horizon during the spring equinox, the world experiences vast changes. Right now we are leaving the Age of Pisces (which brought us the ministry of Jesus) and we are at the dawning of the Age of Aquarius, which will last approximately two thousand years.

As the earth vibrates to the liberating energies of Uranus, we are all affected. Those of us who are making a conscious effort to evolve spiritually will now have the support of Aquarian energy. We've already seen some of the wonders to come in recent astounding technological advances. Computers have revolutionized our world, and soon developing extrasensory perception will open up even more exciting frontiers of communication (will Bill Gates try to trademark telepathy?).

As people look more within themselves for spiritual answers, they'll depend less on materialism—less on selfishness—less on society's approval in terms of status symbols to realize their own worth. Progressive Aquarian tastes that have long been considered "eccentric" may now become the norm, as the planet finally embraces the enormous benefits of alternative medicine, organic living, and, of course, astrology.

Yes, the best is yet to come, and we may yet realize the dream that's been in all our hearts: to see the races working together to create a true brotherhood of man.

We all have the potential to reach this enlightened state. If we start out together now, with love and compassion for everyone on this planet, I promise the journey will be as wondrous as the destination.

> *Harmony and understanding*
> *Sympathy and trust abounding*
> *No more falsehoods or derisions*
> *Golden living dreams of visions*
> *Mystic crystal revelation*
> *And the mind's true liberation.*
> *This is the dawning of the age of Aquarius*
> *Aquarius! Aquarius!*

Decanates

Take two lovers born under the sign of Aquarius and they can be radically different. One is able to work for compromise in a relationship, the other is so self-involved that a try at communication ends up being a monologue. Why are they like day and night? Studying decanates can explain a lot of the differences.

You see, every sign in the zodiac is divided into three parts. Each sign spans thirty days, and each day represents one degree. The decanates encompass ten degrees each. While the first ten degrees reflect the nature of the sign itself, the other decanates have different planets as sub-rulers. So, while Aquarius is ruled by Saturn and Uranus, people can also be sub-ruled by Mercury or Venus, dependent on the date they were born.

Is your Aquarius a mirror-image of the sign? Is there a sub-ruler that will modify your lover's behavior? It's all right here . . .

January 21 to January 30

These exciting lovers will entertain you with stories about how they drove their parents and teachers crazy when they were kids. Of course, they were just reacting to their sub-ruler, Uranus, and flexing their fledgling stubborn and individualistic muscles. It's only after growing up and attaining self-discipline that Aquarians begin to reach their brilliant potential. They're still radical. They're still stubborn. However, when people witness the way they can solve problems with unconventional and never-before-dreamed-of solutions, they receive recognition and the rewards of their dedication. If Uranus is strongly placed in their horoscope, they are even capable of showing genius.

However, it's not easy working with these lightning rods, and it's not always easy loving them. They can be so devoted to their work that they appear aloof. Insist on downtime together to just enjoy life and explore feelings. Stay flexible because whatever happens in your relationship, you can expect the unexpected. The only rules these lovers play by are their own, so life promises to be very exciting, with new and incredibly exciting horizons around every turn. Just fasten your seatbelt!

January 31 to February 9

Transporting your lover to the realms of sexual nirvana may be one of the few times you get him or her to be quiet! Mercury, the planet of communication, fills their heads with ideas and they want to talk about them, dream about them, and talk, talk some more! The problem with these Aquarians is that they risk living only in their imagination and becoming members of Dreamers, Inc.

Yes, they may originate an innovative and fabulous idea, but do they have the self-discipline to get it all together and make it a reality? Perhaps that's where you can give some practical advice in the beginning: financial support if they need it, and encouragement every step of the way.

These lovers have an insatiable curiosity about the world and the people who inhabit it. They will be students of human nature, and they can even tell a lot about someone just by using their intuition. The world of psychic phenomena fascinates them and they may possibly explore their own psychic ability. This is someone people like because they their own minds wake up to the stimulus of just being around them.

February 10 to February 19

Your lover's sub-ruler is Venus, and this planet heightens his or her compassion and love for people, especially the underdog. If material things in life are essential to your happiness, you might find life with this lover frustrating, because the car, the boat, the vacation, and the other 24K gold goodies are way down on this lover's list of what's important.

However, if your share his or her desire to help make a difference in the world, your life together can be extremely fulfilling. You'll find that Venus has gifted your lover with exquisite aesthetic taste (that's why they love you, of course!), and they might even have artistic talent of their own to express.

Just watch out for that old Aquarius inclination to live more in their minds and become too impersonal in your own relationship. If that happens, talk to your lover about it. Besides becoming a battered spouse, a starving child, an abused dog, a recovering alcoholic, or a single mother with five kids being denied welfare—ask your lover what you can do to get attention. That should get him or her to listen.

The Aquarius Lover

January 21 to February 19

The Good

Visionary

Humanitarian

Open-minded

Reformer

Illuminating

The Bad

Radical

Detached

Eccentric

Iconoclast

Tactless

The Ugly

Anarchist

Cold

Bizarre

Nihilist

Disruptive

"And in the end . . . the love you take is equal to the love you make."
—PAUL MCCARTNEY

Pisces

February 20 to March 20

Sex and Pisces

The last water sign in the zodiac is Pisces, ruled by Neptune, the planet of illusion, and symbolized by two fish tied together, yet swimming in opposite directions. You should be able to tell from just these opening lines that your lover is someone out of the ordinary. In fact, there are some who think Pisces is on another astral plane! Aquarius might be the genius who *knows*, but Pisces is the mystic who *feels*. Aquarius might march to the beat of a different drummer, but Pisces flows through life to celestial music that only he or she can hear.

Some astrologers believe the two fish represent the personality and the soul. The more esoteric meaning is that during their life, Pisces will strive to detach themselves from the ego of personality in their struggle for spirituality. However, a lover of Pisces probably won't need esoteric knowledge to understand how Pisces is often drawn in two directions. Those born under this sign are often outgoing and seemingly content. Then, without warning, they can become depressed and withdrawn. They can be absolutely magnetic lovers who transport you to dreamlike realms of fantasy with sensual play. Then, the tides turn and Pisces can become moody, distant, and sex is about as appetizing to them as last night's pizza.

Keep your eye on the prize

Before we delve into the watery depths of the conflicted Pisces, I want to introduce you to someone who will make all your caring worth the effort: the mature Pisces lover.

By now, you know all too well that to help our lovers reach their potential, we must love them enough to battle many different ogres: everything from infidelity and jealousy to tactlessness and temper. It's a wonder we have enough energy left to enjoy the prize, which is a grownup lover. Now, if you've been very good and eaten your tofu and said your prayers, that lover will be a grownup Pisces—someone who loves with their minds, their hearts, their souls, and asks for nothing but your love in return. How many of us have experienced a truly selfless love? Oh, all right, I see a little Asian lady in Bangkok raise her hand. Is that all? Well, pure and selfless love is what a mature and evolved Pisces is all about. If it was possible to grow a lover, organically, without chemicals or additives, this Pisces is what you would get.

Sensitive to the touch

The world, with its growing hard-nosed corporate mentality, war, taxes, and television re-runs, can be a harsh place for everyone, and especially for a Pisces who has a strong inner pull to escape beyond this earthly and material world. Whether your lover shows just a glimmer of the desire to transcend reality, or if the flame burns brightly, it often seems as though Pisces landed on earth by mistake and is just waiting to catch the next spaceship out. You see, Neptune rules the astral plane and it transports Pisces to higher mystical realms we can only imagine. When Pisces develops his or her psychic sensitivity, you'll often wonder how your lover knew when and how and where you wanted to be touched. They seem to feel and know things that are beyond logic.

Perhaps we can all get a glimpse of the mysterious depths of the Pisceans' soul by gazing into their eyes. For example, Liz Taylor—the quintessential Pisces romantic who would sacrifice all for love—possesses incredibly luminous, violet eyes. Those Piscean eyes hypnotized many a lover and transported them to a realm where magic is reality and dreams always come true.

Just imagine

Like Libra, Pisces enjoys setting the stage for love with candles, incense, and illusion. Pisceans want sex to be multi-layered and imaginative. Have you ever acted out your favorite sexual fantasy? Well, be prepared to throw your inhibitions to the wind, because Pisceans love using their acting abilities in sexual fantasy, and they will go wherever you lead. Although their desire stops at any hint of violence, they're adventurous enough to want to try most anything once.

Just as the first sign in the zodiac, Aries, rules the head, the last sign, Pisces, rules the feet. Many an erotic evening has begun with a simple foot massage, and as the optimists around us like to note: there's nowhere to go but up!

Capricorn, you don't show enough emotion to feed the hungry imagination of Pisces. Sorry, Scorpio, you and Pisces are sexual magnets, but in the end you'll be too controlling for this lover. It's that other water sign, Cancer, who can tune in to the Piscean imagination and begin to sway to that celestial music. The Moon Child gives Pisces the kind of gentle security he or she needs to let his or her imagination fly. Together they promise a sexual nirvana that's probably banned in Utah.

Their saving grace

While Pisceans struggle to find their center and become mature (translation: realistic), their great compassion for people can be easily exploited. They want to save the victims of the world, and in the process, they can become victimized themselves.

The problems begin with Pisceans' own romantic nature. They're always searching for the love of their life—*the real thing!* In the same way they want to surrender themselves to the infinite and merge their consciousness with the divine (while the rest of us just want to go shopping and take in a movie!), they want to completely surrender to love.

There are givers and takers among us, and the takers can sense an altruistic, compassionate, and love-starved Pisces eight city blocks away. There's probably a cave painting somewhere that depicts the original sob story being told to an impressionable Pisces. It comes naturally to Pisceans to put another person's needs before their own, but they should practice saying *enough!* in front of their mirror daily. If they're really weak, they should put *already!* after it.

Until they begin to recognize the signals of those who are troubled lovers—who exude negative emotions like a diesel with an emissions problem—they'll have relationships that drain their energies.

It might be the lover with the "I need alcohol to boost my self-esteem" problem, or the lover with the "I just need one more little loan until I find a job" problem, or the "I need you because I'm just too sensitive to cope" problem, and so on and on and on.

(Note: While you're browsing through this book, read your lover the quotation from Bertrand Russell, which begins the chapter on Cancer. It says it all.)

Lovers in need

I personally hate psycho-babble, but the term "co-dependent" has become part of our language and certainly describes the immature and needy Pisces. It's a dance of mutual need between themselves and equally needy lovers, and there's no celestial music to be heard.

Somehow this confused Pisces always finds the lover who feels like he or she will fall apart if alone. Does Pisces stop to consider whether this person is really a victim or just someone who's very self-destructive? What? Waste a minute and risk losing a truly masochistic experience? So, our compassionate Pisces (*who needs to be needed like a splint needs a fracture*) steps in and becomes the emotional crutch. They feel good about themselves because they see their actions as self-sacrificing and spiritual. It's easy to interpret the other's dependence as *the real thing*. Magically, their feeling of self-worth, before dry and shriveled, now blossoms.

Only there's just one little snag: to keep this feeling alive, Pisces depends on his or her lover's dependence! So what happens when the alcoholic finds the strength to quit, the borrower finds a rich relative, and the emotionally fragmented partner suddenly learns how to cope?

If you recognize this pattern in your Pisces lover, and if his or her past romances have left your lover emotionally ravaged, then talk to your Pisces about his or her own feelings and needs. It's possible that Pisces hasn't confronted either in a long time. Sample questions over your beverage of choice: Why are you not able to make it from Monday to Friday without having to rescue someone in need? Why are you addicted to emotional pain? What's missing in your life? Hopefully, in time, the mature and healthy love you bring to your Pisces will help him or her to heal old wounds.

Yours for the asking

A female client of mine recently felt frustrated: "I'm going out with a new date tonight," she explained, "and naturally, he's going to be on his best behavior. He'll be considerate, sweet, funny, and charming, dammit!"

"What's wrong with that?" I asked.

"Well," she sighed, "I wish I could just hand him a list of questions, and I'd know whether I've met Mr. Wrong again. It would sure save a lot of time!"

So here is the list of questions for all of you who want to make sure that your lover will not be greedily needy and co-dependent.

1. If you're close to someone who's making a mess of his or her life, do you feel that you're somehow responsible?

2. If your partners always ask you to do something that they can very well do themselves, will you think "Enough!" but say "Sure!"?

3. If you really want to see a particular film and your lover mentions one that you've already seen, will you try to please him or her instead of yourself?

4. Do you feel sort of un-needed unless your lover is going through a soap opera crisis?

5. Have most of your relationships ended in your feeling deceived or exploited?

If you get definite maybes to the above, then no matter how appealing he or she may be, you might be over your head in Piscean waters!

Enter the virgin

Yes, Virgo whose symbol is the virgin—illustrating this sign's quest for purity—has many qualities that would benefit your Pisces lover. To name a few: pragmatism, self-analysis, discrimination, efficiency, and perfectionism.

Somewhere out there is probably a lover of Virgo reading about Pisces and thinking "Oh, if only my Virgo lover was as in touch with his or her emotions as much as Pisces, life would be wonderful!" The point is that we can all learn from our polar opposites to become better integrated human beings. For instance, the same way Virgo can benefit from more Piscean emotion, Pisces can benefit from more Virgo discrimination. Virgo can certainly learn to be more accepting of people like Pisces, and submissive Pisces can benefit from some of Virgo's analytic caution. Where do Pisceans turn when they become too dreamy and inactive to finish a project? To the role model of Virgo working tirelessly for perfection, of course!

Although Virgo represents the other half of your lover's potential, it might take you, their better half, to help them to realize it.

Tantalizingly tantric

Since your Pisces is attracted to Eastern mysticism, he or she has probably heard of Tantra sex, the sacred Indian act of love. If not, then I urge you to visit your lover on his or her desert island immediately with a copy of *The Kama Sutra,* the beautiful seventh-century Indian scripture. *Kama* in Sanskrit is a word that means "sex and love are undivided; they are one."

Tantra is defined as a spiritual and sexual science, and it is meant to expand the boundaries of sex, using sexual intimacy to raise our consciousness, allowing us to discover emotional and spiritual facets of ourselves. Tantra sex can be a gateway for Pisceans to explore their mystical nature. However, don't for a minute think that your lover will be in some spiritual limbo cut off from you. He or she will be a heartbeat away. It is said that the orgasms one experiences through Tantra are not only multiple, but explosive. Of course, I cannot verify this because I'm usually so busy with my quilting and stamp collecting, but I hope that you will write and tell me of your incredible journey into Tantric bliss.

Betting it all

Many Pisceans have to rev up their courage to go after love and risk losing *the dream* of it. If those born under this sign suffer as easily from unrequited love as from the common cold, it may be that they're living in a dream world, and perhaps they're afraid that the reality and risk of loving won't measure up to that dream. For instance, Meryl Streep plays a woman on a farm in the film *The Bridges of Madison County.* Her heart is awakened by a visiting charismatic photographer (Clint Eastwood) and they fall passionately in love. When the time comes for him to leave, he begs her to go with him, but she refuses. Was she afraid to lose the magic of their brief affair by committing to the relationship? Afraid to risk the dream by living the reality? (I doubt that even Elizabeth Taylor's acting ability could ever let her play that role with any conviction!)

We all know that love is a risk. It is the consummate gamble on ourselves and our instincts to know what is best for us. Sometimes we're right, and sometimes we end up with a name like Elizabeth Taylor-Hilton-Wilding-Todd-Fisher-Burton-Warner-Fortensky!

However, once in a great while we are given the chance to wrap up our fears and wants and needs and to deliver them into the hands of someone we deeply love. If life blesses us enough to offer that chance, I believe we should say thank you and have the courage to take it, before fate changes its mind!

Money and Pisces

If you're wondering if a sensitive Pisces, with his or her desire to transcend reality, could ever be a success in the material world, the answer is definitely yes!

Although Pisceans love the finer things of life, and are quite willing to pay for them, they prefer not to be nine-to-fivers in the corporate world (that's their idea of unsolitary confinement!). But the world needs their creativity and is willing to pay for it.

It's exactly Pisceans' desire to *touch the source* that enables them to express their creativity in innovative and often unforgettable ways. They have big dreams and it doesn't take long for them to learn that dreams cost money. If they're not born into wealth, as so many Pisces are—or don't marry into it, as so many Pisces do—they will work for whatever it takes to fund the dream machine.

Their dreams can manifest in wondrous ways. For instance, your lover has the unique ability to dramatize a situation (yes, even when not in the bedroom), and since the planet Neptune rules film, many Piscean actors create their magical reality on the screen. Others make our lives considerably more beautiful via photography, painting, dance, and music.

Before success visits and decides to stay, you might marvel at the way Pisces can stretch a dollar. The only problem is that they stretch and stress. It's at these times, when your lover loses sleep over enough money to oil that dream machine, that you should know about a *second* way to get him or her to sleep. You see, music is essential to the inner harmony of this sign. If they've never played a musical instrument, they're long overdue for their own guitar or flute or whatever you can fit into the back seat of a taxi. Surprise them with this gift and I promise they will take to it like the fish takes to water.

The art of healing

There's another art, which you won't see performed on stage or applauded at a Hollywood premiere, that is equally as fascinating to Pisces: the art of healing.

Although Pisces lovers can waste a lot of time trying to heal the wounds of others that are really self-inflicted, they do have a sincere desire to make the sick healthy and the fragmented whole. At this stage of evolvement, you won't find Pisces charging an arm and a leg to treat the rest of you, or rejecting someone because he or she doesn't have insurance. No, Pisces who come into their own power can illustrate ways of healing that border on the miraculous, tapping into energies that are yet to be recognized by mainstream medicine. If you're fortunate enough to love a Pisces who wants to develop his or her healing ability, or is even practicing it, then you might be familiar with various holistic healings for body and mind. Or, if your lover is way, way along the path, he or she might have introduced you to the miracles of psychic healing.

Perhaps one of the most famous Pisces psychic healers was Edgar Cayce. The book, *The Sleeping Prophet*, details his life and his extraordinary ability to channel (receive information from a higher source), and to help people with every conceivable problem from getting rid of a stutter to curing life-threatening diseases. By profession, Cayce was a photographer (another Piscean world of illusion). Though he died over half a century ago, Cayce was ahead of his time as a holistic healer, urging people to actively participate in their physical, mental, and spiritual health.

The only problem with getting Pisceans to play an active role in their own healing is that you have to find them first!

The escape hatch

Neither the creative arts nor the healing arts can protect an immature Pisces from the harsher realities of life. Ouch! That sound was a Pisces butting heads with an inevitable financial setback on the road to success. How does your lover handle money problems? Does Pisces square his or her shoulders and get ready to tackle the problem . . . or order a fifth of courage?

Many a lover has been frustrated with this sign's dependence on alcohol when times become stressful. In the same way an immature Pisces can develop a co-dependent relationship (read the previous chapter), that same addictive behavior can raise its needy head when Pisces faces a career setback.

The fact that there are more alcoholics among Pisces than any other sign is to be taken seriously.

So, if you know that your lover has a weakness in this direction, please do two things. First, teach your partner how to say no, *nein, non,* and *nyet*! That's "no" in a sufficient amount of languages to stop doling out money to people who never pay it back. Yes, Pisces are generous to a fault, and the fault is strictly their own when they find themselves exploited enough to drown their depression in a drink.

Next, include alcohol among the ex-friends you will *never* invite to dinner. If your Pisces balks at this revised guest list, and you're tired of hearing "I can stop anytime I want to," then you must sit down and really communicate. If the situation is beyond the reach of one-on-one communication, don't hesitate to contact one of hundreds of groups and services out there—they're all ready to help you help your lover.

(Note: Since Pisces have such a strong spiritual bent, they may respond to therapy with the help of Zen meditation. Many people who have lost themselves to addictive behavior have found hope attending Zen retreats. Of course, meditation, martial arts, and yoga are all ways people can built their inner strength.)

Promises to keep

It's always inspiring to know that less than mature Pisces lovers, who dream of grandiose acts while passively dragging their feet, may someday metamorphosize into flying butterflies! We don't expect all of them to turn into psychic channelers, compose concertos, or display their art in the Metropolitan Museum in New York. Of course, if that's their dream, we want to help them to realize it, but *they* must try. The Piscean passivity—which, by the way, is a national killer after cigarettes and no seat belts!—can be fatal when it comes to realizing goals. If they choose to express their creativity in the Piscean love of architecture, *they* must try. If they're dreaming of their own catering business, *they* must try. So, let Pisces lovers know that promises to themselves, and to you, have to be turned into tangible resolve.

Pisces is such a fortunate sign because those born under this sign don't have to sacrifice material success in their work for spiritual enlightenment. Or visa versa. Anyone who is artistically gifted knows that just the act of creating is a form of meditation. It brings the person closer and closer to a spiritual state. However, I stress that it is in the *doing* and not the dreaming that Pisces will find success on every level.

The philosopher Thoreau might have been talking to Pisces when he said: "If you have built castles in the air, your work needn't be lost. That is where they should be. Now put the foundation under them!"

Just as Capricorn plugs away climbing that mountain of material success, Pisces have the potential to reach their own summit—or get very close to the top—if only they can muster a tenth of Capricorn's discipline.

Strength in numbers

You might have realized by now that Pisces need strong lovers. They prefer that strength in confident sexual partners, and they want it in the ones who are at their side, helping them to deliver their promises.

However, you may have some promises of your own that you need to keep. Perhaps you didn't take standard marriage vows, but did you make your own when you began to love this ethereal, sensitive, and totally mesmerizing lover? Even if your promises were silent ones, didn't you vow to do everything you could to make you and your lover happy, to make the relationship work?

Aquarius, you might not be able to keep your promise for happiness ever after, because, even though you and Pisces might scorn the material world, your logical way to solve problems is just not the Piscean emotional way. Leo, you may resent having to bolster your lover when he or she is feeling depressed about money and your usual dose of optimism isn't working. Gemini, both you and Pisces need stronger lovers than either of you in order to stay grounded. Virgo, your criticism of Pisces' "did I forget to pay the light bill again?" mentality will crush your lover and promise many Excedrin moments.

Libra and Pisces both love luxury, but the only problem is that neither of these lovers may have the discipline to work hard enough to get it.

It's Cancer, again, who comes the closest to a perfect fit (and all you lovers who have the sign of Cancer strong in your charts!). Although Pisceans may frustrate the Moon Child because of their lack of interest in finances—and Cancer loves to feather the nest with designer feathers—Cancers will be so much in love that they'll happily handle the finances as well. Then they will devote themselves to keeping their promise, to create a safe haven for Pisces where they can create and dream to their heart's content.

A new start

Just remember: The next time your Pisces gets depressed over money and wants to escape into a private dream world, your positive energy can help bring him or her back to reality. Remember that when Pisces are deep in an emotional pit, gazing longingly at the top of the summit, your belief in them will renew their energy for the climb. However, this climb is very hard because the creative and spiritual rewards are so great. You can't do it for them, but it gets a lot easier when one of your hands is holding theirs, and the other is placed firmly and lovingly on the small of their back.

Power and Pisces

Astro-psychologists equate the development stage of Pisces with eighty years of age to the end of life. For those (including myself) who believe that the soul transcends death, the fact that our physical body now weakens may test our faith and courage, but it shouldn't be frightening. This life's journey is coming to an end, but we're preparing to make a greater one—the journey home. It's now, before we enter this doorway to a new dimension of being, that we're capable of attaining great spiritual growth.

Smoke and mirrors

It's the power of Pisceans to bring into reality what they dream. That's pure creativity. However, when a confused and immature lover begins to live in a dream world and deny what's really happening, his or her partner begins to feel powerless.

It all begins with a problem that your lover doesn't want to face, so he or she simply denies its reality. Poof, it's gone! Pisces puts on his or her rose-colored glasses and once more, the world is problem-less and beautiful to see. But the problem keeps resurfacing like the Loch Ness monster, and sooner or later you're going to become aware of it. So you bring it to your lover's attention and . . .

Does Pisces suddenly admit to the problem and take mature steps to solve it? Does the magician admit he's using smoke and mirrors? No, the most you can hope for are baby steps, and you realize they're getting you both nowhere. According to your lover, everyone else—not excluding extraterrestrials—is responsible for the problem. It's clear that Pisces' illusions and delusions have power over your relationship and they're making communication impossible.

The truth hurts

Of course, this is extreme behavior that's as frightening as an IRS audit, and hopefully, you'll never encounter either during your lifetime. But what do you do if you do? What if you have a Pisces lover who just won't face some harsh truths about himself or herself, and clings to a fantasy version of reality—*in the face of all reality?* What if your lover even resorts to self-deception in order to maintain the illusion?

Now is the time to go back to the scene of the crime, when your Pisces had a priceless item stolen. No, he or she didn't tell you about it because it was probably too embarrassing. No, it wasn't their wallet or even a winning lottery ticket. It was the loss of their *self-esteem.* When it happened, they quickly convinced themselves of another version of the truth, one that was easier for them to live with, and so the deception began. In this case Pisces' natural acting ability helped to deceive other people and themselves.

If Pisceans just brood and lie to themselves, that's one thing. When they begin to verbalize the deception, it gets more serious. Each time they say it aloud they reinforce the lie, making it all the more believable to them. For instance, they didn't get a promotion they were hoping for. Suddenly you hear Pisces shrugging it off: "Well, this was obviously just an interim move on management's part. It's all politics, and I'll probably be sitting in that corner office by the beginning of the year."

Of course, when you question them further, you discover that their theory is decidedly Piscean fishy. Since it makes no sense, and you have this silly romantic dream of living in the *real world* together, you point it out to them. They don't want to hear it. If they're really confused, they can even become angry with you. "How dare you sit there and suggest that black isn't red after all? Who are you, the color police? I won't discuss it any further."

Now you're having second thoughts about third party objectivity in the form of counseling. Great idea! But how do you explain what happened? You feel powerless, but you just can't put it into words. Don't worry, because Carl Jung, the great psychoanalyst, said for you: "Where love rules, there is no will to power and where power predominates, there love is lacking. The one is the shadow of the other."

Out of the shadows

When we're stressed out and our resolve dissolves into Jello, wouldn't it be wonderful if we could just "borrow" the qualities we need from other signs? Pisceans want to escape this harsh, cruel world? Okay, in order to cope they need some courage of Aries, the stability of Taurus, the resiliency of Gemini, the analytical ability of Virgo, the balance of Libra, the determination of Capricorn, the detachment of Aquarius . . . and let's not forget the philosophical outlook of Sagittarius! Cancer and Scorpio, Pisces has enough emotion to deal with right now—you'll have your part to play later.

I propose that not only can we borrow these qualities, we can make them our own. Just as an actor plays a role over and over again until he or she begins to live the part, so can your Pisces lover. No smoke. No mirrors. But instead of using his or her acting ability to escape reality—*your lover uses it to create a new reality about himself or herself.*

What you see is what you get

In a previous chapter, Leos were urged to solve problems (and fulfill their love of drama at the same time), by writing their own life's script. Pisces can do the same. But instead of writing the script, why not act it? Why not *become* this integrated, mature, and strong personality they would love to be?

Neptune, the planet of illusion, is your ally here. It gives your lover the ability to lose himself or herself in the dream. So, begin by appealing to your Pisces' vivid imagination.

You: I read something really wild the other day—someone wrote about evolving into the person they wanted to be by acting the part.

Pisces: I don't get it.

You: Well, for instance, say someone just gets overstressed and they take the easy way out, they just want to retreat into a dream world.

Pisces: Is this getting personal?

You: [Plowing right on] And instead, they just *pretend* they can cope. They act the role of someone being strong, unfrazzled, able to leap a tall building in a single bound. [Pause for adoring look on your part] Hey, you have acting ability, this sounds perfect for you.

Pisces: Yes, but how long can you keep this kind of thing going?

You: I don't know, just try crawling under the character's skin for a couple of days, see how it goes.

Pisces: Does this come with a script?

You: Just tell yourself whatever the occasion calls for. For instance, "I will now assert myself and not become emotional, and I will not let myself be taken advantage of."

Pisces: [Interrupting] You're talking about my being a soft touch and lending money to the wrong people, right?

You: Or when you tend to lead with your emotions, you need something like . . . "I will not freak about this, I will react in a calm, mature way."

Pisces: [Getting into the spirit] I am in control, I am self-reliant, I'm a fantastic human being!

You: You got it!

There's a song titled "I Whistle a Happy Tune" from the Broadway show *The King and I* that beautifully illustrates this metamorphosis. These are the lyrics (and whistling is optional):

"Whenever I feel afraid, I hold my head erect, and whistle a happy tune so no one will suspect I'm afraid. The result of this deception is very strange to tell, for when I fool the people I fear I fool myself as well! Make believe you're brave and the trick will take you far . . . you may be as brave as you make believe you are!"

And the truth heals

We can only try to communicate the truth to our lovers. Hopefully, they're already teetering enough on the side of maturity that we can (tenderly, of course) give them a push over. Most often it's just telling someone the truth that's enough to jolt them into awareness. Remember that your truth must always come from love, and that love has to be communicated in your voice, in your eyes, and in your heart. Nothing else works.

When it does work, and you and Pisces are finally communicating without veils of illusion, delusion, or confusion, then it should be a time of pride . . . and forgiveness.

Forgive and forget

Unlike Taureans, who can keep their anger on a low boil until they finally forgive, or Scorpios, who may forgive but never forget, Pisceans see the big picture. They know that all things end and that nothing is forever. That's why they're always forgiving people for being "only human."

So perhaps now is the time to forgive this lover for frequently moving into his or her own magical reality and not leaving a forwarding address. It might also be a good time to experiment with a little role playing of your own. Are you a pragmatic earth sign who always dreams in black and white? Then how about "getting under the skin" of a loving, nurturing Cancer and convincing Pisces that you'll always love him or her, even when Pisces doesn't always love himself or herself? Are you a detached air sign who can be indecisive about commitment? Then try on the passionate intensity of Scorpio and assure Pisces that no matter what the crisis, you will both face it together.

Lovers can become stronger and wiser and braver and more loving than they ever thought possible. Perhaps a little make believe can help us get started, but it's the believing in each other that makes it all possible.

Decanates

Take two lovers born under the sign of Pisces and they can be radically different. One is able to work for compromise in a relationship, the other is so self-involved that a try at communication ends up being a monologue. Why are they like day and night? Studying decanates can explain a lot of the differences.

You see, every sign in the zodiac is divided into three parts. Each sign spans thirty days, and each day represents one degree. The decanates encompass ten degrees each. While the first ten degrees reflect the nature of the sign itself, the other decanates have different planets as sub-rulers. So, while Pisces is ruled by Neptune, people can also be sub-ruled by the Moon or Mars, dependent on the date they were born.

Is your Pisces a mirror-image of the sign? Is there a sub-ruler that will modify your lover's behavior? It's all right here . . .

February 20 to February 28

Neptune rules these lovers and covers them with a veil of illusion. They have a quality about them that people just can't "put their finger on." It's both otherworldly and mes-merizing. These lovers are usually highly creative and, although not necessarily religious, they can be strongly spiritual. Since they have a burning desire to transcend reality and touch *the source*, they're drawn to the metaphysical world. If you're lucky enough to have found a more evolved Pisces, someone who has been on the path long enough to have earned a few spiritual calluses, then Pisces may trust you with some of his or her mystical adventures.

You love this Pisces for his or her great compassion and ability to empathize with your feelings. But sometimes the empathy goes overboard and, suddenly, Pisces is drowning in a sea of emotion. These Pisces must learn to keep calm and use their logic when stressed. Once they learn how to do this, they can make a tremendous contribution, helping other people heal their minds and bodies.

Whatever these Pisces do, they will do it better with your encouragement and support. Life is often too harsh for them, and when they can't cope, they can look for that "escape hatch" in ways that will be self-destructive. It's at those times they need the 100 percent proof and strength of your love.

March 1 to March 10

Compared to this Pisces, the one described above will seem as down to earth as your dentist.

The Moon seems to open a direct line to these Pisces' subconscious feelings. Therefore, they can become moody without explanation and distant without leaving the room. Please be careful what you say to these lovers, because they are hypersensitive. If you feel that

Pisces is brooding over some irrational fear, try to talk about it with him or her. It's the best way to chase the ghosts and goblins from their minds. When they become so immersed in another's negative feelings, or begin a worry pilgrimage back and forth from the bedroom to the bathroom, suggest they just picture themselves sitting by the edge of a river, watching their problems come into view, one behind the other. They don't attempt to hold on to any of them, they just let them go and watch them float by. This is a calming form of meditation that might appeal to your lover.

On the plus side, this Pisces is capable of deep compassion, empathy, and love. Sex can become as close to an out of the body experience as you can imagine, and Pisces will feel your orgasm down to his or her toes.

Hopefully, you are a grounded personality who can keep this Pisces down to earth, except of course in bed, where you both can fly!

March 11 to March 20

The planet Mars steps in to make quite an impact on this lover. Astrologers note that impressionable Pisces is made either very good with the help of Mars, or very bad, compliments of the same planet. Hopefully, you have found a lover who can be a tremendous source of good for both of you.

However, because we don't always get what we deserve, watch out for some danger signals: a willful, unrealistic personality accompanied by a temper that goes out of control. An inflexibility when life's lessons must be learned. If your lover is on the wrong end of the Mars planetary vibration, he or she will refuse to learn them—instead, this Pisces will opt for behavior that is both aggressive and self-destructive.

If you think that your lover is displaying more of these traits then you want to admit, remember that you're always your own best friend. So give yourself some smart advice. You know what that advice is, the smart part is taking it!

Hopefully, you have gotten the partner you deserve and he or she is putting artistic, altruistic, and spiritual ideas into practice as we speak. Neptune gives your lover the visions to create wonders, and Mars adds fuel to make them materialize. Hold his or her hand tightly on the incredible life's journey you will take together, and never look back!

The Pisces Lover

February 20 to March 20

The Good

Spiritual

Selfless

Psychic

Artistic

Sensitive

The Bad

Escapist

Co-dependent

Unrealistic

Indecisive

Passive

The Ugly

Alcoholic

Victim

Delusional

Inactive

Submissive

Appendix

The Moon

Understanding your lover's Sun sign will help your relationship to survive and grow, but to weather the most difficult storms, you need true empathy—the ability to nurture and the patience to listen. For this, we look to *your* Moon sign.

Astrology teaches us that the Moon is related to the feminine principles of emotion and intuition. It's the symbol of the mother. What symbol of love could be better? After all, our mothers are the first to give us the unconditional love we need in order to believe in ourselves. It is our mothers we once ran to (and may still) for emotional support when life becomes difficult. They feed our egos and our self-confidence. Their warmth and caring are vital if we are to grow as children. In the same way, if your adult love is to grow in depth, you must be able to offer your lover these same qualities. You've seen in this book that most of our problems stem from a lack of self-confidence. The truth is that we all carry our child inside us, and it's our lovers who must be there for us when that child is hurting.

There are many of us who excel in the art of understanding, listening, and nurturing. But for others, our own emotional blocks prevent us from really giving.

The sign in which your Moon falls is the secret: it tells a lot about your own mother and how well she nurtured you. You may be enjoying the full wealth of that nurturing today . . . or paying for the lack of it. Other elements in your horoscope further determine your ability to nurture your loved one—but the placement of the Moon will definitely tell you a lot about your emotional self. What better time to learn than right now?

Moon in Aries

We've seen that the Ram wants action and often acts on impulse. This is the opposite of the nurturing Moon, desiring always to be patient and reflecting. Aries will often sum up the problem in record time—give their lovers a locker-room type of pep talk—then become annoyed when immediate action isn't taken. Aries, your positive attitude is uplifting. Your optimism is wonderful. However, this type of abrupt nurturing can be unsettling to lovers, and especially difficult on the sensitive emotions of a Cancer or a Pisces. Remember too, that just because your lover may be a dynamic Leo, he or she may still have many planets in sensitive water signs. So take your time to really listen and be patient. Also, try offering some healing, physical warmth. No, not sex . . . not now . . . but just a loving hug. The great thing about a warm hug is that you get as good as you give!

If you had the type of mother who pushed you out on your own (emotionally speaking), then instead of developing sensitivity to other people's needs, you might have been too busy surviving! Take the time now to learn how to nurture. Time is also what's needed to listen to your lover's feelings. Since your mate knows how much time means to you, and how little of it you have to waste, there's no better way to express how much you truly care. Later, the aggressive action you suggest will mean all the more, for it will be based on real understanding.

Moon in Taurus

Moon in Taurus lovers are the great listeners of the zodiac. Unlike those with Moon in Aries, who must learn to listen without checking their watch, you seem to have all the time in the world. You know how to create a soothing atmosphere—one that is safe and comfortable—and it communicates to a distraught lover that everything is all right in the world after all.

You may need to listen a little harder in order to really be sensitive on an emotional level (that's not always your strength), but when it comes to a soft and stable shoulder, you're there 100 percent. Actually, even if you miss an emotional nuance once in a while, your lover will be given so much time to talk that he or she will probably discover the solution to the problem by the time he or she is finished.

The calm atmosphere you create is made even more wonderful by your natural, earthy desire to hold, to touch, to comfort. Afterward, you'll probably continue to nurture your lover with food.

With your Moon in Taurus, your mother was probably a source of comfort and strength in your life. She might not have been the most exciting or innovative mother in the neighborhood, but she was reliable and loving. She was someone who was always there for you. It's quite possible that you nurture your lover so well today because you grew up knowing your mother's caring touch.

Moon in Gemini

As a Moon in Gemini person, when your lover needs a little support and TLC, you want to help in anyway you can, in theory. However, understanding takes listening. It takes reflection. It takes being quiet! Yes, keeping you quiet long enough to really listen to your lover is a Herculean task. Does the intensity of your lover's emotions frighten you? Do you keep interjecting those glib remarks because you want to keep the situation light? Your partner begins to speak about feelings, and suddenly he or she is in an intellectual debate about feelings! Are you up to your old ploy again of discussing feelings instead of feeling them?

You have simply got to bite the bullet and really, really listen. Force yourself not to ask one question until your lover is through speaking. Then, before you import the information from that formidable data bank in your head, think about what you have just heard. Don't be so anxious to give advice. It may really not be as relevant as you think. Moon in Gemini suggests that your own mother was a bit high strung, possibly a nervous talker who never nurtured you in a quiet and thoughtful way. Is that why you don't know how to focus on feelings today? Do you interject chatter, jokes, and the latest headlines to avoid focusing on feelings? With all that talk going on, perhaps you don't have to listen to your own inner feelings, or anyone else's for that matter. So, it's time to open your ears, your mind, and your heart—shut your mouth tightly—and feel!

Moon in Cancer

You're fortunate to have this ideal placement—or should I say that your lover is fortunate? The Moon rules the sign of Cancer, making you extremely comfortable with your feelings. You're in your element relating to people on an emotional level. It seems that you intuitively know how to listen and empathize, and you communicate feelings of acceptance and unconditional love. What a wonderful gift!

I spoke previously about Cancer's attachment to his or her mother. Of course, the whole picture can only be seen in your complete horoscope, but generally, Moon in Cancer people were listened to and nurtured emotionally as children. The result of that caring is very evident. If you are a male, you might be on an eternal quest for a woman "just like Mom" (and that can be for better or for worse!). If you're a female, your mother's influence might manifest itself in your love of home, children, and nurturing everyone you love, and many you simply don't have the heart to turn away. Most importantly, this Moon placement indicates that you grew up with the capacity to accept your feelings, giving yourself the self-love that so many of us lack.

So even though your entire horoscope may show other challenges for you in terms of nurturing your lover, with the Moon in Cancer, you definitely have a head start in the right direction.

Moon in Leo

You share a bit of the Moon Aries problem: you want your lover to cheer up in the minimum amount of time. However, in your case it's because the "negative vibes"—as you think of them anyway—threaten to drag you down. You always keep up that eternal (infernal?) sunny front, even when life is being royally rotten. Do you expect your lover to do the same? You must learn to take the time to listen to the person who shares your bed, and to validate his or her feelings. You can't brush those feelings away with a quick fix of cheer and "C'mon now, let me see a big smile!"

Moon in Leo suggests that your own mother might have enforced this need to show a cheerful face to the world at all times. Perhaps she encouraged the child entertainer in you to shine—and frowned on a show of unhappiness or a trembling lower lip. Did you win your mother's applause and smiles? Children stick to the behavior that brings them love from parents, and perhaps that's exactly what you did. But your childhood's lack of nurturing may be getting in the way of becoming the sensitive lover you want yourself to be. Certainly, you know all about the need to express yourself. Well, give your lover a bit of that spotlight for a while—as long as it takes for your lover to express his or her feelings. Don't anticipate those feelings with dread or distaste, either. Your mother may have reacted to unhappiness as though it was contagious, but you can do better. Start by listening and doing a lot of loving. Chances are, you won't even catch a cold!

Moon in Virgo

You're the intellectual who will try to help your lover by fully analyzing the problem—while not devoting enough time to your lover's feelings. Then, if you're not careful, you might do what you do too well: criticize. You might think you're pointing out a fault in a gentle way. Forget it. Your lover knows you too well. Also, please believe that your partner realizes what mistakes were made. Now is not the time to rehash them or to suggest how things should have been done. Simply be there to listen. Of course, you're a purist and you want your lover to be ultra-smart and capable of problem-solving. But right now, he or she feels foolish, or dumb, or guilty, or unloved, or all of those things. So, however ridiculous you think they are, validate those feelings. Then, a warm hug and stroking is very much recommended.

Now, it's very possible that your mother was a little anal-retentive in terms of emotions. Perhaps she wanted you to solve too many problems too soon. She might have communicated this desire for you with: do your homework, clean your room, take out the trash, don't give me any problems, and so on. Chances are you got the message. Well, remember how awful it was when your mother made you feel like a problem to her? Don't make your lover feel like a problem that you have to solve. Make him or her feel like a needed, cherished part of your life—one that deserves to be listened to with all your heart and not your head.

Moon in Libra

Libra is the sign of "we"—representing companionship and, ideally, the most harmonious love relationship. This sign seems to have everything: looks, charm, intelligence, etc. However, surprisingly, all too often Moon in Libra lacks the ability to really nurture. Yes, you'll listen to your lover, but extreme emotions can make you uncomfortable. You feel off balance. You may even feel embarrassed—like witnessing someone commit a social blunder at a garden party! In order to restore the harmony you need, you may try to get your lover to see another point of view. You'll use your intellect to get him or her to become more rational—in the Libra balanced way you prefer. It may work, and your lover may look at things more rationally. But even though he or she feels better, something will still be missing. They might not be able to name it, but it's simply a warm, physical display of your caring. Why did your arms remain at your sides when your lover needed to feel them? Why did your most tender thoughts remain unsaid when your lover needed to hear them?

Your mother might have been the type of parent who taught you: "There is a time and a place for everything." Was she acutely aware of social behavior and niceties? In fact, she might have been horrified if an emotional storm brewed during a social situation. Well, you're grown up now and you have a better understanding of what nurturing is all about. There's never a right time and place for it. It should be given with love—anytime and anyplace it's needed.

The next time your lover is angry and hurt, and volatile, messy emotions spill all over the place, reach out and get your hands dirty! Hold your lover as tightly as you can, and to hell with the garden party!

Moon in Scorpio

Since you're an intense, in-depth personality, there's little you do that only skims the surface, which means that when you listen to your lover, you listen completely. You hear nuances that your lover might not even know he or she is verbalizing.

You love to investigate dark areas of the soul, and you can be relentless when it comes to uncovering a truth. Perhaps you could lighten up a bit? Instead of asking questions in a manner that will have your lover convinced you were a CIA operative, take your time coming to conclusions. Most of all, I know that you have an uncanny—and often diabolical—talent to seek out someone's Achilles heel. So, although you may be in love now, promise yourself that you'll resist any urge to use private information you learn in a future argument, no matter how tempting! You're being told something because someone trusts you. Never betray it.

Although your perceptions are laser sharp, understand that not everyone can accept the raw truth without large servings of warmth and love. It's the difference between performing an operation with anesthesia or giving the patient a shot of whiskey and something to bite down on!

Your relationship with your own mother was a complex one. She might have been very controlling and left you little space of your own. If so, it made you more anxious to keep your privacy as an adult, to keep your secrets. Now when you give someone you love advice, take the opportunity to give a little of yourself at the same time. As you shed light on their inner feelings and motivations, give them the gift of sharing some of your feelings as well. It may prove to be an enlightening and mutually healing experience.

Moon in Sagittarius

It's important that when you listen to someone, you don't already have the answers on the tip of your tongue. At least be smart enough to *pretend* that you don't.

Your lover may be afraid to talk to you because you often project the attitude of *knowing it all*. You may be totally unaware of this characteristic, but it may also intimidate your lover from asking for help.

The answer is to make your partner feel as though he or she is actually contributing to the conversation—and asking you something that you don't already have your mind made up about. Your worst fault at these times is that, although your heart may be in the right place, you can sound pretentious and lecture more than listen. What's the worst that can happen? You can inadvertently make your lover feel dumb. That's sort of overkill, because when people are depressed and troubled, they usually feel they've exceeded their dumb quotient for the year!

So, before you try to educate your lover in ways to intellectually overcome his or her problems, try empathizing a bit more. I promise that feelings will never negate intellectual problem-solving, they will just bring you closer together.

Your mother might have been as smart as you, as intellectually astute, and as optimistic. However, was she always as sympathetic and empathetic as you would have liked? Sometimes, especially as kids, we know that we can do better. We even plan to do better. However, there are those moments when we simply want to be held.

Those moments don't vanish with adulthood. So, keep your mind open, Sag, and make sure that your arms are as well.

Moon in Capricorn

Your ability for self-discipline, your steel-like determination to succeed, and your standards of perfectionism are just what you *do not need* when your partner needs a soft shoulder and some serious nurturing. Too often these qualities translate to your partner as a rigidity that will only keep you apart.

The term *unconditional* is one that you must understand before you can really be a supportive lover. It means that you don't have an unspoken list of demands in your head that you mentally check off before your partner can earn your love and support. For instance, you plan to be loving and supportive and wonderful for about an hour. It shouldn't take longer than that to solve the problem, you think. An hour later, your lover is still in a depressed groove, and you're becoming impatient. What do you do?

You try to listen with sympathy instead of keeping your feelings locked away in some impenetrable vault. You try to empathize instead of resenting the time you're taking to listen. Finally, you offer encouragement instead of conveying the feeling that your lover is simply weak. We are all weak at times, and that's the time we put our lovers to the test. Will you pass yours?

Your mother might have left a rigid imprint in your mind. Perhaps she was never as soft and compassionate as you would have liked. Was her love dependent upon you meeting some unreachable requirements? Well, if she set a pattern for your own rigid expectations, then it's never too late to change it. Open the door to that vault, release your feelings, and then throw away the key.

Moon in Aquarius

You tend to intellectualize your partner's feelings, and as with so many brainy lovers, you often forget to nurture with your emotions. It can seem to the person on the receiving end of your advice that you are standing on a lofty plateau, calling down brilliant ideas to them but not really relating.

Nobody can shock someone into a state of enlightenment as well as you can. You're able to take someone completely by surprise with your uncanny perception, which may or may not be easy to digest. But sometimes you hardly wait for them to swallow one truth before you're ready with another. Yes, the truth can set us free, but it can also put us in an unnecessary state of shock. So, in order to avoid ending up with an "enlightened trauma victim," don't you think a gentler approach might do as well?

Even if you know what your lover has to understand before he or she can resolve a problem, take the time to help him or her understand it. Sometimes a truth is far more meaningful if we discover it for ourselves. Besides, we're twice as grateful when someone takes the time to speak to us lovingly and compassionately, especially when we know it really isn't in his or her nature to do so.

Your mother was probably an eclectic and even brilliant personality. However, was she too distant? Was she perhaps (as you often are) too involved in ideas on a global scale and not enough in one-on-one communication? Again, I advise that you can change any pattern once you become aware of it, and if you care enough about someone to try.

Moon in Pisces

You epitomize compassion and deep sensitivity, and at times you show a psychic sensitivity that knows far more than is being said.

Watch out for your desire to *save* people, and to make their problems your own. It's an invitation that too many people will be tempted to accept, and it can leave you emotionally drained. The fact is that you can't live your lover's life or solve all of his or her problems, nor should you even try to. Remember that we're all here to accept life's lessons and to learn from them; there are no shortcuts. So, no matter how much we want to spare someone we love from pain, perhaps it's that very pain that will help him or her to grow. One more suggestion: it's also not necessary to show our love by suffering twice as much as our loved one is suffering! It isn't going to help our partners if they have to give us the shoulder rub and words of comfort that they need themselves.

So, try to keep your objectivity when nurturing someone you love. Let your partner know that you are thinking as well as feeling—*be there now*—and don't become lost in a sea of emotion.

It's possible that your mother was needy in a way that required you to feel her feelings, perhaps you risked losing your own identity in the process, and you might even have felt an uncomfortable responsibility for her emotional happiness. Don't forget that no matter how much you loved your mother, you fought to become your own person, with your own individuality, and with your own needs. It's exactly that strength that your lover needs from you now.

Find Your Moon Sign

The following method for finding your Moon sign was developed by Grant Lewi and writen about in *Astrology for the Millions*, published by Llewellyn Worldwide.

Grant Lewi's System
Step 1:
Find your birth year in the tables on pages 244–251.

Step 2:
Run down the left-hand column and see if your birth date is there. If your birth date is in the left-hand column, run over this line until you come to the column under your birth year. Here you will find a number. This is your base number. Write it down, and go directly to the direction under the heading "What to Do with Your Base Number" on page 240.

Step 3:
If your birth date is not in the left-hand column, get a pencil and paper. Your birth date falls between two numbers in the left-hand column. Look at the date closest to the one after your birth date; run across this line to your birth year. Write down the number you find there, and label it "top number." Directly beneath it on your piece of paper write the number printed just above it in the table. Label this "bottom number." Subtract the bottom number from the top number. If the top number is smaller, add 360 and subtract. The result is your difference.

Step 4:
Go back to the left-hand column and find the date before your birth date. Determine the number of days between this date and your birth date. Write this down and label it "intervening days."

Step 5:
Note which group your difference falls in.

Difference	Daily Motion
80–87	12 degrees
88–94	13 degrees
95–101	14 degrees
102–106	15 degrees

Note: If you were born in a leap year and use the difference between February 26 and March 5, then the daily motion is slightly different. If you fall into this category use the figures below.

Difference	Daily Motion
94–99	12 degrees
100–108	13 degrees
109–115	14 degrees
116–122	15 degrees

Step 6:
Write down the "daily motion" corresponding to your place in the proper table of difference above. Multiply daily motion by the number labeled "intervening days" (found at step 5).

Step 7:
Add the result of step 6 to your bottom number. This is your base number. If it is more than 360, subtract 360 from it and call the result your base number.

What to Do with Your Base Number

Locate your base number in the Table of Base Numbers on page 241. At the top of the column you will find the sign your Moon was in. In the far left-hand column you will find the degree the Moon occupied at 7:00 A.M. on your birth date if you were born under Eastern Standard Time (EST). Refer to the time zone conversion chart (see pages 242–243) to adjust information for your time zone.

If you don't know the hour of your birth, accept this as your Moon's sign and degree. If you do know the hour of your birth, get the exact degree as follows:

If you were born after 7:00 A.M. EST, determine the number of hours after the time that you were born. Divide this by two, rounding up if necessary. Add this to your base number, and the result in the table will be the exact degree and sign of the Moon on the year, month, date, and hour of your birth.

If you were born before 7:00 A.M. EST, determine the number of hours before the time that you were born. Divide this by two. Subtract this from your base number, and the result in the table will be the exact degree and sign of the Moon on the year, month, date, and hour of your birth.

Table of Base Numbers

	♈ (13)	♉ (14)	♊ (15)	♋ (16)	♌ (17)	♍ (18)	♎ (19)	♏ (20)	♐ (21)	♑ (22)	♒ (23)	♓ (24)
0°	0	30	60	90	120	150	180	210	240	270	300	330
1°	1	31	61	91	121	151	181	211	241	271	301	331
2°	2	32	62	92	122	152	182	212	242	272	302	332
3°	3	33	63	93	123	153	183	213	243	273	303	333
4°	4	34	64	94	124	154	184	214	244	274	304	334
5°	5	35	65	95	125	155	185	215	245	275	305	335
6°	6	36	66	96	126	156	186	216	246	276	306	336
7°	7	37	67	97	127	157	187	217	247	277	307	337
8°	8	38	68	98	128	158	188	218	248	278	308	338
9°	9	39	69	99	129	159	189	219	249	279	309	339
10°	10	40	70	100	130	160	190	220	250	280	310	340
11°	11	41	71	101	131	161	191	221	251	281	311	341
12°	12	42	72	102	132	162	192	222	252	282	312	342
13°	13	43	73	103	133	163	193	223	253	283	313	343
14°	14	44	74	104	134	164	194	224	254	284	314	344
15°	15	45	75	105	135	165	195	225	255	285	315	345
16°	16	46	76	106	136	166	196	226	256	286	316	346
17°	17	47	77	107	137	167	197	227	257	287	317	347
18°	18	48	78	108	138	168	198	228	258	288	318	248
19°	19	49	79	109	139	169	199	229	259	289	319	349
20°	20	50	80	110	140	170	200	230	260	290	320	350
21°	21	51	81	111	141	171	201	231	261	291	321	351
22°	22	52	82	112	142	172	202	232	262	292	322	352
23°	23	53	83	113	143	173	203	233	263	293	323	353
24°	24	54	84	114	144	174	204	234	264	294	324	354
25°	25	55	85	115	145	175	205	235	265	295	325	355
26°	26	56	86	116	146	176	206	236	266	296	326	356
27°	27	57	87	117	147	177	207	237	267	297	327	357
28°	28	58	88	118	148	178	208	238	268	298	328	358
29°	29	59	89	119	149	179	209	239	269	299	329	359

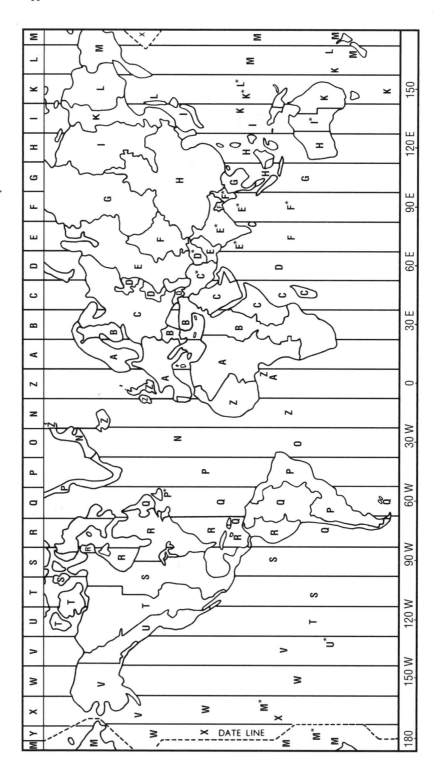

Time Zone Conversions
World Time Zones Compared to Eastern Time

(R)	EST—Used		(C⋆)	Add 8½ hours
(S)	CST—Subtract 1 hour		(D)	Add 9 hours
(T)	MST—Subtract 2 hours		(D⋆)	Add 9½ hours
(U)	PST—Subtract 3 hours		(E)	Add 10 hours
(V)	Subtract 4 hours		(E⋆)	Add 10½ hours
(U⋆)	Subtract 4½ hours		(F)	Add 11 hours
(W)	Subtract 5 hours		(F⋆)	Add 11½ hours
(X)	Subtract 6 hours		(G)	Add 12 hours
(Y)	Subtract 7 hours		(H)	Add 13 hours
(Q)	Add 1 hour		(I)	Add 14 hours
(P)	Add 2 hours		(I⋆)	Add 14½ hours
(P⋆)	Add 2½ hours		(K)	Add 15 hours
(O)	Add 3 hours		(K⋆)	Add 15½ hours
(N)	Add 4 hours		(L)	Add 16 hours
(Z)	Add 5 hours		(L⋆)	Add 16½ hours
(A)	Add 6 hours		(M)	Add 17 hours
(B)	Add 7 hours		(M⋆)	Add 17½ hours
(C)	Add 8 hours			

Important!

All times given are set in Eastern Time. The conversions shown here are for standard times only. Use the Time Zone Conversions map and table to calculate the difference in your time zone. You must make the adjustment for your time zone and adjust for Daylight Saving Time where applicable.

Chart for Finding Moon Sign from 1931 to Present

Month	Date	1931	1932	1933	1934	1935	1936	1937	1938	1939	1940
Jan.	1	60	196	346	107	231	8	156	277	41	181
Jan.	8	162	294	70	193	333	104	240	4	144	275
Jan.	15	257	20	158	294	68	190	329	104	239	360
Jan.	22	342	108	255	32	152	278	67	202	323	88
Jan.	29	68	207	353	116	239	19	163	286	49	191
Feb.	5	171	302	78	203	342	113	248	14	153	284
Feb.	12	267	28	168	302	78	198	339	113	248	8
Feb.	19	351	116	266	40	161	286	78	210	332	96
Feb.	26	77	217	1	124	248	29	171	294	59	200
Mar.	5	179	324	86	213	350	135	256	25	161	306
Mar.	12	276	48	176	311	86	218	347	123	256	29
Mar.	19	360	137	277	48	170	308	89	218	340	119
Mar.	26	86	241	10	132	258	52	180	302	69	223
Apr.	2	187	334	94	223	358	144	264	34	169	315
Apr.	9	285	57	185	321	95	227	355	133	264	38
Apr.	16	9	146	287	56	178	317	99	226	349	128
Apr.	23	96	250	18	140	268	61	189	310	80	231
Apr.	30	196	343	102	232	7	153	273	43	179	323
May	7	293	66	193	332	103	237	4	144	272	47
May	14	17	155	297	64	187	327	108	235	357	139
May	21	107	258	28	148	278	69	198	318	90	239
May	28	205	351	111	241	17	161	282	51	189	331
Jun.	4	301	75	201	343	111	245	13	154	280	55
Jun.	11	25	165	306	73	195	337	117	244	5	150
Jun.	18	117	267	37	157	288	78	207	327	99	248
Jun.	25	215	360	120	249	28	169	291	60	200	339
Jul.	2	309	84	211	353	119	254	23	164	289	64
Jul.	9	33	176	315	82	203	348	125	253	13	160
Jul.	16	126	276	46	165	297	87	216	336	108	258
Jul.	23	226	8	130	258	38	177	300	69	210	347
Jul.	30	317	92	221	2	128	262	33	173	298	72
Aug.	6	41	187	323	91	211	359	133	261	21	170
Aug.	13	135	285	54	175	305	97	224	346	116	268
Aug.	20	237	16	138	267	49	185	308	78	220	355
Aug.	27	326	100	232	10	136	270	44	181	307	80
Sep.	3	49	197	331	100	220	8	142	270	31	179
Sep.	10	143	295	62	184	314	107	232	355	125	278
Sep.	17	247	24	147	277	58	194	317	89	228	4
Sep.	24	335	108	243	18	145	278	55	189	316	88
Oct.	1	58	206	341	108	229	17	152	278	40	188
Oct.	8	151	306	70	193	322	117	240	4	134	288
Oct.	15	256	32	155	287	66	203	324	100	236	13
Oct.	22	344	116	253	27	154	287	64	198	324	98
Oct.	29	68	214	350	116	239	25	162	286	49	196
Nov.	5	161	316	78	201	332	126	248	12	145	297
Nov.	12	264	41	162	298	74	212	333	111	244	22
Nov.	19	353	125	262	36	162	296	73	207	332	108
Nov.	26	77	222	0	124	248	33	172	294	58	205
Dec.	3	171	325	87	209	343	135	257	19	156	305
Dec.	10	272	50	171	309	82	220	341	120	253	30
Dec.	17	1	135	271	45	170	306	81	217	340	118
Dec.	24	86	231	10	132	256	43	181	302	66	214
Dec.	31	182	333	95	217	354	142	265	27	167	313

Month	Date	1941	1942	1943	1944	1945	1946	1947	1948	1949	1950
Jan.	1	325	88	211	353	135	258	22	165	305	68
Jan.	8	50	176	315	85	219	348	126	256	29	160
Jan.	15	141	276	50	169	312	87	220	340	123	258
Jan.	22	239	12	133	258	52	182	303	69	224	352
Jan.	29	333	96	221	2	143	266	32	174	314	75
Feb.	5	57	186	323	95	227	358	134	265	37	170
Feb.	12	150	285	58	178	320	96	228	349	131	268
Feb.	19	250	20	142	267	62	190	312	78	234	359
Feb.	26	342	104	231	11	152	274	43	182	323	83
Mar.	5	65	196	331	116	236	8	142	286	46	179
Mar.	12	158	295	66	199	328	107	236	10	139	279
Mar.	19	261	28	150	290	72	198	320	102	243	8
Mar.	26	351	112	242	34	161	281	53	204	332	91
Apr.	2	74	205	340	125	244	16	152	294	55	187
Apr.	9	166	306	74	208	337	117	244	19	148	289
Apr.	16	270	36	158	300	81	206	328	112	252	17
Apr.	23	360	120	252	42	170	290	63	212	340	100
Apr.	30	83	214	350	133	254	25	162	302	64	195
May	7	174	316	82	217	346	127	252	27	158	299
May	14	279	45	166	311	90	215	336	123	260	26
May	21	9	128	261	50	179	299	72	221	349	110
May	28	92	222	1	141	263	33	173	310	73	204
Jun.	4	184	326	91	226	356	137	261	36	168	307
Jun.	11	287	54	174	322	98	224	344	134	268	34
Jun.	18	17	137	270	60	187	308	81	231	357	119
Jun.	25	102	231	11	149	272	42	183	318	82	213
Jul.	2	194	335	99	234	7	145	269	44	179	316
Jul.	9	296	63	183	332	106	233	353	144	277	43
Jul.	16	25	147	279	70	195	318	89	241	5	129
Jul.	23	110	240	21	157	280	52	192	327	91	224
Jul.	30	205	343	108	242	18	153	278	52	190	324
Aug.	6	304	71	192	341	115	241	3	153	286	51
Aug.	13	33	156	287	80	203	327	98	251	13	138
Aug.	20	119	250	30	165	289	63	201	336	99	235
Aug.	27	216	351	117	250	28	162	287	61	200	332
Sep.	3	314	80	201	350	125	249	13	161	296	59
Sep.	10	41	165	296	90	211	336	108	260	21	146
Sep.	17	127	261	39	174	297	74	209	345	107	246
Sep.	24	226	359	126	259	38	170	295	70	209	341
Oct.	1	323	88	211	358	135	257	22	170	306	67
Oct.	8	49	174	306	99	220	344	118	269	30	154
Oct.	15	135	272	47	183	305	84	217	353	116	256
Oct.	22	236	8	134	269	47	180	303	80	217	351
Oct.	29	333	95	220	7	144	265	31	179	315	75
Nov.	5	58	181	317	107	229	352	129	277	39	162
Nov.	12	143	283	55	192	314	94	225	1	125	265
Nov.	19	244	18	141	279	55	189	311	90	225	0
Nov.	26	343	104	229	16	153	274	39	189	323	84
Dec.	3	67	189	328	115	237	360	140	284	47	171
Dec.	10	153	292	64	200	324	103	234	9	136	274
Dec.	17	252	28	149	289	63	199	319	100	234	9
Dec.	24	351	112	237	27	161	282	47	199	331	93
Dec.	31	76	198	338	123	246	9	150	293	55	180

Month	Date	1951	1952	1953	1954	1955	1956	1957	1958	1959	1960
Jan.	1	194	336	115	238	6	147	285	47	178	317
Jan.	8	297	67	199	331	107	237	9	143	278	47
Jan.	15	30	150	294	70	200	320	104	242	9	131
Jan.	22	114	240	35	161	284	51	207	331	94	223
Jan.	29	204	344	124	245	17	155	294	55	189	325
Feb.	5	305	76	207	341	116	246	18	152	287	56
Feb.	12	38	159	302	80	208	330	112	252	17	140
Feb.	19	122	249	45	169	292	61	216	340	102	233
Feb.	26	215	352	133	253	27	163	303	63	199	333
Mar.	5	314	96	216	350	125	266	27	161	297	75
Mar.	12	46	180	310	91	216	351	121	262	25	161
Mar.	19	130	274	54	178	300	86	224	349	110	259
Mar.	26	225	14	142	262	37	185	312	72	208	356
Apr.	2	324	104	226	358	135	274	37	169	307	83
Apr.	9	54	189	319	100	224	360	131	271	34	170
Apr.	16	138	285	62	187	308	97	232	357	118	269
Apr.	23	235	23	150	271	46	194	320	82	217	5
Apr.	30	334	112	235	6	146	282	48	177	317	91
May	7	62	197	330	109	232	8	142	279	42	177
May	14	146	296	70	196	316	107	240	6	127	279
May	21	243	32	158	280	54	204	328	91	225	15
May	28	344	120	244	15	155	290	55	187	326	100
Jun.	4	71	205	341	117	241	16	153	288	51	186
Jun.	11	155	306	79	204	325	117	249	14	137	288
Jun.	18	252	42	166	290	63	214	336	101	234	25
Jun.	25	354	128	253	26	164	298	63	198	335	109
Jul.	2	80	214	351	125	250	24	164	296	60	195
Jul.	9	164	315	88	212	335	126	259	22	147	297
Jul.	16	260	52	174	299	72	223	344	110	243	34
Jul.	23	3	137	261	37	173	307	71	209	343	118
Jul.	30	89	222	2	134	258	33	174	304	68	205
Aug.	6	174	324	97	220	345	134	268	30	156	305
Aug.	13	270	62	182	308	82	232	353	118	254	42
Aug.	20	11	146	269	48	181	316	79	220	351	126
Aug.	27	97	232	11	143	267	43	183	314	76	215
Sep.	3	184	332	107	228	355	143	278	38	166	314
Sep.	10	280	71	191	316	92	241	2	127	265	50
Sep.	17	19	155	278	58	189	325	88	230	359	135
Sep.	24	105	242	20	152	274	54	191	323	84	225
Oct.	1	193	341	116	237	4	152	287	47	174	324
Oct.	8	291	79	200	324	103	249	11	135	276	58
Oct.	15	27	163	287	68	198	333	98	239	8	143
Oct.	22	113	252	28	162	282	64	199	332	92	235
Oct.	29	201	350	125	245	12	162	295	56	182	334
Nov.	5	302	87	209	333	114	256	19	144	286	66
Nov.	12	36	171	297	76	207	341	109	247	17	150
Nov.	19	121	262	37	171	291	73	208	341	101	244
Nov.	26	209	0	133	254	20	173	303	65	190	345
Dec.	3	312	95	217	342	124	265	27	154	295	75
Dec.	10	45	179	307	84	216	348	119	255	27	158
Dec.	17	129	271	46	180	299	82	218	350	110	252
Dec.	24	217	11	141	263	28	184	311	73	199	355
Dec.	31	321	103	225	352	132	273	35	164	303	84

Month	Date	1961	1962	1963	1964	1965	1966	1967	1968	1969	1970
Jan.	1	96	217	350	128	266	27	163	298	76	197
Jan.	8	179	315	89	217	350	126	260	27	161	297
Jan.	15	275	54	179	302	86	225	349	112	257	36
Jan.	22	18	141	264	35	189	311	74	207	359	122
Jan.	29	105	225	1	136	275	35	173	306	85	206
Feb.	5	188	323	99	225	360	134	270	35	171	305
Feb.	12	284	64	187	310	95	235	357	121	267	45
Feb.	19	26	150	272	46	197	320	81	218	7	130
Feb.	26	113	234	11	144	283	45	182	315	93	216
Mar.	5	198	331	109	245	9	142	280	54	180	313
Mar.	12	293	73	195	332	105	244	5	142	277	54
Mar.	19	34	159	280	71	205	329	90	243	15	139
Mar.	26	122	243	19	167	291	54	190	338	101	226
Apr.	2	208	340	119	253	18	151	290	63	189	323
Apr.	9	303	82	204	340	116	252	14	150	288	62
Apr.	16	42	167	288	81	213	337	99	253	23	147
Apr.	23	130	253	28	176	299	64	198	347	109	235
Apr.	30	216	349	128	261	27	161	298	71	197	333
May	7	314	90	213	348	127	260	23	158	299	70
May	14	51	176	298	91	222	345	109	262	32	155
May	21	137	263	36	186	307	74	207	357	117	245
May	28	225	359	137	270	35	172	307	80	205	344
Jun.	4	325	98	222	357	137	268	31	168	309	78
Jun.	11	60	184	308	99	231	353	119	270	42	163
Jun.	18	146	272	45	195	315	82	217	6	126	253
Jun.	25	233	10	145	279	43	183	315	89	214	355
Jul.	2	336	106	230	6	147	276	40	178	318	87
Jul.	9	70	191	318	108	241	1	129	279	51	171
Jul.	16	154	281	56	204	324	91	227	14	135	261
Jul.	23	241	21	153	288	52	193	323	98	223	5
Jul.	30	345	115	238	16	156	286	47	188	327	97
Aug.	6	79	200	327	116	250	10	138	288	60	180
Aug.	13	163	289	66	212	333	99	238	22	144	270
Aug.	20	250	32	161	296	61	203	331	106	233	14
Aug.	27	353	124	246	27	164	295	55	199	335	106
Sep.	3	88	208	336	126	259	19	147	297	68	189
Sep.	10	172	297	77	220	342	108	249	30	152	279
Sep.	17	260	41	170	304	72	212	340	114	244	23
Sep.	24	1	134	254	37	172	304	64	208	344	115
Oct.	1	97	217	344	136	267	28	155	308	76	198
Oct.	8	180	306	88	228	351	117	259	38	161	289
Oct.	15	270	50	179	312	82	220	350	122	254	31
Oct.	22	10	143	262	47	182	313	73	217	353	123
Oct.	29	105	226	352	146	275	37	163	318	84	207
Nov.	5	189	315	97	237	359	127	268	47	168	299
Nov.	12	281	58	188	320	93	228	359	130	264	39
Nov.	19	19	151	271	55	191	321	82	225	3	131
Nov.	26	113	235	1	157	282	45	172	328	92	215
Dec.	3	197	326	105	245	7	138	276	55	176	310
Dec.	10	291	66	197	328	102	237	7	139	273	48
Dec.	17	30	159	280	63	202	329	91	234	13	139
Dec.	24	121	243	11	167	291	53	183	337	101	223
Dec.	31	204	336	113	254	14	149	284	64	184	320

Month	Date	1971	1972	1973	1974	1975	1976	1977	1978	1979	1980
Jan.	1	335	109	246	8	147	279	56	179	318	90
Jan.	8	71	197	332	108	243	6	144	278	54	176
Jan.	15	158	283	69	207	328	93	240	18	139	263
Jan.	22	244	20	169	292	54	192	339	102	224	4
Jan.	29	344	117	255	17	156	288	64	188	327	99
Feb.	5	81	204	342	116	253	14	153	287	63	184
Feb.	12	167	291	79	216	337	101	251	26	147	271
Feb.	19	252	31	177	300	62	203	347	110	233	14
Feb.	26	353	126	263	27	164	297	72	199	334	109
Mar.	5	91	224	351	124	262	34	162	296	72	204
Mar.	12	176	312	90	224	346	122	262	34	156	203
Mar.	19	261	55	185	309	72	226	356	118	243	37
Mar.	26	1	149	270	37	172	320	80	208	343	130
Apr.	2	100	233	360	134	270	43	170	307	80	213
Apr.	9	184	320	101	232	355	131	273	42	164	302
Apr.	16	271	64	194	317	82	235	5	126	254	46
Apr.	23	9	158	278	47	181	329	88	217	352	139
Apr.	30	109	242	8	145	278	52	178	318	88	222
May	7	193	329	111	240	3	141	282	50	173	312
May	14	281	73	203	324	92	243	14	134	264	54
May	21	19	167	287	55	191	337	97	226	3	147
May	28	117	251	16	156	286	61	187	328	96	231
Jun.	4	201	339	120	249	11	151	291	59	180	323
Jun.	11	291	81	213	333	102	252	23	143	273	63
Jun.	18	29	176	296	64	201	346	106	234	13	155
Jun.	25	125	260	25	167	295	69	196	338	105	239
Jul.	2	209	349	129	258	19	162	299	68	188	334
Jul.	9	300	90	222	341	111	261	32	152	282	72
Jul.	16	40	184	305	72	212	354	115	243	24	163
Jul.	23	133	268	35	176	303	78	206	347	114	248
Jul.	30	217	0	137	267	27	172	308	77	197	344
Aug.	6	309	99	230	350	120	271	40	161	290	83
Aug.	13	51	192	314	81	223	2	124	252	34	171
Aug.	20	142	276	45	185	312	86	217	356	123	256
Aug.	27	225	10	146	276	36	182	317	86	206	353
Sep.	3	317	109	238	360	128	281	48	170	299	93
Sep.	10	61	200	322	90	232	10	132	262	43	180
Sep.	17	151	284	56	193	321	94	228	4	132	264
Sep.	24	234	20	155	284	45	191	326	94	215	2
Oct.	1	325	120	246	9	136	291	56	179	308	103
Oct.	8	70	208	330	101	241	19	140	273	51	189
Oct.	15	160	292	66	202	330	102	238	12	140	273
Oct.	22	243	28	165	292	54	199	336	102	225	10
Oct.	29	334	130	254	17	146	301	64	187	318	112
Nov.	5	79	217	338	112	249	27	148	284	59	197
Nov.	12	169	300	76	210	339	111	247	21	148	282
Nov.	19	253	36	175	300	63	207	347	110	234	18
Nov.	26	344	139	262	25	156	310	73	195	329	120
Dec.	3	87	226	346	122	257	36	157	294	67	206
Dec.	10	177	310	84	220	347	121	255	31	156	292
Dec.	17	261	45	185	308	72	216	356	118	242	28
Dec.	24	355	148	271	33	167	318	81	203	340	128
Dec.	31	95	235	355	132	265	44	166	303	76	214

Month	Date	1981	1982	1983	1984	1985	1986	1987	1988	1989	1990
Jan.	1	226	350	129	260	36	162	300	71	205	333
Jan.	8	315	89	225	346	126	260	36	156	297	72
Jan.	15	53	188	309	73	225	358	119	243	37	168
Jan.	22	149	272	35	176	319	82	206	348	129	252
Jan.	29	234	0	137	270	43	172	308	81	213	343
Feb.	5	324	98	234	354	135	270	44	164	306	82
Feb.	12	64	196	317	81	236	6	128	252	48	175
Feb.	19	157	280	45	185	328	90	217	356	138	260
Feb.	26	242	10	145	279	51	182	316	90	222	353
Mar.	5	332	108	242	15	143	280	52	185	313	93
Mar.	12	74	204	326	104	246	14	136	275	57	184
Mar.	19	166	288	55	208	337	97	227	19	147	268
Mar.	26	250	20	154	300	60	191	326	111	230	1
Apr.	2	340	119	250	24	151	291	60	194	322	103
Apr.	9	84	212	334	114	255	22	144	286	66	192
Apr.	16	175	296	66	216	346	106	237	27	156	276
Apr.	23	259	28	164	309	69	199	336	119	240	9
Apr.	30	349	130	258	33	160	302	68	203	331	113
May	7	93	221	342	124	264	31	152	297	75	201
May	14	184	304	75	225	114	246	36	165	285	
May	21	268	36	175	317	78	207	347	127	249	18
May	28	358	140	266	41	170	311	76	211	341	122
Jun.	4	102	230	350	135	272	40	160	307	83	210
Jun.	11	193	313	84	234	3	123	255	45	173	294
Jun.	18	277	45	185	325	87	216	357	135	258	27
Jun.	25	8	149	275	49	180	320	85	219	352	130
Jul.	2	110	239	359	146	281	49	169	317	92	219
Jul.	9	201	322	93	244	11	133	263	55	181	304
Jul.	16	286	54	196	333	96	225	7	143	266	37
Jul.	23	19	158	284	57	191	328	94	227	3	138
Jul.	30	119	248	7	155	290	57	178	327	101	227
Aug.	6	210	331	101	254	19	142	272	66	189	313
Aug.	13	294	64	205	341	104	236	16	152	274	48
Aug.	20	30	166	293	66	202	337	103	236	13	147
Aug.	27	128	256	17	164	299	65	187	335	111	235
Sep.	3	218	340	110	264	27	151	281	75	197	321
Sep.	10	302	75	214	350	112	247	24	160	282	59
Sep.	17	40	174	302	74	212	345	112	245	23	156
Sep.	24	138	264	26	172	309	73	197	343	121	243
Oct.	1	226	349	119	274	36	159	292	84	206	329
Oct.	8	310	86	222	359	120	258	32	169	291	70
Oct.	15	50	183	310	84	220	354	120	255	31	165
Oct.	22	148	272	35	181	319	81	206	352	130	251
Oct.	29	234	357	130	282	44	167	303	92	214	337
Nov.	5	318	96	230	8	129	268	40	178	300	79
Nov.	12	58	193	318	93	229	4	128	265	39	175
Nov.	19	158	280	44	190	329	90	214	2	139	260
Nov.	26	243	5	141	290	53	175	314	100	223	345
Dec.	3	327	106	238	16	139	277	49	185	310	88
Dec.	10	66	203	326	103	237	14	136	274	48	185
Dec.	17	167	288	52	200	337	98	222	12	147	269
Dec.	24	252	13	152	298	62	184	324	108	232	355
Dec.	31	337	114	248	24	149	285	59	193	320	96

Month	Date	1991	1992	1993	1994	1995	1996	1997	1998	1999	2000
Jan.	1	111	242	15	145	281	53	185	317	92	223
Jan.	8	206	326	108	244	16	136	279	56	186	307
Jan.	15	289	54	210	337	99	225	21	147	270	37
Jan.	22	18	158	299	61	190	329	110	231	2	140
Jan.	29	119	252	23	155	290	62	193	326	101	232
Feb.	5	214	335	116	254	24	145	287	66	193	315
Feb.	12	298	63	220	345	108	235	31	155	278	47
Feb.	19	29	166	308	69	201	337	119	239	12	148
Feb.	26	128	260	32	164	299	70	202	335	111	240
Mar.	5	222	356	124	265	32	166	295	76	201	337
Mar.	12	306	87	229	354	116	259	39	164	285	72
Mar.	19	39	189	317	77	211	360	128	248	22	170
Mar.	26	138	280	41	172	310	90	212	343	121	260
Apr.	2	230	5	133	275	40	175	305	86	210	345
Apr.	9	314	98	237	3	123	270	47	173	294	83
Apr.	16	49	198	326	86	220	9	136	257	31	180
Apr.	23	148	288	50	180	320	98	221	351	132	268
Apr.	30	238	13	143	284	48	183	315	95	218	353
May	7	322	109	245	12	132	281	55	182	302	93
May	14	57	207	335	95	228	18	144	267	39	190
May	21	158	296	59	189	330	106	230	1	141	276
May	28	247	21	154	292	57	191	326	103	227	1
Jun.	4	330	119	253	21	141	291	64	190	311	102
Jun.	11	66	217	343	105	236	28	152	276	48	199
Jun.	18	168	304	68	199	340	114	238	11	150	285
Jun.	25	256	29	165	300	66	199	337	111	236	10
Jul.	2	339	129	262	29	150	300	73	198	321	111
Jul.	9	74	227	351	114	245	38	160	285	57	209
Jul.	16	177	313	76	210	348	123	246	22	158	293
Jul.	23	265	38	175	309	75	208	347	120	245	19
Jul.	30	349	137	272	37	160	308	83	206	331	119
Aug.	6	83	237	359	123	255	48	169	293	67	218
Aug.	13	186	322	84	221	356	132	254	33	166	302
Aug.	20	273	47	185	318	83	218	356	129	253	29
Aug.	27	358	146	282	45	169	317	93	214	340	128
Sep.	3	93	246	7	131	265	56	177	301	78	226
Sep.	10	194	331	92	231	4	141	263	43	174	311
Sep.	17	281	56	194	327	91	228	5	138	261	39
Sep.	24	8	154	292	53	178	326	102	223	349	137
Oct.	1	104	254	16	139	276	64	186	310	89	234
Oct.	8	202	339	101	241	13	149	273	53	183	319
Oct.	15	289	66	202	337	99	238	13	148	269	49
Oct.	22	16	164	301	61	187	336	111	231	357	148
Oct.	29	115	262	25	148	287	72	195	318	100	242
Nov.	5	211	347	111	250	22	157	283	61	193	326
Nov.	12	297	76	211	346	107	247	22	157	277	58
Nov.	19	24	174	309	70	194	346	119	240	5	159
Nov.	26	126	270	33	156	297	80	203	328	109	251
Dec.	3	220	355	121	258	31	165	293	69	202	334
Dec.	10	305	85	220	355	115	256	31	165	286	67
Dec.	17	32	185	317	79	203	357	127	249	13	169
Dec.	24	135	278	41	166	306	89	211	338	117	260
Dec.	31	230	3	131	266	41	173	303	78	211	343

Month	Year	2001	2002	2003	2004	2005	2006	2007	2008	2009	2010
Jan.	1	355	128	263	33	165	300	74	203	336	111
Jan.	8	89	228	355	117	260	39	165	288	71	211
Jan.	15	193	317	79	209	4	127	249	20	174	297
Jan.	22	280	41	174	310	91	211	346	121	261	21
Jan.	29	4	137	273	42	175	308	84	211	345	119
Feb.	5	97	238	3	126	268	49	173	296	80	221
Feb.	12	202	326	87	219	12	136	257	31	182	306
Feb.	19	289	49	184	319	99	220	356	130	269	31
Feb.	26	13	145	283	49	184	316	94	219	355	127
Mar.	5	106	248	11	147	278	59	181	317	90	229
Mar.	12	210	334	95	244	20	145	265	56	190	315
Mar.	19	298	58	193	342	107	229	4	153	277	40
Mar.	26	23	153	293	69	193	325	104	239	4	136
Apr.	2	116	257	20	155	289	67	190	325	101	237
Apr.	9	218	343	104	255	28	154	274	67	198	323
Apr.	16	306	68	202	351	115	239	12	162	285	50
Apr.	23	32	162	303	77	202	334	114	247	12	146
Apr.	30	127	265	29	163	300	75	199	333	112	245
May	7	226	352	113	264	37	162	284	76	207	331
May	14	314	77	210	1	123	248	21	172	293	59
May	21	40	173	312	86	210	345	122	256	20	157
May	28	138	273	38	171	311	83	207	342	123	254
Jun.	4	235	0	122	273	46	170	294	84	217	339
Jun.	11	322	87	219	11	132	257	30	181	302	68
Jun.	18	48	183	320	95	218	356	130	265	29	168
Jun.	25	149	281	46	181	321	92	216	352	132	262
Jul.	2	245	8	132	281	56	178	304	93	227	347
Jul.	9	330	95	229	20	140	266	41	190	310	76
Jul.	16	56	195	328	104	227	7	138	274	38	179
Jul.	23	158	290	54	191	330	101	224	2	140	272
Jul.	30	254	16	142	290	65	186	313	101	236	356
Aug.	6	339	103	239	28	149	274	52	198	319	84
Aug.	13	65	205	336	112	236	17	147	282	47	188
Aug.	20	167	299	62	201	338	110	232	12	149	281
Aug.	27	264	24	151	299	74	194	321	111	245	5
Sep.	3	348	112	250	36	158	282	63	206	328	93
Sep.	10	74	215	345	120	246	26	156	290	58	197
Sep.	17	176	309	70	211	347	120	240	22	157	290
Sep.	24	273	33	159	309	83	203	330	122	253	14
Oct.	1	356	120	261	44	167	291	73	214	336	103
Oct.	8	84	224	354	128	256	34	165	298	68	205
Oct.	15	184	318	78	220	355	129	248	31	167	299
Oct.	22	281	42	167	320	91	212	338	132	261	23
Oct.	29	5	129	271	52	175	301	82	222	344	113
Nov.	5	95	232	4	136	266	42	174	306	78	213
Nov.	12	193	327	87	229	5	137	257	40	177	307
Nov.	19	289	51	176	331	99	221	346	143	268	31
Nov.	26	13	139	280	61	183	312	91	231	352	123
Dec.	3	105	240	13	144	276	51	183	315	87	223
Dec.	10	203	335	96	237	15	145	267	48	188	315
Dec.	17	297	59	185	341	107	229	356	152	277	39
Dec.	24	21	150	288	70	190	322	98	240	0	134
Dec.	31	114	249	22	153	285	60	191	324	96	232

☽ LLEWELLYN ORDERING INFORMATION

Order Online:
Visit our website at www.llewellyn.com, select your books, and order them on our secure server.

Order by Phone:
- Call toll-free within the U.S. at 1-877-NEW-WRLD (1-877-639-9753). Call toll-free within Canada at 1-866-NEW-WRLD (1-866-639-9753)
- We accept VISA, MasterCard, and American Express

Order by Mail:
Send the full price of your order (MN residents add 7% sales tax) in U.S. funds, plus postage & handling to:

Llewellyn Worldwide
2143 Wooddale Drive, Dept. 0-7387-0853-4
Woodbury, Minnesota 55125-2989, U.S.A.

Postage & Handling:

Standard (U.S., Mexico, & Canada). If your order is:
$49.99 and under, add $3.00
$50.00 and over, FREE STANDARD SHIPPING

AK, HI, PR: $15.00 for one book plus $1.00 for each additional book.

International Orders (airmail only):
$16.00 for one book plus $3.00 for each additional book

Orders are processed within 2 business days. Please allow for normal shipping time.
Postage and handling rates subject to change.